THE STORM PASSED BY

The Condor at Sea, adapted from a painting by Helen Mladek

TREVOR ALLEN

THE STORM PASSED BY

Ireland and the Battle of the Atlantic,
1940–41

IRISH ACADEMIC PRESS

This book was typeset
in 11 on 13 Ehrhardt by
Woodcote Typesetters
and first published in 1996 by
IRISH ACADEMIC PRESS
Kill Lane, Blackrock, Co. Dublin, Ireland
and in North America by
IRISH ACADEMIC PRESS
c/o International Specialized Book Services,
5804 NE Hassalo Street, Portland, OR 97213.

A catalogue record for this title
is available from the British Library

ISBN 0-7165-2616-6

To Sally, David and Roger

Printed in Great Britain by Hartnolls Ltd, Cornwall

CONTENTS

LIST OF ILLUSTRATIONS

CREDITS

Anne O'Hara 1; Dr E.M. Patterson 2; National Maritime Museum 3, 4, 10; Bundesarchiv 5, 6, 12, 17, 19, 21, 22, 23, 26; U-Boat-Archiv 7, 13, 14; US National Archives 8, 25; Bernard & Graefe 9, 15, 16, 27; Imperial War Museum 11; Siegfried Röthke 18; Joachim Herrforth 24; Walther Siber 20

PREFACE

The material for this book was obtained from a number of bodies and individuals.

I gratefully made use of the facilities of the following institutions whose staffs were without exception helpful and courteous: Imperial War Museum, London; Guildhall Library, London; National Maritime Museum, Greenwich; Meteorological Office, Bracknell; Meteorological Service, Dublin; Public Record Office, Kew; Public Record Office of Northern Ireland; Linenhall Library, Belfast; Belfast Central Library; University of Ulster at Coleraine; Irish Military Archives, Dublin – especially Commandant Peter Young and his staff; US National Archives and Records Administration, Washington; Bundesarchiv, Koblenz; Bundesarchiv-Militärarchiv, Freiburg; Auswärtiges Amt, Bonn; Deutsche Dienstelle, Berlin; Volksbund Deutsche Kriegsgräberfürsorge e.V., Kassel (the staffs of the two last-mentioned bodies made long searches in the records of German war dead); U-Boot Archiv, Cuxhaven, where Horst Bredow gave me the benefit of his wide experience and his hospitality.

I acquired invaluable material on a little-known topic from the late Heinz Nowarra and from his book *Focke-Wulf Fw200 Condor*. I regret that I was unable to fully express my thanks to him before his death but I express them to his publishers Bernard & Graefe of Koblenz for permission to reproduce photographs from his book.

The published books referred to in the bibliography contained relevant information on a variety of subjects. Two of them were indispensable. The information gained from John M. Young's *Britain's Sea War* was so extensive that it was impossible to attribute each incident individually in the notes. In the case of Peter Stahl's *Bomber Pilot between the Arctic and the Sahara* the content is simply unique. Brian Barton's *The Blitz. Belfast in the War Years* provided a comprehensive overview of the bombing of Belfast from several standpoints.

I am deeply grateful to the individuals who gave me material and their precious time during my research. Some of them are mentioned in the key to the notes. Others who supplied photographs are also named but all, whether mentioned or not, have my thanks.

In view of the fragmentary nature of surviving Luftwaffe records I cannot thank enough all those former German airmen who went to the trouble of giving me the kind of first-hand accounts of those events of long ago which sadly will become more and more difficult to obtain. Among them, very special mention must be made of Walther Siber and Georg Aigner whose generosity went far beyond merely supplying information.

I must also specifically acknowledge the professionalism of my publishers and their expert guidance. Military historian Richard Doherty kindly read the first draft of the manuscript. For his wise counsel and spontaneous encouragement, my most sincere thanks.

Finally, to my wife Sally, who bore a long ordeal with fortitude, my deepest gratitude.

INTRODUCTION

*The only history worth reading is that written at the time of which it treats,
the history of what was done and seen, heard out of the mouths of the men who
did and saw.*   John Ruskin, 1853

When Hitler made what was to prove to be his greatest mistake and invaded
the Soviet Union on 22 June 1941, exactly a year to the day had elapsed since
the signing of the Franco-German Armistice which formalized the capitula-
tion of France. As that year began, few doubted that all the might of a seemingly
invincible war machine would now be turned against Britain. In fact, this did
not happen. The planned seaborne invasion, code-named *Operation Sealion*,
was abandoned in face of overwhelming British sea power and the Luftwaffe's
failure to gain command of the skies over Southern England.

Instead, the German High Command resorted to a night aerial bombardment of British cities and a repetition of the First World War attempt to
strangle the country economically by destroying its merchant fleet. The first
objective achieved little in strategic terms and the German Navy's inability
to secure the second by the summer of 1941, in fact, signified its failure.

This phase of the conflict had barely begun before it became obvious that
the island of Ireland would inevitably be caught up in the pursuit of both
these objectives. In the north, its indispensable ports and airfields were a
concomitant of belligerent status but at the same time they attracted its evils,
one of which was the bombing of Belfast. The story of those attacks and their
grievous consequences in the spring of 1941 seems to have an enduring
fascination for those who lived through them which is not always easy to
explain. But what is even less easy to explain is the apparent curiosity of
children choosing the theme of 'The Blitz' as an optional subject in school
examinations two generations later.

But what of the men who dropped the bombs on Belfast? Many of them
did not survive the war and died in savage battles on the Russian front. Some
became fighter pilots during the last desperate days of the Third Reich. There
is a record of some having been drafted into infantry units and thrown into
futile attempts to stem the tide of the Red Army when there was no fuel left
for their aircraft. Fortunately, a few of those who did survive it all seemed
glad to shed their anonymity and leaf through old logbooks or dredge their
memories to relive their flights to Belfast more than fifty years before. Their
stories may help to dispel some myths.

South of the Irish border, the policy of neutrality adopted by the Dublin government on the outbreak of war created a situation for which there was no precedent. Initially, it was thought that the effect of neutrality would favour Germany and in the year in question British resentment was centered on the issue of her former naval bases in Ireland of which she was now deprived. A number of complex factors may have motivated Eire's often anomalous policy but perhaps the fact that a mere twenty years had elapsed since the Anglo-Irish war and the bloody Civil War that followed it may go some way towards explaining the apparent ambivalence that so enraged Churchill. The denial to Britain of ports and airfields in Eire in the year after the fall of France may have given the German U-boats and long-range aircraft an indeterminate advantage but any more far-reaching benefits which Germany may have expected to derive from having access to a neutral country on Britain's back doorstep did not materialize.

Ireland's significance in the early days of the Battle of the Atlantic was assured once the Germans had, for tactical and logistic reasons, chosen to wage it in the North West Approaches. The North Channel became the focal point for all the ocean-going traffic upon which Britain depended for survival. A strict censorship regime concealed the deteriorating situation which rapidly developed from an already nervous British public. There was much to conceal. Figures quoted by Winston Churchill after the war disclosed that a total of 543 Allied ships had been lost to enemy action in the six months ended 31 December 1940, that is, an average of three a day. A large proportion of them went down within sight of the Irish coast or a few hours' sailing distance away. The passage of time may have obscured the impact of these frightening losses and of the suffering of seamen but for Britain's war leaders at the time it must have been difficult to see how it could go on.

The further the Second World War recedes into the past, the more difficult it becomes to apply John Ruskin's test of authenticity in describing the events of 1940–1. The narrative in the following chapters is, as far as possible, based on either the personal recollections of men who were there or on the official accounts written by their contemporaries. Any emphasis on German material is an attempt to throw light on previously neglected sources of information. A lack of detailed material concerning British or Allied personnel in the events described simply stems from the fact that in general such information has always been, and still is, more easily accessible. It does not imply a lesser estimation of any of the individuals involved.

STORM WARNING

In July 1940, the transition from 'phoney war' to something much more menacing was well under way in Britain. A feeling of alarm-and uncertainty predominated. Hitler had returned to Berlin in triumph after having been photographed and filmed in front of the Eiffel Tower. On the nineteenth, he made a speech to the Reichstag which, he said, contained 'a last appeal to reason.' It was addressed to the British government but it was doomed to fall on deaf ears even before it was delivered.

In Northern Ireland, the traditional holiday season was marred by poor weather. Records for July frequently refer to heavy rain and gale force winds. On the 'twelfth' (the traditional Orange demonstration was cancelled), the rain was almost continuous. The unsettled conditions matched the public mood as daily life gradually took on a warlike appearance. Troop movements were conspicuous and in Belfast Lough naval vessels were to be seen in increasing numbers. Several French merchant ships were anchored there while their owners and crews chose whether to give allegiance to the new Vichy government or to de Gaulle.[1]

At the mouth of the lough, the seaside town of Bangor was destined to play a major role in the war at sea. The offshore waters were designated a convoy assembly and dispersal point. Movements were controlled from the Royal Hotel on the seafront and throughout the war naval personnel could be seen signalling to ships in the bay by Aldis lamp from the upper floors.

Already the German Luftwaffe was surreptitiously monitoring the movement of shipping in and around the lough from its newly-acquired bases in occupied France and the Channel Islands: Junkers Ju88 aircraft from the 2nd Staffel of the reconnaissance unit, Aufklärungsgruppe 122 (2.(F)/122), had moved into St Helier airport in Jersey and were engaged in these operations on a daily basis. How important this entire area had become can be seen from a mission report filed by another reconnaissance unit, 3.(F)/123, which began operating from Dinard airfield in Brittany at the same time. This discloses that on one sortie in July, a total of 43 ships had been observed – 20 of them lying at anchor off Bangor and another 23 steaming in that direction.[2] A concentration of this magnitude pointed to the formation of a large convoy.

1 The Royal Hotel, Bangor

On the same night as Hitler made his 'last appeal', German aircraft were positively identified over Belfast Lough for the first time. At 0110 hours, troops of the 525th (Antrim) Coast Regiment, on guard at the coastal defence site at Greypoint on the south side of the lough, saw at least four parachutes being dropped from an aircraft.[3] The following morning, the Royal Navy's Flag Officer in Charge (FOIC) at Belfast reported to the Admiralty that two enemy aircraft were known to have laid an estimated eight mines in the lough during the hours of darkness.[4] All available minesweepers were deployed to clear channels in what were considered to be the most vulnerable areas. One channel was to provide safe access to the lough close to the Co. Down shoreline.

The mines being laid by German aircraft at this stage were of the 'influence' type, that is, they were detonated either by the magnetic pull of a ship's hull or acoustically by the sound of propellers. The latter was a particularly sophisticated device. Its detonator could be programmed to lie dormant for weeks or even longer and 'ignore' the noise from a given number of ships before 'selecting' one for attack.

German minelaying by parachute had proved extremely effective since the outbreak of war, particularly in the Thames Estuary. It called for a high degree of airmanship and navigational skill on the part of the aircrews involved. They had to familiarize themselves with the format of nautical charts and study the behaviour of tides and currents. The random scattering of these valuable devices was strictly forbidden and accuracy was therefore essential. A gradual descent to a predetermined release point, usually over inshore waters where the path taken by ships entering and leaving harbours was predictable, had to be made with engines throttled back to minimize the risk of detection from the shore. The mines were released from a height of between 400 and 800 metres and were calculated to fall into water having a minimum depth of five to eight metres at ebb tide. The parachutes, green in colour, were attached to the mine casing by a firm solution of salt which dissolved in the water. This allowed the parachute to float away and so avoid revealing the precise location of the mine.

On the afternoon of 20 July, shortly after the FOIC Belfast had reported the minelaying to the Admiralty, the tramp steamer *Troutpool* (4886 tons), owned by Sir R. Ropner & Co, was lying at anchor about a mile off the Bangor pier light. She had been steaming down the North Channel on the way from ports on the River Plate with a cargo of maize and bran for Avonmouth when her master, Captain Muitt, was instructed to put into Belfast Lough for degaussing. This was a process designed to neutralize the influence of magnetic mines by passing electric current through a cable round a ship's hull.

When the degaussing had been completed, the *Troutpool*'s engines were

2 The *Troutpool* shortly after sinking with anti-submarine trawler in attendance

started and she was swung for compass adjustment. Almost immediately, at 1352 hours, she was struck by a mine under her bows and, about two minutes later, by a second slightly further aft. Eleven members of the crew were killed in the explosions. According to the Royal Navy's report of the incident, the ship had been lying to the northward of the swept channel.[5] She sank slowly in seven fathoms, coming to rest on the sea bed with her superstructure and masts visible at low tide.

The explosions had been heard over a wide area and witnessed by many people in Bangor. A U-boat attack was considered to be a possible cause and anti-submarine trawlers from Belfast and Larne were dispatched to the scene. Evidently sabotage was also thought to be a possibility and a party of soldiers from the 145th Field Regiment, Royal Artillery, who had just arrived in Bangor, were put on board to investigate. However, when it was eventually realized that the explosions had occurred immediately after the ship's engines were started up, acoustically-detonated mines were presumed to be the cause.

Four nights after the *Troutpool* sank, a German 4-engined Focke-Wulf Fw200C Condor aircraft belonging, to the 1st Staffel of Kampfgeschwader 40 (I/KG 40), was loaded with four 500kg LMA sea mines at Brest-Langveoc airfield in Brittany. The destination of the mines was Belfast Lough.

The Condor was being utilized at this early stage for delivering sea mines against the wishes of the unit's commanding officer, Major Edgar Petersen. The aircraft was the Luftwaffe's only 4-engined machine in operational service and Petersen believed that its true role lay in maritime reconnaissance and in support of the U-boat fleet. He was to be proved correct and Kampfgeschwader 40 eventually earned the appellation of 'the scourge of the Atlantic' by no less a person than Winston Churchill.

After the fall of France, the airfield at Bordeaux-Merignac had been chosen as the operational base for I/KG 40. Strategically placed on the Bay of Biscay, it would provide a convenient terminal point for long flights over the Atlantic. For minelaying in the Irish Sea, however, when the fuel load had to be curtailed in order to carry mines weighing 2000 kg, an airfield closer to the target area was necessary. Brest was chosen for the purpose and both I/KG 40 and Kampfgruppe 126 (KGr126), a unit equipped with the twin-engined Heinkel He111H-5, began nightly sorties over the Irish Sea.[6]

The Condor bound for Belfast (identification code F8+BH) took-off at 0030 hours local time (2330 hours BST). It had a crew of five and was commanded by Hauptmann Volkmar Zenker. They had flown a similar sortie on the night of the 19th–20th and, although it cannot be confirmed from the records, there is a strong possibility that theirs was the aircraft observed from the Greypoint gun site and – by the same token – the one responsible for sinking the *Troutpool*.

The flight to the entrance of Belfast Lough seems to have been uneventful. Shortly after 0200 hours, the Condor made its descent through the cloud base to the release point close to Black Head at the southern end of Islandmagee. When the release mechanism was activated, however, only three of the mines left the bomb racks. Zenker immediately opened the throttles fully and made a climbing turn to come round again to try and get rid of the remaining mine.[7] The first drop was, in fact, observed by the gunners at Greypoint and the time logged in the regimental war diary was 0220 hours.[8]

Zenker apparently decided to make the second attempt from the very low level of 15 metres although it was obvious that, from this height, the para-chute would not open. This time, the remaining mine left the racks but when the throttle levers were advanced to climb the aircraft away, both port engines failed to respond and the aircraft yawed violently to the left. At such a low level, Zenker had no time to adjust to this critical situation. He lost control and the aircraft crashed into the sea. Zenker and two of the crew, Unteroffizier Heinz Höcker and Gefreiter Lothar Hohmann, were able to scramble clear with a rubber float but Feldwebel Willi Andreas, aged 26, and Unteroffizier Rudolf Wagner, aged 25, went down with the aircraft. There is no record of their bodies ever being recovered.

Shortly afterwards, the anti-submarine trawler HMT *Paynter* picked up the three survivors close to the Black Head light and landed them at Larne.[9] They were taken to the Olderfleet Hotel, overlooking the harbour, which had been requisitioned by the Naval Officer in Charge at Larne (NOIC) as his headquarters. Under initial interrogation, the prisoners stated that they were members of the crew of an He111 which had been engaged in reconnaissance. The reason for the attempted deception about their aircraft type probably lay in the fact that the Condor was a newcomer to the battlefront and the Germans wanted to conceal its presence as long as possible.

There is nothing in any British record to indicate the exact position where the Condor crashed but the Luftwaffe's daily loss reports[10] put it at '15 miles north-east of Belfast' which would be near to the point where the three airmen were picked up. How the Luftwaffe obtained this information is not known. Although there was little time for it, it is possible that the Condor was able to transmit a distress signal either before it crashed or before it sank. One other aircraft, probably an He111 of KGr126, was minelaying in the Irish Sea area and it may have been aware of the incident. At 0257 hours, three-quarters of an hour after the Condor crashed, the RAF Wireless Intelligence unit (known as 'Y' Service) intercepted a message on the frequency 4665 kilocycles (kc/s), transmitted either to or from Zwischenahn Radio in North-ern Germany, which read 'attentions aircraft in distress at sea'.[11]

Petersen was angered by the loss of another of his valuable aeroplanes (the second in two weeks) and another experienced crew along with it. He protested again to General Hans Jeschonnek, the Chief of the Air Staff, and this time he was successful. The Condors were withdrawn from minelaying and deployed in an increasing number of low-level attacks on shipping, most of them close to the Irish coast.

The mining of Belfast Lough and the approaches to it nevertheless continued unabated. It was something that was very difficult, if not impossible, to counter. Single aircraft broke through the cloud base without warning, dropped their mines and climbed out over the sea in a matter of minutes. Three aircraft were known to be operating on the night of 27 July. The following day, a mine was exploded off Whitehead by the minesweeper *Souvenir* and two days later another was dealt with a mile and a half off Greypoint. It was clear that the Germans had now identified the anchorage at Bangor as a terminal point for convoys.

The threat posed by this aerial mining was all too obvious and the three Belfast-based minesweepers *Gloamin*, *Harvest Reaper* and *Jewel* were reinforced. By the end of July, at least six were operating, including the magnetic ship *Burlington* and three converted net drifters, *Ocean Swell*, *Norbreeze* and *Pecheur*.

Enemy action was not confined to laying mines but the public was largely insulated from these hostile activities by a censor who might have been vigilant but not always consistent. On 27 July, the *Belfast News Letter* contained an item, based on eyewitness reports, about an air attack on a convoy. Residents of a Co. Down seaside town (it was, in fact, Bangor) were awakened the previous morning by heavy gunfire, a few miles from the shore. RAF fighters were seen making for the scene. However, in the following day's issue, it was stated (probably under instructions) that authoritative sources in London had denied that there was any truth in the report. The newspaper peevishly pointed out that the report had been based on the statements of reputable persons and that, in any event, the censor had passed it.

Eight hundred kilometres due east of Belfast, at the former Dutch military airfield of Soesterberg, near Utrecht, a Luftwaffe bomber group forming part of Kampfgeschwader 4 was assigned, as one of its tasks, the mining of Belfast Lough and its approaches. After completing an intensive course of training on aerial mining techniques at Varel, near the Baltic coast, I Gruppe began operating from Soesterberg in the middle of July 1940.

In the context of aircraft performance at this early stage of the war, Belfast was a long way from Soesterberg and, not for the last time, the Luftwaffe would regret the lack of a 4-engined bomber such as the RAF would soon put into service. The aircraft with which I Gruppe was equipped was the twin-engined H-4 variant of the Heinkel He111. It was a reliable aeroplane, popular with the crews, but when loaded with 2000 kg of mines or bombs, along with full fuel tanks and a crew of four, its range limitations could become critical when attacking targets 800 kilometres away.

The mines, which were of two types, the 500kg LMA and the 1000kg LMB, were slung externally under the fuselage. The heavy all-up weight made take-off precarious and every metre of the long runways at Soesterberg was needed to attain the speed of 150 km/h (90 mph) at which the aircraft left the ground. After take-off, the rate of climb was little more than 50 metres per minute.

When these missions started, crews were under instructions to bring the mines back if the target was not found or if a serious technical fault made it impossible to continue. The mines were certainly valuable but it soon became apparent that following these orders could lead to disaster. On 1 August, the day after I Gruppe had completed its move to Soesterberg, an aircraft which had been unable to find the assigned dropping zone returned with its two 1000kg mines still on board. The pilot made a heavy landing and the undercarriage collapsed. The mines were thrown clear by the impact and the timing mechanism activated. A devastating explosion threatened but the Gruppe's ordnance officer, one Leutnant Honey, immediately set to work and was said to have defused the mines with minutes to spare.

As a result of this and other emergencies, aircraft returning with mines were in future to drop them into Aalsmeer Lake, just outside the boundary of Schiphol airport at Amsterdam, for possible recovery.[12] For its part, the RAF gave notice of future problems that the minelayers would encounter. On the night of 2 August, a lone Blenheim swooped through the low cloud and dropped a few bombs on the airfield, badly damaging three aircraft and injuring five airmen.

A few nights later, on 7 August, an He111 commanded by Leutnant Artur Zeiss with a crew of three, took off with two 1000kg mines for Belfast Lough.[13] At about 0130 hours BST, while on a gradual descent to the release point, the aircraft hit the summit of the 2331-foot Cairnsmore of Fleet in Kirkcudbrightshire. It disintegrated and all four on board died instantly. The exact cause of the accident is not known but clearly the aircraft should not have been at such a low altitude at that stage of the approach.

On the night of 11/12 August, a mine was seen from Greypoint to explode prematurely in mid-air. A report from FOIC Liverpool to his counterpart in Belfast at this time advised that the minelayers invariably came from an easterly direction, thus suggesting that I/KG 4 was now chiefly responsible for the mines being laid in the approaches to Belfast. The navy's records reveal that this activity intensified markedly in August. There was scarcely a night when enemy aircraft were not over the lough. Nevertheless, the rigidly controlled media saw to it that the public at large had no inkling of what was going on. Knowledge that German bombers were able to mine Belfast Lough would have led to the realization that the city itself was within range. As yet, the popular notion was that this was not feasible.

The daily entries in the log of the FOIC Belfast as September opened indicate that the danger to shipping in the lough showed no sign of abating. In the first ten days, six mines were detected and detonated. However, intensive sweeping seems to have brought some improvement for the FOIC's summary for the period 1–14 September recorded that vessels might now anchor in safety within a specified area off Kilroot on the northern side of the lough as well as in Bangor Bay.[14]

There was now a noticeable increase in hostile air activity by day as well. It was no accident that this coincided with I/KG 40's withdrawal from minelaying operations. The unit's fortunes in the long Battle of the Atlantic would inevitably be linked to Ireland. The island occupied a pivotal position in German anti-shipping operations throughout the war. Measured against the comparatively small number of aircraft involved at any one time its losses were heavy. Some of the crews are buried in the republic and many others were interned there after their aircraft had crashed on Irish soil or in the surrounding waters.

One early casualty was the Condor commanded by Oberleutnant Kurt Mollenhauer. On 20 August 1940, Mollenhauer became disoriented in bad weather off the west coast of Ireland. While flying in cloud and without any warning, the aircraft ground to a stop in level flight on the slopes of Mount Brandon in Co. Kerry. It had, in effect, made an unintentional wheels-up landing. In the field of aviation accidents it would be difficult to imagine a more bizarre happening. Mollenhauer and the co-pilot Stabsfeldwebel Robert Beumer suffered only minor injuries and along with the rest of the crew became the first German airmen to be interned in the Curragh in the Second World War.

PERIL IN HOME WATERS

Attacks on vessels off the Ulster coast escalated significantly in September. On the fifth, a Condor bombed the Greek-registered *Aedeon* close to the entrance of Belfast Lough causing some damage. A week later, another Condor dropped what are presumed to be the first bombs to fall on Northern Ireland soil since the outbreak of war. (In an obscure incident which was said to have occurred on 30 June, two bombs from an He111 aimed at harbour installations in Belfast had apparently fallen into the harbour basin or into the adjoining lough.) Against the background of the Battle of Britain, which was now reaching its climax, the incident was relatively unimportant. It was, however, symptomatic of the menacing trend in the war at sea. Once the Germans had become aware that the Royal Navy had mined the southern reaches of the Irish Sea the North Channel was quickly identified as Britain's most important waterway. The U-boats and Focke-Wulf Condors were deployed accordingly.

In the early hours of 13 September, ships of convoy HX 70 from Halifax, Nova Scotia dropped anchor in Bangor Bay after what the navy described as an uneventful crossing of the Atlantic. Its arrival was nevertheless known to the enemy. During the hours of darkness, the RAF's 'Y' service monitors had been following the progress of a Luftwaffe *Zenit* flight (call-sign L7L) which had been in two-way communication with its base at Bordeaux-Merignac. A *Zenit* flight was one which combined weather reconnaissance with surveillance or low-level attacks on shipping. The aircraft in question (the name of its commander is not recorded in the Luftwaffe records) was airborne at Bordeaux at 0104 hours BST.[1] Its task was 'armed and weather reconnaissance to the north and west of Ireland.' In addition to the residue of HX 70, there were ships waiting to join the outbound Halifax convoy OB 213, the main body of which was just leaving Liverpool. Among the latter was the Ellerman Lines flagship *City of Benares* (11081 tons) with 406 passengers on board, including 100 children being evacuated to Canada. The *City of Benares* was fated to become the focal point of one of the most infamous episodes of the Battle of the Atlantic. On 17 September, when approximately 450 miles west of Donegal, she was sunk by torpedoes from *U-48*, at that time under the command of Kapitänleutnant Heinrich Bleichrodt. Two hundred and fifty-six people on the ship were lost. One of the escort destroyers, HMS *Hurricane*, picked up 105 survivors the following day. Eight days later, on 25 September, the remaining survivors in lifeboats were sighted by a Sunderland flying boat of 10 Squadron, Royal Australian Air Force. The information was passed to another Sunderland of 210 Squadron, which directed the destroyer HMS *Anthony* to the scene. A further 45 people were rescued in this way but the harrowing story of how many children had died from exposure in the open boats (only seven out of the 100 survived) provoked a wave of revulsion and anger throughout Britain.[2] Bleichrodt himself was said to have been shocked and distressed when he learned the consequences of his action. In his book *Humanity in the war at sea*, the German naval historian Helmut Schmoeckel writes:

> Although no reproach could be levelled against him in international law (the ship was armed and sailing in an escorted convoy) Bleichrodt suffered much in later years as a result of his sinking of this childrens' transport. This came out again and again in conversations with colleagues.

The incident formed the basis of one of the charges of war crimes brought against Admiral Doenitz before the Nuremberg International Military Tribunal after the war but Schmoeckel also cites another, later incident involving Bleichrodt when he was in command of a different U-boat. On 6 September 1942, the *Tuscan Star*, 11449 tons (Blue Star Line), was sunk off the coast of West Africa by *U-109*. Schmoeckel writes that in 1984 he had correspondence with a surviving crew member of the *Tuscan Star* who recalled that after the sinking Bleichrodt brought the U-boat alongside lifeboats containing survivors and gave them tinned milk and food and advised them of the course they should steer to reach the coast. The U-boat's bo'sun was said to have dived into the water to rescue the freighter's badly injured wireless operator. He was taken on board the submarine where he was given medical attention and eventually landed in France.

More than half a century later, it is possible to view the sinking of the *City of Benares* as a tragic but unintended consequence of total war but at the time it appeared that the conflict was descending to the level of barbarism.

According to the Luftwaffe account of the events of 13 September at Bangor the Condor arrived over the entrance to Belfast Lough between 0700 and 0710 hours BST. It then seems to have flown south and attacked the anti-submarine trawler, HMT *Arctic Pioneer* with machine-gun fire, five kilometres east of Ballywalter. A few minutes later, it turned its attention to the ships anchored in Bangor Bay. The Royal Navy's record gives no details of the number of ships present but the Condor's crew reported that there were 35 cargo vessels, 10 destroyers and '3 fast guard ships'. An armed cargo

3 The sinking of the *City of Benares* shocked world opinion

ship of approximately 6,000 tons was singled out for attack with four SC250 kg bombs. One bomb was seen to fall about two metres from the ship and some damage was presumed. No other damage could be observed from the aircraft because of heavy defensive fire.

The attack was clearly seen from the shore. One witness said that he saw a pilot boat go out to one of the ships and after the pilot had gone on board an aircraft came out of the clouds and dropped a bomb which missed its mark. The aircraft then came back and dropped another bomb which came much closer and shook the vessel.[3] Another witness stated that, after the attack on the ship, the machine flew across the seafront in the direction of Bangor railway station. As this witness watched, he saw an object fall from the aircraft but unaccountably disappear in mid-air.[4] What he had seen was almost certainly an *Abwurf* container for incendiary bombs. The Luftwaffe used the container in a variety of sizes. An example frequently encountered held twenty-four 2kg incendiaries. It was of light alloy construction and contained a small explosive charge which was set to blow it apart at a predetermined height above the ground. It could be aimed and the effect was calculated to prevent the bombs falling over a wide area. On this occasion, several bombs fell in the forecourt of the station and in business premises in Main Street causing some damage.

The Ministry of Public Security report of the incident stated that 22 incendiary bombs had fallen and that after the attack the aircraft flew towards Clandeboye where it turned in the direction of Newtownards. As soon as the attack had commenced, three Hurricane fighters of 245 Squadron at Alder-grove were scrambled but, not surprisingly, by the time they had arrived over Bangor there was no sign of the raider.[5] An hour and a half later, at 0835 hours, a message was intercepted, probably from the same aircraft, in which an attack was reported on a medium-sized cargo vessel a few miles south-west of the Ailsa Craig, off the Ayrshire coast.

German air activity round the coast of Northern Ireland was now only limited by the number of available Focke-Wulf Condors. While the Helll and the Ju88 had the range to reach the area, they did not have the endurance to carry out a protracted search for targets. Only the Condors could do this and provide the U-boats lurking outside the North Channel with adequate information about convoys forming in the Irish Sea and Admiral Karl Doenitz, the commander of the U-boat fleet, was continually calling for more of them.

As darkness fell on the evening of 15 September, the British India Steam Navigation Company's passenger-cargo liner *Aska* (8,323 tons) was coming within sight of the coast of Donegal on the final stage of a voyage from West Africa to Liverpool. She had left Bathhurst (now Banjul) on 7 September with general cargo and 350 French colonial troops, some of whom wanted to

4 The *Aska*, attacked while rounding Rathlin Island

join the Free Free French forces in Britain. The remainder wished to be repatriated to France.[6]

The ship was capable of making 20 knots and considered fast enough to travel alone. The voyage was uneventful until the morning of 15 September, when a position due south-west of Ireland had been reached. A submarine's periscope was sighted but no attempt at an attack was made which was probably due to the sudden appearance of an RAF patrol aircraft. The ship continued on a northerly course and passed Malin Head some time after midnight. At about 0200 hours, she passed north of Rathlin Island and entered the North Channel.

Earlier in the evening two Focke-Wulf Condors had taken off from Bordeaux-Merignac on armed reconnaissance over the Irish Sea. One was airborne at 1940 hours BST. The aircraft commander's identity is not known but the second aircraft, which was airborne at 1949 hours,[7] was commanded by Oberleutnant Fritz Fliegel, the Staffelkapitän, or squadron leader, of 2nd Staffel I/KG 40. Fliegel's mission report states that between 0130 and 0140 hours BST, he sighted a large passenger steamer close to Rathlin Island, steering a course of approximately 160 degrees. Visibility was good and he attacked it with two SC250kg bombs and saw one hit the foredeck and the other the afterdeck. This standard of accuracy was common in this type of low-level attack. Instead of a conventional bomb-sight operated by a bomb-aimer, the pilot himself lined the target up through a simple device on the nose of the aircraft called a '*Revi* sight'. The ship was approached diagonally from the stern at little more than mast height and presented such a large target (so large that the German crews christened it the *Steckrübe* or 'turnip tactic') that at least one direct hit was probable. As merchant ships became more heavily armed however the tactic became increasingly hazardous. Condor losses became unsustainable and this method was abandoned.

On board the *Aska*, the Condor had been seen approaching from the direction of the Maiden's Rocks in a zigzagging fashion. It was at first thought to be friendly but almost immediately two heavy calibre bombs hit the ship. Although Fliegel's report simply stated that two bombs were dropped, the *Aska*'s master said that the aircraft in fact made two separate passes over the ship, dropping one bomb in each. The first exploded just above the engine room after which a fierce fire broke out. According to the master's report, six European crew members, including the third and fourth engineers, were killed in the explosion together with six Indian seamen.

Several of the numerous vessels in the area went to the assistance of the stricken ship,[8] including the minesweeper *Jason* which later signalled that she had 440 survivors on board. The Dutch motor vessel *Prinses Irene* rescued a further 25 and landed them at Larne. The anti-submarine trawler *St Zeno* had 18 survivors on board but was ordered to remain in the vicinity as the burning vessel constituted a serious danger to shipping. She drifted helplessly in a north-westerly direction and finally ran aground on Cara Island.

About 30 minutes after the attack on the *Aska*, the other Condor, which had also been operating over the North Channel, flew past the burning ship in a southerly direction. South of Portpatrick, the crew sighted a destroyer and a submarine travelling north-west on a course of 330 degrees. They were ignored as merchant ships were considered of greater importance to the British war economy and thus more worthy of attack. A few minutes later, however, at 0215 hours, the Condor made out the shapes of two ships steaming south in a position 13 kilometres east of Ballyquintin Point at the southern tip of the Ards Peninsula. One was a large freighter and the other a destroyer. The cargo vessel was in fact the Ellerman Line *City of Mobile* (6,124 tons) en route from Glasgow to Liverpool with military and general stores, including 30 tons of petroleum as deck cargo. She had been ordered to sail close to the Irish coast in order to stay clear of a northbound convoy out of Liverpool. The destroyer was HMS *Sabre*.

The Condor made a single pass over the freighter, dropping one bomb which hit the stern. The German crew report filed on return to Bordeaux stated that the effect was not observed but damage was presumed. This claim proved to be modest as the blow turned out to be a mortal one. At 0220 hours, the *Sabre* radioed that the freighter was sinking and that immediate assistance was required. A short time later, FOIC Belfast confirmed that the ship had sunk in 48 fathoms but that the crew of thirty-two had been rescued by the fishing trawler *Skikker*.

The movement of shipping in the waters around the north of Ireland was now fraught with danger. Just over 24 hours after the sinking of the *Aska* and the *City of Mobile*, the Greek-registered *Kalliopi* (5132 tons) was hit by two bombs from a Condor at 0530 hours on the 17th as she rounded Tory Island off the Donegal coast. She was a straggler from the convoy HX 70 which had arrived in Bangor on the 13th and which had earlier been reported by the FOIC Belfast as having suffered no losses. Once again, the Dutch *Prinses Irene* appears to have been on hand and she landed the *Kalliopi*'s master and 28 of her crew at Londonderry. When last seen, the ship was still afloat and the records do not say whether she subsequently sank. This incident was an early and ominous sign that the German leadership had reappraised its policy toward neutral vessels. This development would have particular significance for ships flying the Irish flag which by force of circumstance were unable to avoid sailing into and out of British ports.

On 26 September, the crew of a Condor engaged in surveillance witnessed what was an historic event as five First World War US destroyers, *Caldwell*, *Campbelltown*, *Castleton*, *Chelsea* and *Clare*, flying the White Ensign, sailed into Belfast to tie up in the Victoria Channel. They were the first of fifty destroyers delivered to Britain under what was known as the 'Destroyers-for-Bases Deal'.[9] In return, the United States received 99-year leases of land in Newfoundland, Bermuda and the Caribbean for the purpose of establishing naval and air bases. Although the ships were old, they were fast and and could be used as convoy escorts. Sorely needed, they left Belfast for Plymouth the next day to take up operational duties.

Viewed in retrospect, September 1940 would prove to be a watershed in the year when Britain fought alone for survival. As the month ended, there was no way then of knowing that the great daylight battles in the skies over Southern England would not be repeated. What was known, however, was that the Luftwaffe's aura of invincibility had been seriously blemished. Neither was it known that the alarming losses in shipping would begin to show a slight (but temporary) decline. In June, 125 vessels representing 571496 tons of British, Allied and neutral ships had been lost. In September, a total of 90 ships representing 442634 tons, had been sunk by enemy action. Although the number of ships sunk in October rose to 97, the gross tonnage showed a fall and by December the loss totalled 357314 tons.[10]

In the context of the Battle of the Atlantic, the Irish Sea assumed unparalleled importance for Britain when shipping using her east coast ports became hopelessly vulnerable to air attack from newly-established German air bases in France and the Low Countries. A minefield laid from Cornwall to the Irish coast as an anti-invasion measure meant that ocean-going traffic using ports on the west coast had to be routed northabout through the North Channel, that narrow stretch of water separating Scotland from Northern Ireland. In a minute dated 5 August 1940, in which he urged the Admiralty to pursue the laying of the minefield, Churchill said that the sector of the Irish Sea from Cornwall north to the Mull of Kintyre could henceforth be considered the least vulnerable to seaborne invasion. This enabled the land-based defences to be concentrated on areas more directly threatened.

In August and September, public attention in Britain and throughout the world was fixed on the titanic air battles being fought over Southern England but in the waters to the north and west of Ireland an equally dire threat was taking shape. It took the form of a recapitulation of the submarine menace of the First World War.

Its proximity to the North Channel assured Northern Ireland's place in the history of the Battle of the Atlantic but after the fall of France the true scale of the appalling shipping losses had to be concealed in order to limit the acute public anxiety at Britain's sudden isolation. It is only when the contemporary British and German records are analysed that the ferocity of the battle close to the shores of Ireland and the suffering it occasioned can be grasped.

In the autumn of 1940, one other related factor made these waters the focal point of the war at sea. The German U-boat fleet at this early stage was largely composed of the smaller short-range Type II boats of 250 tons whose optimum operating range coincided with the North West Approaches. The larger medium-range Type VIIs were Doenitz's most effective weapon but there were not enough of them.

Promoted to Konteradmiral (Rear Admiral), in 1939, Karl Doenitz was to play a dominant role in the war at sea. He had been a submariner in the First World War and had seen at first hand how an island nation such as Britain could be brought to the brink of starvation by underwater warfare. In the 1930s he had advocated the creation of a U-boat fleet of 300 boats but he was frustrated in this by the traditionalists in the German Navy who continued to see the need as one for surface ships. The result was that Doenitz went to war in 1939 with 57 boats, approximately two-thirds of which only were operational.[11] In view of the havoc caused by a force of this size in the winter of 1940/41, Doenitz's failure to achieve his original target had fortunate consequences for Britain.

The initial successes of the U-boat fleet were dramatic enough but the fall of France opened up a whole range of new opportunities. All the approaches to the British Isles were now within easy reach of the coast of Brittany where Doenitz speedily established fortified bases for his boats. This advantage, which had fortuitously fallen into his lap, was accompanied by a radical change in German policy which would have serious consequences for seafarers of all nationalities trading with Britain.

The destructive power of the submarine had been demonstrated in the First World War and in 1930 the principal maritime powers (not including Germany) attempted to address the threat. On 22 April of that year the International Treaty for the Limitation and Reduction of Naval Armaments[12] was concluded. The measure was principally concerned with surface vessels and armaments, but Part IV dealt with the conduct of submarine warfare. It provided that a warship was not entitled to sink or render incapable of navigation a merchant ship unless the crew, passengers and ship's papers were first placed in a place of safety. The ship's lifeboats were not to be regarded as a place of safety unless the safety of the passengers and crew was assured, in the existing sea and weather conditions, by the proximity of land or the presence of another vessel which was in a position to take them on board.

The Treaty was not ratified by all the signatories but the insidious threat posed by the submarine was considered to be sufficiently important to make a further attempt to reach agreement. Accordingly, the Treaty was superseded by a Protocol entitled 'Procès-Verbal relating to the Rules of Submarine Warfare'[13] which was signed in London on 6 November 1936. Its sole provision was a repetition of Part IV of the Treaty and the declared intention was that it should have the force of international law. The signatories were the same powers which had subscribed to the earlier accord but the United

Kingdom government was expressly requested to invite the accession of those powers which had not signed the Treaty. An invitation extended to Germany was formally accepted and she became bound in international law. However, in spite of its well-intentioned motivation the measure was naive and unworkable.

When war broke out the German Navy's actions against merchant ships were also governed by a code of its own known as the *Prisenordnung*[14] (formulated on 28 August 1939) which was based on the ancient doctrine of prize, that is, the seizure of ships and their cargoes at sea in time of war. Provided they were unarmed, the rules applied to the ships of belligerents and those of neutrals which were making for enemy harbours or into enemy waters. The use of weapons against a ship was forbidden until a prize crew had first been put on board and had ascertained the nature of the cargo and its destination. However, sailing in a convoy was regarded as a hostile act, as was travelling at night without lights or zigzagging. Adopting any of these measures would remove immunity.

In the early days of the war, the commanders of German surface ships and U-boats by and large acted correctly and observed the terms of both the London Protocol and the rules relating to prize. However, in the case of submarines, there was no solution to the problem of how to place the crew and passengers in a safe place. Unlike surface ships, there was no room to take them on board. In practice, the ship was ordered to stop and they were simply allowed to take to the boats before it was sunk. There were some infamous exceptions to the general rule, however. One took place on 3 September 1939, the very day that Britain declared war, when Oberleutnant Fritz-Julius Lemp in *U-30* sank the passenger liner *Athenia*, 13582 tons (Donaldson Line) en route to Montreal with the loss of 112 lives. Lemp's explanation was that the liner had been sailing on a zigzag course without lights and that he had mistaken her for an armed merchant cruiser.

For the second time in 25 years, Germany saw Britain's dependence on overseas trade as her greatest weakness and sought to exploit it to the full. But to continue to wage the war at sea in accordance with international law and usage would be too long-drawn out to fit in with Hitler's plans. On 1 August 1940, he issued instructions for the intensification of the sea and air war by imposing a complete blockade on all shipping trading with Britain. The orders were embodied in an order of the High Command (*Weisung Nr. 17*) and one of its most far-reaching provisions was the effect that it would have on ships of neutral countries. It would, of course, have made nonsense of the blockade if neutral ships were to be allowed to continue entering and leaving British ports. Accordingly, with effect from 17 August, a large area of the waters surrounding the British Isles westward to the 20 degrees meridian (approximately 350 nautical miles west of Ireland) were declared to be an area where all ships would be subject to attack without warning. Many neutral countries could choose to avoid the area but Irish ships, for obvious reasons, had no such choice.

In common with other neutrals, Irish ships had to comply with the British *Navicert* system. This meant that if they were sailing between Ireland and countries other than Britain they had to obtain a *Navicert* which entailed calling at a designated British port (Bangor was one of them) for examination. Germany regarded any use of the *Navicert* procedure as a hostile act and on 17 September the Naval War Staff (Sk1) declared:

> Germany takes the view that in international law the provision and acceptance of English navicerts is to be regarded as an unneutral act in support of the belligerent which utilizes them. On the grounds of political expediency (the political necessity of special treatment of the USA) neutrals are not to be notified of this interpretation of the law.
>
> Operational units including those engaged further afield will therefore be issued with guide-lines for dealing with neutral ships with English navicerts.[15]

In concealing his intentions, Hitler had shrunk from incurring the wrath of the United States which would certainly have reacted violently to the sinking of its merchant ships. However, small countries like Eire would now be treated as belligerents.

All neutral countries had been notified that *Weisung Nr.17* would come into effect on 17 August and in little more than two weeks an Irish ship became a victim of the spread of hostilities. On 4 September the Limerick Steamship Company's *Luimneach*, 1074 tons, was stopped by a U-boat travelling on the surface 260 miles south of Kinsale. The ship was on the way from Huelva in Spain to Drogheda with a cargo of iron pyrites and had the word 'Eire' painted in large letters on her side.[15] The U-boat, which was the *U-46*, was commanded by Oberleutnant zur See Englebert Endrass and two shots were fired across the *Luimneach*'s bows. The crew was ordered to take to the boats and after they were clear the ship was sunk by gunfire. According to the submarine's war diary, Endrass gave the crew provisions along with tobacco and a bottle of rum for each of the two lifeboats. The survivors were picked up by a French trawler two days later and eventually arrived home by way of Spain and Liverpool. In view of the fact that not only had the ship been neutral but that it had been en route from one neutral country to another, its sinking was contrary to international law but with the introduction of their new directive the Germans would have argued that there was no guarantee that the cargo would not have been transshipped to a British port. In fact, Doenitz subsequently confirmed that the U-boat captain had acted in accordance with standing instructions.

3

AN ORDER TO SCATTER

As September progressed, the outlook for Britain looked bleak as shipping losses in the North West Approaches rose alarmingly. A relatively small number of U-boats was causing an altogether disproportionate amount of destruction. The war diary of the Skl indicates that on a typical day no more than six boats may have been in the operational area with a further six either heading for it or back to their bases for refuelling and rearming.[1] The Admiralty reports on inbound and outbound convoys shows that there was no lack of targets for them.

On 18 September, Luftwaffe air reconnaissance reported that a convoy, presumed to be HX 71, had been sighted 300 nautical miles west of the Hebrides and heading for the North Channel. It consisted of 31 cargo ships, two destroyers and four other escort vessels. The Skl diary entry for the following day makes no mention of this convoy but discloses that five U-boats (*U-43*, *U-48*, *U-65*, *U-99* and *U-100*) were being deployed for an attack on another homeward-bound convoy sighted by *U-47*, 540 miles west of the Hebrides. The story of the remainder of this convoy's voyage says a great deal about the precarious state of Britain's lifeline at the time.

In his book, *The Second World War*, Winston Churchill revealed his fears about the course of the war at sea:

> The week ending 22 September showed the highest rate of loss since the beginning of the war and was in fact greater than any we had suffered in a similar period in 1917. Twenty-seven ships, of nearly 160,000 tons were sunk, many of them in a Halifax convoy.[2]

Churchill's deep concern was based on a report he had received from the Commander-in-Chief, Western Approaches dated 15 October 1940. This report, which drew on information supplied by FOIC Belfast, read:

> The most serious loss of ships in convoy since the beginning of the war occurred when 12 out of 42 ships were lost. This was scarcely compensated for by the possible destruction of one U-boat.[3]

The convoy in question was the HX 72, the main section of which,

5 Admiral Karl Doenitz

comprising 21 ships, left Halifax, Nova Scotia, at 1430 hours on 9 September. It was joined by 11 ships of the Sydney (Nova Scotia) section on the eleventh and by a further 11 of the Bermuda section on the thirteenth. The total was reduced to 42 when one ship had to turn back for an undisclosed reason. Based on the average speed of all the ships, the convoy travelled at seven and a half knots. Its local escorts were the destroyer HMCS *Saguanay* and the patrol vessel HMCS *French*. The armed merchant cruiser HMS *Jervis Bay* would provide the ocean escort until UK-based warships could take over protection. Less than two months later, the *Jervis Bay*, under the command of Captain Fogarty Fegan RN engaged the German pocket-battleship *Admiral Scheer* in an gallant act of self-sacrifice in order to protect convoy HX 84. She was sunk with the loss of more than 200 officers and men. Fegan was postumously awarded the Victoria Cross.

The U-boat which first made visual contact with the convoy was *U-47* under the command of none other than Korvettenkapitän Günther Prien who had achieved fame early in the war when he sank the battleship *Royal Oak* in Scapa Flow on 14 October 1939. Prien received orders from U-boat head-quarters (BdU) at Lorient by radio to shadow the convoy and report its progress until the other boats reached the area.[4] He was approaching the end of his seventh war cruise which had commenced on 28 August. During it he had sunk six ships and he had now no torpedoes left.

According to German records, the first attack on the convoy was made by Bleichrodt's *U-48* on the evening of the twentieth. The freighters *Broompark* (5136 tons, J.& J. Denholm) and *Blairangus* (4409 tons, G. Nisbet & Co) were both torpedoed but only the latter sank.[5] A position report earlier in the day from *U-47* had been monitored by *U-99*. This boat was commanded by an officer who was probably the most famous of all the U-boat commanders of the Second World War, Otto Kretschmer. On learning that the convoy was steaming in a south-easterly direction at 7 knots, Kretschmer estimated that he could intercept it around midnight. The U-boat's war diary describes what followed:

0125   Convoy in sight, emerging from a squall. The moon is on the wrong side of the boat. When the moon is obscured by a dark cloud an attack is made on the largest ship, a tanker. During the attack the moon again appears so that the torpedo will have to be fired from a greater range.

0212   Single torpedo from 1350 metres. Direct hit for'ard. Tanker veers away from the convoy and stops, sinking for'ard with fo'c'sle down to waterline. Crew leaving. A coup de grace will probably be required. It emerges that she is the *Invershannon* (9154 tons).

0319   Single torpedo at a heavily-laden freighter from 580 metres.
Direct hit amidships. Ship breaks in two and sinks in 40 seconds.
It is the *Baron Blythwood* (3668 tons), with, as later established, a
cargo of iron ore.

0347   Single torpedo at the largest freighter from 1,000 metres. Direct
hit amidships. Ship veers away and stops with heavy list to
starboard. She transmits her name and position by radio. She is
the *Elmbank* (5156 tons).[6]

All *U-99's* torpedos had been fired when the submarine had been on the
surface and according to the Admiralty's report of the attack no escort vessel
was present at the time.

The circumstances surrounding the sinking of the *Elmbank* and *Invershannon* as recorded in Kretschmer's journal have an element of farce about them.
The *Elmbank* had been bound for Belfast with a cargo of timber, some of which
was being carried as deck cargo. After the crew had taken to the lifeboats and
were clear of the ship, Kretschmer decided to sink her by gunfire. He fired 41
shells into her but she refused to sink. While this was going on, Prien arrived
in *U-47*. He joined in but had no more success than Kretschmer and after
expending his remaining ammunition he set course back to Lorient.
Kretschmer then realized that the ship was floating on its own cargo of timber
and he decided to use another torpedo. This was defective, however, and ran
too close to the surface before hitting some of the floating timber and exploding
harmlessly. Totally exasperated, Kretschmer then returned to the *Invershannon* which was now half-submerged. All the ammunition for his deck gun had
been exhausted and his 2 cm anti-aircraft gun proved useless.

The Admiralty records relating to the incident contain a statement from
the second officer of the *Invershannon*.[7] He said that *U-99* came alongside his
lifeboat and Kretschmer told him that he was going to put men on board to
set time fuses. He later heard two explosions from the side of the tanker furthest
away from him and assumed that this had in fact been done. Kretschmer's account
makes no mention of the conversation with the second officer but confirms
that he intended to put time-bombs on board. He sent his first officer and a
seaman in a dinghy to board the vessel but the dinghy overturned and they
had to be rescued. Another torpedo was then fired and although it, too,
surfaced several times before it reached the target, it hit the tanker amidships.
Loud explosions followed and the ship began to break up and sink. There was
still the *Elmbank* to attend to and on returning to the scene, Kretschmer found
that she was still afloat. He used his last torpedo and saw the ship sink stern
first. It was 1510 hours on the afternoon of 21 September and, with all his
ammunition gone, Kretschmer set course for Lorient at the end of an operational cruise lasting 23 days during which he had sunk a total of eleven ships.

6 Otto Kretschmer

The second attack on HX 72 came soon after the onset of darkness on the 21st. The Admiralty narrative records that the convoy now consisted of 36 ships and that at 2000 hours its position was 280 miles west of Aran Island.[8] After Prien's departure, Doenitz's headquarters (BdU) ordered *U-100* to take over the duty of shadower. She was commanded by another of the outstanding U-boat captains of the war, the charismatic Joachim Schepke. In his first war cruise as commander of *U-100* he had sunk seven ships belonging to convoys, HX 65, HX 66 and OB 205. He had left Lorient on his tenth cruise on 11 September. When he first sighted the convoy, late on the twenty-first, Schepke estimated that it was approximately 300 miles due west of Malin Head. His war diary takes up the story:

2150   Silhouette of convoy in sight. Boat is on its starboard side. In order to get inside the convoy I decided first to create a gap. Attack on the three largest ships. Explosions clearly seen from first three hits. The fourth shot (Tube 5) hit a 4–5000 ton steamer which quickly sank. The tanker *Torinia* was among the first three. The other two steamers were of a similar size *Canonesa – Dalcairn*.

2225   Shot from Tube 4. Missed. Three tubes immediately reloaded.

2322   Torpedo at tanker. Hit after 105 seconds. *Empire Airman*.

2323   Torpedo at steamer. Missed.

2350   Torpedo at steamer. Hit after 53 seconds. Steamer burning. *Scholar*. Turned back toward the foremost column and reloaded.

0053   Double shot at tanker. After 65 seconds first hit for'ard, second aft. Two very violent explosions, massive tongue of flame and the deck completely splits open. I personally have never seen such a violent and imposing direct hit. The ship sinks stern first very quickly. *Frederick S. Fales*.

0114   Torpedo at freighter. Explosion after seconds. Direct hit for'ard. Despite its great size the ship slides under bow first and soon disappears. *Simla*.

0157   Torpedo fired from Tube 1. (Last torpedo) – Missed. Ship turned away. Torpedo wake passes about 30 metres in front. Suddenly the steamer begins to shoot. We are lying stationary behind him in the moonlight at 600 metres range. The shot passes over conning tower. I turn away with full power and rudder. The ship fires very slowly. The next shot falls short and the third goes over and wide. After this he stops firing.[9]

7 Kapitänleutnant Joachim Schepke who was killed in action on 17 March 1941

All his torpedoes expended, Schepke terminated his patrol and set course for Lorient where he arrived late on 25 September. In a period of 4 hours he had sunk seven ships* from convoy HX 72. It was a remarkable achievement but he seems to have met no opposition from escorting warships. The merchant ship that had fired on him was the only opposition he had encountered. It was, in fact, the convoy commodore's vessel, the *Harlingen* (5415 tons, J. & C. Harrison).

At first light, it was found that several ships had strayed from the convoy and were now very vulnerable. One such ship was the *Pacific Grove* (7117 tons, Furness Withy) which was located by the escorting sloop *Lowestoft* and ordered to proceed to Belfast forthwith. A short distance away, the freighter *Collegian* (7886 tons), which had witnessed the sinking of five ships during the previous two nights was attacked by a U-boat 220 miles west of Erris Head. Oberleutnant z. S. Hans Jenisch in *U-32* had only just arrived in the operational area a few hours earlier with orders to seek out HX 72. According to the convoy commodore's report, it was 0550 hours when a U-boat on the surface opened fire on him with its deck gun. The *Collegian* immediately turned its stern towards the source of the fire in order to present a smaller target The U-boat fired a total of 25 shells none of which seem to have hit the ship which replied with 10 rounds from its own gun. In their respective reports of the engagement both the U-boat and the freighter agree on the number of shots exchanged but Jenisch stated that he had also fired one torpedo which missed.

There was now intense activity among escort vessels in the vicinity. The *Collegian*'s SOS had brought no less than four warships to the scene, the destroyers *Skate* and *Shakari* along with the corvettes *Lowestoft* and *Heartease*.[10] A depth charge attack was launched but the submarine escaped by diving to 60 metres and making off in a westerly direction. The *Collegian* escaped in the confusion and proceeded to Belfast.

Shortly afterwards, the *Skate* in company with another destroyer, the *Scimitar*, picked up 45 survivors from the *Scholar*. Not far away, the destroyers sighted another of Schepke's victims, the tanker *Torinia*, which was lying stationary with her back broken. Fifty-seven survivors from her were also taken on board the *Skate* which then headed for Londonderry at full speed where they were landed.

During the daylight hours of the twenty-second the anxious search for

*(1) *Torinia* (10,364 tons, Anglo Saxon Petrol Co);
 (2) *Scholar* (3940 tons, T. & J. Harrison);
 (3) *Canonesa* (8286 tons, Furness-Houlder Argentine Lines);
 (4) *Empire Airman* (8586 tons, Ministry of Shipping);
 (5) *Dalcairn* (4608 tons, Mongo Campbell & Co);
 (6) *Frederick S. Fales* (10,525 tons, Oriental Tankers);
 (7) *Simla* (6031 tons, Norwegian-owned).

U-boats continued as the convoy edged its way painfully slowly towards the North Channel. In view of the destruction of the two preceding nights, the Admiralty apparently concluded that another night would further decimate the convoy. Accordingly, soon after darkness fell, at 2225 hours, the order for the convoy to disperse was given presumably on the basis that the U-boats would no longer have a convenient focus for their attacks. In fact, several of them had had to return to their bases at the end of their operational cruises and the Skl war diary for 22 September discloses that only two boats, *U-32* and *U-138*, were still operating in the North West Approaches. Consequently, the surviving ships of the much-mauled HX 72 were able to reach the North Channel, one by one, several of them dropping anchor, no doubt gratefully, in Bangor Bay.

Before they reached the sanctuary of the Irish Sea, however, some of their crews saw further evidence of the danger that lurked in these waters. Some fifty miles north of the entrance to Lough Foyle, survivors from ships belonging to an outbound convoy were still being pulled from the sea.

Six ships forming the nucleus of convoy OB 216 had left Liverpool on 19 September to be joined by one from Belfast and eight from the Clyde. The total was made up to 19 by the addition of four more from undisclosed locations.[11] The convoy steamed north of Rathlin Island and when it had reached a position 50 miles north of Lough Foyle at 2026 hours on the evening of the 20th, a loud explosion was heard in the convoy, followed by three more 12 minutes later. One of the escort vessels, the destroyer *Vanquisher* quickly located lifeboats from the whale factory ship *New Sevilla*, (13801 tons, C. Salvesen & Co) and the freighter *Boka* (owner unknown). Shortly afterwards, lifeboats from the *Empire Adventure* (5145 tons, Ministry of Shipping) were also sighted. All three ships sank at varying intervals after being attacked. A total of 107 survivors were picked up and taken to Londonderry by another of the escorts, the corvette *Arabis*.

The convoy continued on course but at 0140 hours, the *City of Simla* (10138 tons, Ellerman Lines) was struck by a single torpedo and abandoned about 50 miles north-west of Malin Head. The *Vanquisher* reported the next morning that the ship was still afloat at 0720 hours. She sank almost two hours later and the *Vanquisher* took survivors from her to Lough Foyle. That afternoon, the convoy amalgamated with convoy OA 216, made up of ships from east coast ports, and continued to Halifax where it arrived on 29 September. All four of its ships which were sunk off the Ulster coast had fallen victim to *U-138* under the command of Oberleutnant z.S. Wolfgang Lueth.[12]

As September ended, the daily losses in ships and vital materials continued. A total of 90 British, Allied and neutral vessels were lost,[13] or, an average of three every day over the course of the month. The hazards and hardships endured by merchant seamen that these figures represent is exemplified by the experience (which is by no means exceptional) of some of the crew of the *Invershannon*, torpedoed by *U-99* on the twenty-first. After spending eight days in an open boat in atrocious weather conditions, they were landed at Belfast after being picked up in poor condition by the anti-submarine trawler *Fandango* 30 miles from Tory Island in Co. Donegal.

4

THIN ON THE GROUND

Throughout the summer, the meagre defence resources that could be allocated to Northern Ireland were spread thinly throughout the area. In July, the 61st Division joined the 53rd (Welsh) Division to augment troop numbers and the RAF spared a squadron of precious Hurricane fighters, No. 245, which took up residence at Aldergrove.

Inevitably, it was Belfast and its harbour complex that was given priority in defence planning. A plan entitled 'Defence Scheme for the Belfast dock area' was formulated.[1] The manpower and equipment made available to it were pitifully inadequate, however. The 7th Battalion Gloucestershire Regiment was designated 'The Dock Battalion' and took up billets in hastily-erected Nissen huts in Victoria Park on the Sydenham airfield boundary. One of its duties was the provision of guards for French ships moored in the lough. Those whose masters had refused to give an undertaking that they would serve the Allied cause and instead declared allegiance to Vichy were prevented from sailing.

Responsibility for the ground defence of the lough shores was given to the Commanding Officer of 525th (Antrim) Coast Regiment at Greypoint and he was designated 'Commander Fixed Defence Belfast Lough'. The 5th Bn. Royal Inniskilling Fusiliers was placed under his command for the purpose.

Equipment of all kinds was chronically scarce. For example, there were not even enough rifles to equip the newly-formed Local Defence Volunteers (later to become the Ulster Home Guard) until some of the first instalment of half a million .30 calibre rifles that Britain had obtained from the United States arrived in Belfast. But the shortage of anti-aircraft guns was particularly serious in view of the likelihood of air attacks. The 102nd Heavy Anti-Aircraft Regiment had six gun sites ranged round the city with a total establishment of twenty-four 3.7-inch guns but all batteries were under strength. However, it was the low-level attacks and dive-bombing by the Luftwaffe in support of ground forces in France and the Low Countries that was fresh in everyone's memory and perceived as a particular threat to Belfast's shipbuilding and aircraft construction installations. Defence against this threat was the concern of 175 and 176 Light Anti-Aircraft Batteries but records indicate that they had not more than five or six 40mm Bofors light guns dispersed throughout the harbour area. The heavy losses in this excellent weapon incurred during the retreat to Dunkirk were sorely felt. Two obsolescent 3-inch high-angle guns were positioned close to the Twin Islands power station but they were totally unsuitable for engaging fast low-flying aircraft. The dire state of the anti-aircraft defences is illustrated by the fact that Sydenham airfield had 12 ancient Lewis machine-guns of First World War vintage ranged round its perimeter.

Over at Greypoint, the Commander Fixed Defence Belfast Lough fared no better in the distribution and efficacy of equipment. In addition to the Greypoint battery itself, 6-inch coastal defence guns were installed at Larne and Orlock as well as two surveillance searchlights at Kilroot but even the most uninitiated observer at the time would have discounted a German seaborne invasion of Belfast Lough. Another of the elderly 3-inch high-angle guns was installed at Greypoint and it actually fired one round at a German minelaying aircraft on 4 August. From its vantage point overlooking the lough, the unit performed valuable observation work and its war diary provides a good record of the mines that were laid during this period.

Belfast (and Northern Ireland, in general) differed in one important respect from regions in Great Britain in the implementation of defensive measures. There was a greater danger of sabotage. The perennial problem of the IRA had now taken on a new dimension and there was a belief in security circles that the organisation would not be slow to take advantage of Britain's plight. This is demonstrated by the following passage in the 'Defence scheme for the Belfast dock area':

> There is a likelihood of enemy action by sea land and air against Belfast assisted by a Fifth Column. The IRA is expected to cooperate or act independently against our forces.

Events would show that the expectation was well founded. Although the IRA's contribution to the Nazi war effort never amounted to anything, the sparse and ambiguous evidence from German espionage sources indicates that there was in 1940 an intention at least to create links between republican activists and German spies who had already landed in Ireland. These events are described in Enno Stephan's book *Spies in Ireland*.[2]

Whether or not the perceived threat from the IRA would crystallize in overt action, the organisation's reputation alone was sufficient to cause the security authorities concern. In the atmosphere of crisis that surrounded the evacuation of Dunkirk, the Stormont government gave serious consideration to a proposal to convert the RUC into a combatant force under direct military control.[3] The proposal was not adopted but the role of the police was re-defined to meet the changing situation and their long experience with subversion would be invaluable in forestalling sabotage. An illustration of co-operation between the RUC and the RAF is to be found in the Operations Record Book of one of the squadrons that maintained patrols over Northern Ireland throughout the summer with ageing Fairey Battle fighter-bombers. This stated that surveillance was being carried out over an area in mid-Tyrone which was said to be a meeting ground for subversive elements.[4]

As the month of October began, the port of Belfast and its approaches became increasingly caught up in the Battle of the Atlantic. An ominous indication of how the battle was progressing was the growing number of survivors being landed from stricken ships. It was what the American war historian Edwin P. Hoyt has called 'the golden age of the U-boats'. On 3 August, Winston Churchill had noted in a message to the First Sea Lord, Sir Dudley Pound, that 'our repeated severe losses in the North West Approaches are most grievous'. On 20 October, Churchill wrote to President Roosevelt:

> You will have seen what heavy losses we have suffered in the North West Approaches to our last two convoys ...

In this case, he was referring to the frightening loss of thirty-three ships between 17 and 19 October. These figures included twenty ships from one convoy, the SC 7 from Sydney, Nova Scotia.

A report from one of the unglamorous but dogged little anti-submarine trawlers based at Belfast and Larne at this time puts the substance of Churchill's message to Roosevelt into context. The log of HMT *Blackfly*[5] shows that she left Pollock Basin East at 1900 BST[*] hours on 15 October in company with HMT *Lady Elsa*. Both ships anchored in Bangor Bay at 2015 hours to await the assembly of convoy OB 229 for Halifax, the main body of which was sailing from Liverpool. The completed convoy sailed the next day into waters north-west of Donegal that were littered with flotsam and lifeboats packed with shipwrecked seamen. The *Blackfly* returned to Belfast crammed to capacity with the hapless survivors of no less than four ships.

In spite of their small numbers the Condors of I/KG40 were making a telling contribution to this havoc. After making a wide sweep to the west of Ireland, they often continued in a northerly direction to land at Stavanger in Norway, making the return journey to Bordeaux the following day. This increased the search area that could be covered.

On one such sortie on 8 October, a major British disaster was narrowly averted. At 0312 hours, a Condor commanded by Oberleutnant Edmund Daser, one of KG40's most outstanding fliers, took off from Bordeaux and flew north. At 0915 hours, he sighted two heavy cruisers, a destroyer and a troop transport on a northerly course close to the island of Berneray in the

*By Order in Council British Summer Time now applied throughout the year.[6]

Outer Hebrides. No attack was made. Instead, the Condor turned south-west towards the Irish coast and at 1000 hours, five fully-laden troopships were sighted north-west of Malin Head. Daser selected the largest vessel, which was the passenger liner *Oronsay* (20043 tons) with 3100 troops on board. He made a low-level attack, dropping four SC250kg bombs. At least one of the bombs hit the ship but because of heavy defensive fire, the Condor had to turn away without observing the extent of the damage. A short time later, one of the aircraft's radio operators (two were carried) intercepted a distress call from the liner to say that both its engines had stopped. The ship was now a stationary target for U-boats and FOIC Belfast hurriedly dispatched the anti-aircraft cruiser HMS *Cairo*. which had been lying at Victoria Wharf Belfast. along with the destroyer HMS *Sabre* from Londonderry. Two further destroyers arrived at the scene and the crippled ship was taken in tow and successfully brought into Greenock. The casualties were mercifully small, consisting of 3 soldiers and 1 crew member killed and 11 soldiers and 1 crew wounded.

Meanwhile, the mining of Belfast Lough and the approaches to Larne Harbour continued to disrupt traffic and the port of Belfast had to be closed periodically until swept channels were provided. On 17 October, the armed merchant cruiser HMS *Cheshire*, which had been torpedoed outside the North Channel, was towed laboriously into the suspect waters of the lough preceded by minesweepers. Three days earlier, the ship had been engaged in convoy escort duty off the Donegal coast. At 2000 hours, she sighted a large quantity of wreckage and began searching for survivors. U-boats were known to be in the area and as a precautionary measure she was steering a zigzag course in a westerly direction. At 2028 hours, when approximately 120 miles north-west of Erris Head, she was struck by a torpedo which tore a hole in her starboard side 36 feet long. Three of her holds were flooded but with the pumps working at full capacity, the ship was able to stay afloat and maintain a very slow speed. A course was set for the perilous journey to the Irish coast with the destroyer HMCS *Skeena* and the corvette HMS *Gladiolas* providing a screen.

More than 24 hours after the attack, the *Cheshire* reached the comparative safety of the North Channel and, after passing the Altacarry Light on Rathlin Island, she was met by the salvage vessel *Ranger* and towed into Belfast Lough. Towing had to be suspended when an enemy aircraft was sighted but no attack materialized. The gaping hole in her side clearly visible from the shore, she was beached at Kilroot to await a berth in the hard-pressed repair yard at Harland and Wolff's.

The enemy aircraft sighted was probably the highflying reconnaissance aircraft belonging to Luftflotte 5, based in Norway or Denmark, which was taking advantage of clear skies and good visibility to take a series of superb aerial photographs of Belfast and the surrounding area, including Larne and

Newtownards. The photos of the Belfast harbour complex show clearly the new aircraft carrier HMS *Formidable* lying at the Thompson Wharf.[7] The ship was nearing completion in the Belfast shipyard and was due to leave on trials in a few weeks' time. The Germans were particularly interested in aircraft carriers (possibly because they had none of their own) and although their intelligence would have known about the stage reached in the *Formidable*'s construction, the photos provided confirmation that she would soon be entering service.

Three minelaying aircraft were operating over the lough on the night of 24/25 October and an unknown number on two successive nights. As a result, FOIC Belfast issued a warning on the 25th that no ships could anchor in the lough except in Bangor Bay, south of the swept channel. In an attempt to stem the nightly incursions of the minelayers, the first four balloons of the Belfast Lough Balloon Barrage were flown from lighters on the 26th.[8] Nevertheless, that night a low-flying aircraft, obviously minelaying, was observed by troops of the Greypoint battery who opened fire with a 3-inch gun. It was now accepted that these nocturnal incursions were solely for minelaying purposes and consequently no air raid warnings were sounded in Belfast. However, enemy aircraft were identified in the area on the afternoon of the 29th and again on the 30th. On both these occasions, a 'Red' alert was issued and the sirens sounded. No attacks on land targets materialized and the presumption was that reconnaissance or anti-shipping sorties were involved.

A few days later, on 1 November, the Dutch motor vessel *Santa Lucia* (379 tons) hit a mine and sank directly opposite the Greypoint gun emplacement. The next day, another mine was exploded by a minesweeper in the middle of the lough, near the Pile Light. When, on the following day, an unidentified aircraft flew low over the Blackhead Light just after nightfall and two unexplained explosions were heard, the port of Belfast was promptly closed for 18 hours to enable intensive sweeping to take place. Clearly, the situation was serious and people living within sight of the lough could not have failed to be aware of it. Away from the lough, however, the wider public was screened from the worrying trend by a watchful censor. There was no doubt a genuine belief among people with sensitive information that gratuitous gossip harmed the national interest. The Ministry of Information constantly exhorted the public to be discreet with slogans such as 'Careless talk costs lives' and 'Beat Hitler by silence'.

In a wider context, and seen from a strategic standpoint, German sea and air operations around the coasts of Ireland were generating a feeling of acute alarm within the British defence establishment. In his book *The Second World War* Winston Churchill wrote:

> The only thing that ever really frightened me during the war was the U-boat peril.

8 Luftwaffe reconnaissance photo showing the *Formidable* nearing completion

In the last three months of 1940, only an inadequate number of U-boats at his disposal (sometimes not more than 10 ocean-going boats) frustrated Doenitz in his bid to strangle Britain economically. But what he did with the small number at his disposal was remarkable. It seemed that Churchill's worst fears were becoming reality. Although much of this momentous battle for survival was taking place just out of sight of the coasts of Antrim and Londonderry, people walking on the seafront at Portrush could often hear the muffled sound of depth charges far out to sea and sense the desperation.

Ironically, it was not a submarine, but an aircraft which made the biggest single contribution to this catalogue of destruction. At 0309 hours GMT on the morning of 26 October, an Fw 200C Condor took off from Bordeaux-Merignac airfield on an armed reconnaissance which would take it to the west and north of Ireland. It had a crew of six and was commanded by 26-year old Oberleutnant Bernhard Jope from Leipzig. Its armament included six SC250 kg bombs and it carried just over 8000 litres of fuel. Subject to opportunities that might present themselves, Jope's orders were to skirt the west coast of Ireland and then reconnoitre the approaches to the North Channel before returning to Bordeaux.[9]

According to the mission report sent to Luftwaffe headquarters by IV Fliegerkorps, it was when they were more than five hours into the flight that the Condor's crew sighted what appeared to be a large merchant ship, approximately 140 kilometres west of Aran Island on an easterly course. It was, in fact, the Canadian Pacific Steamship Company's *Empress of Britain* (42348 tons). She was on her way from Capetown to Liverpool on charter to the British government as a troopship. Lloyd's register discloses that she was armed and carried a crew of 416 with 205 passengers and 2 gunners. The cargo included 300 tons of sugar and 300 tons of general stores.

Jope was reported to have said afterwards that as he approached the ship he was staggered by the sheer size of it, never having seen anything like it from the air before. During what is believed to be three separate runs over the ship the defensive fire from its armament was intense and the Condor was hit by machine gun fire and rocked by near misses from light anti-aircraft guns. At least two of the Condor's bombs hit the ship with catastrophic results. From the aircraft the crew could see that a fierce fire had started amidships.

The FOIC *Belfast* received a distress call reporting that passengers and crew were taking to the boats. The Royal Navy destroyer HMS *Echo* and the Polish destroyer *Burza* were dispatched to pick up survivors. Lloyd's casualty report states that of the the 623 persons board, 25 crew and 20 passengers lost their lives.[10]

The following day, another Condor reported that the giant ship was burning from end to end '220 kilometres west of Londonderry'. Her entire

9 Bernard Jope, who sank the *Empress of Britain*

exterior was blackened and a pall of smoke rose from her to a height of 1100 metres. Two destroyers, six tugs and four small vessels were in attendance but at this particular time no tow lines were seen to be attached.

The tugs *Marauder* and *Thames* later took the liner in tow but she was torpedoed by *U-32* under the command of Oberleutnant z. S. Hans Jenisch and sank 75 miles west of Malin Head. Some of the survivors were landed at Belfast.

Two days later, *U-32* was herself sunk by the destroyers *Highlander* and *Harvester* by depth charges. Jenisch and all but six of the crew were rescued. Notwithstanding that torpedoes were the ultimate cause of the sinking, Jope was credited with her destruction. She is believed to be the largest merchant ship sunk by air attack in the Second World War. Jope himself survived the war and ended his flying career as a senior captain with Lufthansa.

A feeling of despondency and dread now gripped Britain. The shrinking hours of daylight brought confirmation that, after its defeat in the titanic daylight battles of the late summer, the Luftwaffe was now going to try and overcome the obstinate island by night bombing. While it was industrial centres in Great Britain that were occupying the enemy's attention at this stage, Northern Ireland's geographical importance was recognized by the German leadership. Although the waters off the northern coast had become the focal point in a savage battle, the Irish Sea itself had been comparatively safe for merchant ships. A shortage of U-boats and the high risk involved in negotiating the North Channel provided some immunity for convoys starting and finishing their voyages. Some U-boat commanders apparently took the risk, however. On 12 August, an unidentified submarine had been reported two miles south-east of Guns Island near the entrance to Strangford Lough. Three anti-submarine trawlers from Belfast were ordered to investigate but no contact was made. A week later, on 19 August, the anti-submarine trawlers *British Guiana* and *Guava* attacked a contact in the anti-submarine nets at the entrance to Belfast Lough with negative results.

Although the Irish Sea itself was in the main free of U-boats, its importance to Britain at the time was afterwards recalled by Churchill in stark terms:

> As November and December drew on the entrances and estuaries of the Mersey and the Clyde far surpassed in mortal significance all other factors in the war.[11]

On another occasion, he said:[12]

> The Mersey, the Clyde were the lungs through which we breathed.

Attacks by Condors became commonplace in the Irish Sea. On 27 October at 0945 hours, one of them made two attacks on outbound convoy OB 234 outside Belfast Lough damaging the freighter *Alfred Jones** (5,013 tons, Elder

* The *Alfred Jones* was eventually sunk by *U-107* near Freetown, West Africa on 1 June 1941.

10 A pre-war photograph of the *Empress of Britain*

Dempster Lines) and killing 12 members of the crew. An escorting destroyer, HMS *Amazon* fired on the aircraft which was thought to have sustained some hits.

The Condor was not of robust construction. It had been designed as a long-range passenger aircraft and had set several records for long non-stop flights with Lufthansa before the war. The military derivative was produced in haste and with little regard for crew protection. Casualties were common and many mission reports speak of aircraft returning to Bordeaux with dead or injured aboard Aircraft which ostensibly escaped unscathed in attacks on convoys may, in fact, have been mortally disabled. A case in point was that of Oberleutnant Theo Schuldt.

Schuldt took off from Bordeaux just before dawn on 22 October on a 'Zenit' armed reconnaissance and meteorological sortie over the North Channel and the northern coast of Ulster. The visibility over the Irish Sea was poor and no contacts seem to have been made. Evidently the Condor then attacked at least one armed merchant ship off the coast of Donegal but nothing more is known about it. The aircraft failed to return to Bordeaux and a few days later the bodies of the 27-year old Schuldt and that of meteorologist Dr Hans Sturm were washed ashore in Co. Galway at Aillebrack and Dynich Island respectively.[13] Schuldt is buried in the German Military Cemetery in Glencree, Co. Wicklow. There is no record of the bodies of any of the other four crew members having been found.

Paradoxically, the increasing level of German air activity around Ireland in October and November was achieved in spite of a chronic shortage of aircraft and crews trained in maritime operations. The German Naval Staff (Skl) war diary discloses that a British aircraft carrier had been sighted in the North Sea on 22 September and, although this was a prime target in German eyes and conditions were favourable, no attack could be made because there were no aircraft available.[14] The same source provides the interesting information that the RAF Coastal Command operations from Aldergrove were proving particularly troublesome to Doenitz's U-boats about this time and he made a request that it be attacked in an effort to cause disruption.[15] Nothing came of the proposal – very likely because of a lack of aircraft but an aerial photograph of the airfield taken on 8 December suggests that an attack was seriously considered.

The dearth of suitable aircraft was aggravated by petty inter-service rivalry. There was endless bickering between the naval and air staffs and the flying units which came under the direct command of the Commander in Chief of the German Navy, Grand Admiral Erich Raeder, seemed to come off worse. The problem was not helped by Goering's desire to have a say in the direction of all flying operations. His attitude was – as one officer put it – 'everything that flies belongs to me'. The result was that the coastal flying units (Küstenfliegergruppen) were being continually transferred from naval to Luftwaffe command and back again.

The crash of a flying-boat belonging to one of these coastal units created difficulties in Irish-German relations and resulted in acrimonious exchanges between the two governments. On 28 November, officers of the Irish army G2 intelligence branch went to Dunmore Head in County Kerry and took into custody a German naval officer, Oberleutnant z.S. Konrad Neymeyer, who had come ashore in a curach from Great Blasket Island. He stated that his aircraft had had engine trouble and came down on the shore of the uninhabited island of Inishvickillane, about three miles south of the Blaskets. He and his crew of four had rowed to Great Blasket in two rubber dinghies. The crew had remained there and Neymeyer had come over to the mainland alone. He was taken to Tralee and the crew were later removed to Valentia in the Irish naval patrol vessel *Fort Rannoch*.

Although Neymeyer did not divulge the type of the aircraft or the identity of his unit, it was, in fact, a Blohm and Voss BV 138 flying boat attached to 2.Staffel of Küstenfliegergruppe 906 (2./906). The unit had only recently been equipped with the type and contemporary records indicate that persistent problems with the engines made it unsuitable for long-range reconnaissance.

The German legation in Dublin became involved and the question arose as to whether the aircraft had come down within Irish territorial waters. Neymeyer claimed that it had not. According to the German view, the uninhabited Inishvickillane lay outside the recognized three-mile territorial limit but the Irish authorities apparently relied instead on the Fisheries Protection Act 1933 which, it was claimed, extended the limit to six miles in a southerly direction from Great Blasket Island. The importance of this dispute lay in the fact that if the aircraft had come down outside the territorial limit the crew would have had to be released. Otherwise they would be interned.

The German consul in Dublin, Dr Eduard Hempel, did not agree with the Irish contention and asked Berlin for instructions. On 18 January 1941 the Foreign Office replied to say that Germany would not recognize an extension of the limit beyond three miles as attempts by Germany to extend her territorial limit in the past had been opposed. The Germans were also quick to point out that British sailors shipwrecked from the *Empress of Britain* (sunk on 26 October) had not been interned. The Irish reply to this allegation was that it had been intended to intern the sailors but that they were, in the interim, picked up by British destroyers.[16] The Germans were probably not very impressed with this explanation but one of their officials acknowledged that eye witnesses would claim that the aircraft was unquestionably over territorial waters north-west of Great Blasket Island immediately before it came down. It was clear that the Germans had no hope of winning the argument and the aircraft's crew were accordingly interned in the Curragh. Neymeyer himself proved to be a troublesome internee. Both Allied and German personnel in the Curragh were allowed to leave the camp provided they signed an 'honour book' pledging themselves to return. Apart from a Canadian officer about whom there seemed to be some misunderstanding, Neymeyer was said to be the only internee during the course of the war to break his pledge. He stowed away on a ship at Dublin docks bound for Barry in South Wales but was apprehended there while trying to board a ship for Lisbon.

NEUTRALITY HAS MIXED
BLESSINGS

On 21 November, the newly-completed HMS *Formidable* left Belfast for sea trials.[1] In view of the presence of U-boats outside the North Channel and the German desire to sink an aircraft carrier (their repeated claims to have sunk the *Ark Royal* were becoming embarrassing) an atmosphere of anxiety must have surrounded her departure. Two days before she sailed, the anti-submarine trawler HMT *King Sol* had attacked an underwater contact inside the North Channel, just north of Rathlin as if to emphasize the menace.

The restricted area in which the trials were carried out is an indication of the concern felt for the ship's safety. The log discloses that, during the 11 days of the trials, she was no further north than the Firth of Clyde nor further south than Anglesey.[2] There is a gap in the operational records of I/KG 40 at this time but undoubtedly the Condors and aircraft from other reconnaissance units had kept the carrier under observation.

The danger to the *Formidable* was not confined to U-boats and Condors. The day after the carrier entered the Irish Sea, a sister ship of the *Troutpool*, the *Pikepool* (3683 tons), sank after hitting a mine south of the Isle of Man. Outside the North Channel, conditions could not have been much worse. Fifty miles north-west of Malin Head, *U-103* under the command of Korvettenkapitän Schütze was sinking the *Daydawn* (4768 tons, Claymore Shipping Co.), en route from Barry to Santiago with a cargo of coal. The Canadian destroyers *Skeena* and *St Laurent* on escort duty with eastbound convoy SC 11 went to pick up survivors. A little further south, the *Cree* (4701 tons, Muir Young Ltd), bound for Workington from Pepel with iron ore, was sunk with all hands by *U-123*, commanded by Kapitänleutnant Moehle.

It was the approach of convoy SC 11 to the North Channel[3] which accounted for the intense U-boat activity in the area. The convoy had left Sydney, Nova Scotia on 9 November and when fully constituted it comprised 33 ships. Two of them, the *Bruse* and the *Salonika* had been sunk 100 miles north-west of Erris Head. Survivors were picked up by another of the escorts, the sloop HMS *Enchantress*, but the toll was not completely one-sided. *U-104* under the command of Leutnant z. S. Juerst was intercepted by the corvette HMS *Rhododendrum* and sunk with depth charges. There were no survivors.

11 HMS *Formidable*

In an atmosphere of deep crisis at the Admiralty, the alarming losses in merchant ships continued. Joachim Schepke in *U-100* evaded the convoy escorts and sank the *Justitia* (4562 tons, Chellew Steamship Management Co.) bound for London from Savannah and the *Bradfyne* (4740 tons, Sir W. Reardon Smith & Sons) also bound for London with grain from Montreal. West of Rockall, Moehle's *U-123* sank the *Oakcrest* (5407 tons, Crest Shipping Co.) which was outward bound from Liverpool to New York and then sailed westwards at full speed to intercept an outbound convoy and sink two more ships, the *King Idwal* (5115 tons, Dodd Thompson & Co.) on the way to Baltimore from Liverpool and the *Tymeric* (5228 tons, A. Weir & Co.) from Hull to Buenos Aires with coal.

As the embattled SC 11 entered the North Channel, the freighter *Leise Maersk* (3136 tons, ex-Danish flag) inbound from Three Rivers, Michigan, was torpedoed by Schepke in *U-100*. Two of the escorts, HMS *Vesper* and HMS *Malcolm* reported sonar contacts and the *Malcolm* made an attack with depth charges just beyond the entrance to Lough Foyle with no apparent success.

The *Formidable* returned to Belfast unscathed on 2 December. About the same time as she entered Belfast Lough, a Coastal Command aircraft was attacking a U-boat on the surface just off the County Antrim coast at Portrush as if to emphasize the potential danger the carrier had been in. One hit was claimed before the submarine crash-dived.

Apart from the U-boat menace, the twin threat from aerial minelayers and the Condors of I/KG 40 dominated British defence planning in home waters. RAF Intelligence estimated that up to 100 German bombers were being used for minelaying, a large number of them operating from Dutch airfields. Attempts to intercept them en route had met with no success and consideration was given to attacking them in the vicinity of their bases. Twin-engined fighters were needed for this task but the Blenheim I was the only suitable aircraft that Fighter Command had available. It soon became apparent, however, that when operating from bases in East Anglia they had insufficient endurance to remain in the vicinity of enemy airfields long enough to be effective.[4] The problem would remain until the RAF had enough night fighters equipped with airborne interception (AI) radar.

Dealing with the Condors was a similarly unrewarding business. Intercepting them was given top priority but up to the end of 1940 none had been accounted for in this way. At Aldergrove, the Hurricane pilots of 245 Squadron, in particular, suffered from this frustration with the knowledge that Condors were frequently reported—too late—to be within range of their base. A memo from the RAF 'Y' Service dated 28 October gives details of the movement of four Condors in the period 17 to 27 October including the times of take off at Bordeaux and arrival over various points on the Irish coast, including Waterford, Cork and Foynes. What is perhaps most interesting about this Memo is that it concludes by stating:

> This information received from the Irish observer organisation was useful.

This was one example of the co-operation from the Irish defence authorities which came to light after the war. However, first-rate intelligence like this failed to prevent the Condors from eluding interception. A measure of British perplexity is shown by the fact that at one stage a leading academic mathematician was asked to try and calculate the most likely positions where interceptors might converge with them. This proved fruitless and it was, in fact, not until convoy escort carriers with fighter aircraft were introduced in sufficient numbers that the Condors were seriously threatened.

In spite of their success, or perhaps because of it, the Condors of I/KG40 also became the subject of inter-service rivalry. Up to the end of 1940 they had been operating as part of the Luftwaffe's IV Fliegerkorps and thus under the command of Hermann Goering as Commander-in-Chief. Although the information they gained about shipping movements was supposed to be made available to Doenitz, it was of a random nature. What Doenitz wanted was to have operational control over aircraft specifically dedicated to work with his boats. Goering strenuously opposed the suggestion, regarding it as something that would diminish his authority. Doenitz was supported by Admiral Raeder, however, who saw to it that the request was brought to Hitler's personal attention during Goering's absence on a hunting trip. The Führer approved the plan.

It was no accident that the decision to transfer control of the Condors was made in Goering's absence. In his diary, Erhard Milch, the Inspector-General of the Luftwaffe and de facto second-in-command, describes how Goering had informed him that he intended to take six weeks' leave and give him temporary command of the Luftwaffe. He was, according to Milch, very depressed and had seemingly lost interest in the war since the Luftwaffe's defeat in the Battle of Britain.[5] His discomfiture was aggravated when Hitler, for the first time, openly criticized him for his failure to deliver the victory he had categorically promised. Doenitz had got his way and increasingly made use of his new weapon to learn of the movement of convoys, particularly the eastbound ones. and use the advance warning to deploy his boats much sooner.

For its part, the Admiralty was also very much occupied with the North West Approaches. Consideration was given to the laying of a carpet of contact mines across the approaches to the North Channel. Thousands of them would be anchored to the sea bed reaching up to 35 feet of the surface thus allowing ships to pass but denying entry to submarines. Events would overtake this plan however and in a few months time the focal point of the battle was destined to move away westwards.

Meanwhile, the little island of Rathlin continued to be at the centre of a logistic operation on which the survival of Britain depended. There was a striking similarity between the prevailing circumstances and those of 25 years earlier during the First World War. Then too, the North Channel assumed a singular importance when the German U-boat armada threatened to literally starve Britain into submission. In 1917, that was seen as a real possibility. Already before the end of 1914, German U-boats had penetrated the Irish Sea and sunk several ships. As a result, the North Channel Net Barrage was conceived. Suspended from a fleet of drifters and stretching from a point near Fair Head to the Mull of Kintyre, the nets were laid north of Rathlin and, in the main, proved an effective obstacle.[6] In the Second World War, the advances made in anti-submarine warfare techniques made U-boat operations inside the North Channel much more hazardous. Instead, the U-boats preferred to remain in the North West Approaches and rely on what information they could obtain from aerial reconnaissance and other intelligence-gathering sources.

The traffic in the narrow waterways around Rathlin was dense in the extreme. Admiralty records from the late 1940s set out in detail the navigational coordinates to be followed by convoys entering and leaving the North Channel.[7] The presence of such large numbers of ships at the same time meant that station-keeping and accurate navigation was crucial. All ships were to pass to the east of the island; northbound and southbound traffic had to pass to the east of the Altnacarry Light at a distance of eight and six nautical miles respectively. A separation of two miles left little margin for error, especially in bad visibility. This placed a heavy burden on the Royal Navy's escort vessels and the Belfast and Larne-based trawlers of the Irish Sea Trawler Force played an indispensable role in this work.

Back in Belfast, the fitting out of the *Formidable* for operational duty was completed and she finally left for Scapa Flow on 9 December. Bad weather provided a certain amount of protective cover for the voyage and no enemy air activity was reported.[8]

A week later, the weather had improved sufficiently for the Condors to resume low-level attacks. On the sixteenth, the *Sandra* (1,028 tons) was bombed and machine-gunned 15 miles north-east of Rathlin. The aircraft appears to have dropped six bombs in the attack and all missed. On the twenty-second, the tug *Superman* was attacked by a Condor three miles north of the island after reportedly taking on board the crew of the *Armbjorn Hersir*. The nationality of this ship and the reason or the circumstances in which the crew were taken off are not recorded.

Further south, in waters within range of German twin-engined bombers, a series of incidents about the same time illustrate the ever-present danger to the crews of the small coasters that stubbornly continued to ply between the various Irish Sea ports as well as elsewhere in Eire. Among them were the little colliers belonging to John Kelly Ltd of Belfast, whose often dangerous but unrenowned work in wartime is recalled in the company's publication *A Collier Fleet at War.*

At 0900 hours on 18 December, the small tanker *Osage* (1,010 tons, Anglo-American Oil Co.) was bombed and sunk by an aircraft 4 miles north-east of Arklow while on passage from Belfast to Foynes. The crew was rescued. Thirty-five minutes later, the *Tweed* (2697 tons) was also bombed and machine-gunned 45 miles east of Drogheda Bay. Yet another incident occurred a little later in the same general area. When an hour out from Kingstown (now Dun Laoghaire) the London Midland & Scottish passenger ferry *Cambria* was damaged when a German aircraft attacked it with three or four bombs. The aircraft was driven off by the ship's armament but it returned and raked the decks with machine gun fire. The third officer was badly injured in this last attack and died shortly afterwards.

The next day, an even more serious incident occurred, exemplifying the perils of sailing under a neutral flag. An aircraft attacked the Irish-registered *Isolda* (734 tons) a tender owned and operated by the Commissioner of Irish Lights, off the Wexford coast, three miles from the Coningbeg light vessel. Six men were killed and seven wounded.[9] An attack on a vessel serving lighthouses with the words 'Lighthouse Service' painted on the hull in large letters would have been difficult to explain. According to Hitler's formulation of the rules, neutral ships trading with Britain were aiding the British war economy but a lightship tender could hardly be said to be *trading* with anyone.

This sinking and many others like it serves to highlight the difficulties faced by Irish shipping throughout the Second World War. Unlike many neutral countries, geography dictated that Ireland had no alternative but to trade with Britain. Its small merchant fleet could maintain only a minimal trade with other countries in wartime and that, in itself, raised a further problem in the shape of the stark choice that faced Irish shipowners: They could sail independently and rely on their neutral status, thereby running the risk that a U-boat or aircraft would consider that they came within the scope of Hitler's directive and sink them. Alternatively, they could sail in British convoys, This course carried obvious dangers but apparently Irish sailors were overwhelmingly in favour of it. It had the advantage for shipowners that insurance premiums were halved.

The aircraft involved in many of the attacks in the Irish Sea at this time are not identified in the existing British or German records but it seems probable that some, at least, were carried out by Ju88s belonging to the coastal unit Küstenfliegergruppe 806 (KGr806). Based at Nantes, the crews were composed of a combination of naval and Luftwaffe personnel. Most of the aircraft commanders were naval officers. One of them was Paul Just, who was active in the Irish Sea area in the winter of 1940/41. His description of the high-speed attacks on coastal shipping carried out at 'zero altitude' are contained in a book he wrote after the war.[10] Just completed his eventful career by transferring to the U-boat service later in the war and managed to live to tell the tale.

NO CAUSE FOR REJOICING

In Britain, the approach of Christmas 1940 promised little in the way of peace and goodwill. To city dwellers, spending their nights in air raid shelters, the festive season must have seemed an irrelevance. No respite was in sight and the stress that stemmed from wondering where the next blow would fall was creating severe tensions throughout the country. A civil population had never before been called upon to endure the demoralizing effects of prolonged night bombing on such a scale. (At this stage, the weight of the bombs being dropped on Germany by the RAF fell far short of the corresponding amount dropped by the Luftwaffe.)

Events would show, however, that a sustained aerial bombardment, by itself, will not necessarily break public morale and can, in fact, stiffen it. This would be demonstrated in an even more striking fashion before the war was over as German cities were reduced to dust and ashes.

Records for the period show that several incidents during December served to focus the thoughts of Belfast people on the city's continuing immunity. On the evening of 14 December a 'Red' alert was issued and shortly afterwards, at 2235 hours, three batteries of 102nd Heavy Anti-Aircraft Regiment (102nd HAA) opened fire on a hostile aircraft over the city. The guns at the U3 site at Lisnabreeny in the Castlereagh Hills fired one round and those at Balmoral (U4) and Sunningdale Park (U6) fired two each. The three-inch guns at Greypoint also opened fire. No attack developed but the sirens sounded again at 0022 hours and this time flares were seen to the north of the city by RAF crews manning the balloon barrage.

By the middle of December, the No. 968 Balloon Squadron, which had arrived in the province in September, had established a large number of sites in and around Belfast.[1] These included 30 waterborne sites (not all of which were in commission) in Belfast Lough. A variety of vessels were being used for this purpose, including four Belgian trawlers which had escaped before Antwerp fell to the Germans. The presence of these waterborne balloons could account for the fall in the number of suspected minelaying flights over the lough since November. To date, most minelaying seems to have taken place from low level but the presence of balloons would have made this a very risky practice. RAF intelligence had observed that mines were sometimes being dropped from 10,000 feet or above and this naturally had an effect on accuracy. The men of 968 Squadron's 'E' flight at Bangor heard a violent explosion in mid-air about this time which was attributed to a prematurely detonated mine dropped from high altitude.

In the early morning of 18 December, an enemy aircraft was known to be over the coasts of Antrim and Down and at 0400 hours two bombs, which were positively identified as German, fell into a field near Waringstown causing no material damage.[2] There was widespread fog over England and Wales that night and a raider may have jettisoned his bombs when he realized that he was hopelessly lost.

Two nights later, at 2215 hours on the twentieth, two parachute mines were dropped over open country, five miles west of Larne. One exploded in mid-air and the other exploded on impact near a place called Topping's Hill.[3] This incident presumably resulted from an attempt to mine the approaches to Larne harbour and it was probably an He111 of KG4 that was responsible. The weather records for the night show that a strong easterly wind was blowing over the Irish Sea, which, if not adequately compensated for, would have caused the parachutes to drift inland. Minelayers frequently operated under cover of air raids along their route, making their destination even more difficult to plot. The tactic may have been employed on this occasion when KG4 was engaged in a major attack on Liverpool and Birkenhead.

The heavy attack on Liverpool was repeated on the following night. When Manchester was subjected to major attacks on two successive nights commencing 22 December a suspension of bombing over the Christmas period seemed unlikely. Field Marshal Erhard Milch deals with the background to these events in his diary. He pointed out that the Luftwaffe's unremitting attacks had provoked calls in England for reprisal raids against German cities. This was perhaps inevitable and after Sheffield was heavily bombed on the night of 15/16 December, the RAF embarked on a series of raids against Mannheim in the Ruhr. On three different nights between 16 and 23 December, the city was singled out for major attacks. It was an important rail communications centre but no special effort seems to have been made to confine the bombing to industrial targets and serious damage and casualties occurred in residential areas.

Each side was now engaged in a propaganda battle aimed at denigrating the other's tactics while, at the same time, justifying his own. What was indisputable was that, given the available navigation and target-finding aids, heavy civilian casualties were unavoidable. Sometimes, the anxiety to score points precipitated explanations that were transparently inaccurate and unconvincing. After Sheffield had been heavily bombed on the night of the fifteenth, there was little or no German activity for three nights. The British authorities immediately ascribed this to the RAF's crippling of Luftwaffe airfields. The truth was that low cloud and fog over much of England and Wales had made operations by the Luftwaffe virtually impossible.

According to Milch, he eventually received a telephone instruction from Hitler that all offensive aerial operations against Britain were to be halted for the duration of the Christmas period.[4] As a result, night bombing did not resume until the twenty-eighth. The same diary entries disclose interesting information on an unrelated subject. Milch was summoned to a meeting with Hitler on Christmas Eve and, as the Führer showed him to the door at the end of it, he said that the Russians were preparing to attack Germany and that consequently he was planning to launch a pre-emptive strike against the Soviet Union.[5] The diary does not state whether Milch was surprised by this casual announcement but no doubt he deduced from it that the bombing campaign he was conducting against Britain had an uncertain future. He would also have recalled that Germany had concluded a non-agression pact with the Soviet Union just 16 months earlier.

The pages of the Belfast daily papers of the time convey the impression that Christmas would be observed more in form than in spirit. The *Belfast Telegraph* said that there was 'as much bustle and bargaining about the Belfast Christmas markets as ever' but predictably made no mention of the prevailing mood of apprehension heightened by the long hours of darkness. A representative of the same paper flew over the city in an RAF training aircraft to view the effectiveness of the black-out and found it 'anything but perfect'. The situation at Bangor was much more satisfactory, only one spot of light having been observed.[6]

On the evening of 20 December, two incidents occurred south of the border which did nothing to allay the feeling of nervousness in Belfast.[7] At 1930 hours, the residents of Dun Laoghaire heard an aircraft flying over the town and saw what were described as 'blinding flares'. Moments later a bomb fell into the roadway followed by another 100 yards from Sandycove Railway Station. Three people were injured. About half an hour later, two large bombs fell in the townland of Shantonagh, near Carrickmacross in County Monaghan injuring one person. The dropping of flares in the first incident could have been explained by an aircraft trying to establish its position. A large force of Luftflotte 3 aircraft based in Northern France flew up the Irish Sea that night to attack Liverpool and if a navigator had not allowed sufficient drift for the strong easterly wind an aircraft could have arrived over Dun Laoghaire and mistook the harbour for Liverpool. Dublin was 200 kilometres west of Liverpool but navigational errors of this magnitude were not uncommon in the difficult weather conditions existing over the British Isles in winter, particularly if the winds aloft were not correctly forecast.

Liverpool was again the target the following night and this time the Irish defence forces on the east coast made a number of positive observations. Their report stated that between the hours of 1900 and 0030, aircraft were seen at various points along the coast with lights showing at different times during the period. The report goes on:

> From information received, generally it is thought that British aircraft do not show lights or fire pyrotechnics. In fact, they are forbidden to do so. It is thought that these aircraft were German proceeding to Liverpool, keeping in touch with one another.[8]

It was alleged that in some instances Irish airspace had been penetrated to a distance of a few miles. One aircraft had been reported inland at a point between Slane and Drogheda.

Two major attacks on Manchester took place before the brief Christmas lull but before this momentous year closed London suffered two more devastating attacks. The second, on the night of 29/30 December, turned the commercial heart of the city into an inferno.

On the other side of the Irish Sea, 1941 began with a series of incomprehensible incidents in which bombs were dropped in the eastern counties of Eire causing damage and loss of life. The first occurred on New Year's Day at 2143 hours when eight bombs were dropped in County Meath, five of them at Duleek and three at Julianstown. Some slight damage to houses occurred but there were no injuries.

The following morning, at 0610 hours, two bombs fell in Terenure, Dublin, demolishing two houses and damaging several others. Seven people were trapped in the wreckage but rescued without serious injury. Three bombs dropped at Ballymurrin, Co. Wexford caused no damage or injury. Two other bombs fell on waste ground in Fortfield Road, Dublin damaging several houses but causing no casualties. A more serious incident occurred at Borris in County Carlow where three persons were killed and two seriously injured. At the Curragh racecourse, three high explosives were dropped along with a number of incendiaries. One unexploded incendiary bomb was found to be of German origin. Magnetic mines were also reported dropped in Co. Wicklow without having exploded. These and fragments of bombs found there were also of German manufacture. The next day, 3 January, the city of Dublin was subjected to yet another of these baffling attacks. At 0355 hours, a bomb fell on the densely populated South Circular Road area, destroying two houses and injuring 20 people.[9]

The earliest recorded occasion on which bombs fell in Eire had been at Campile in Co. Wexford in August when a creamery was destroyed and three girls killed. On 25 October, high-explosives and incendiaries had fallen near Rathdrum in Co. Wicklow. These and the incidents of 20/21 December were generally regarded as isolated and the result of inaccurate navigation but this latest series was open to a more sinister interpretation. There was a suspicion that the bombings were in some way connected with diplomatic exchanges which had been taking place between Dublin and Berlin on the subject of augmenting the German consular staff in Dublin.

The text of diplomatic telegrams passing between the German Foreign Office and its Dublin Consulate, released after the war, disclose that the question of providing additional staff became a serious issue. On 6 December the German consul, Dr Eduard Hempel, sent a telegam[10] to Berlin advising against the appointment of a German military attache in Dublin. He said that it was not in Germany's interest to do so at this time and that, in any case, his assistant Henning Thomsen was himself a reserve officer and could perform this function.

The Foreign Office took Hempel's advice in that the appointment of a military attache, as such, was not pursued but they then embarked on an even more ambitious plan. On 18 December, Hempel was informed by Berlin[11] that three serving members of the German army were to be sent to Ireland in the guise of consular officials. It was pointed out that Dublin was now regarded as an important observation location for surveillance of British military and maritime activity. They would be flown to 'Limerick' (Hempel wanted to know if it was Rineanna (now Shannon Airport) or the flying-boat base at Foynes that was meant) as soon as possible. They were named as Major Fiedler, Hauptmann Boehm-Tettelbach, his wife, and a radio operator called Hartmann. In order to stress the 'innocent' nature of the undertaking, the party would be carried in a Lufthansa airliner. By way of further proof of authenticity, the aircraft's civil registration was furnished (D-AGAK) together with the names of the three civilian crew members, namely, Naumann, Mitscher and Amtblatt. The Irish authorities were to be asked to provide details of available radio beacons and frequencies.

In a long telegram dated 21 December,[12] Hempel said that Irish Minister for External Affairs Joseph Walshe had seemed very worried about the proposal and urged that it be postponed. He used the fact that the Taoiseach, Eamon de Valera, was in hospital for an eye operation as a pretext for delay. He was very agitated and asked the Germans to consider the furore that would ensue in England and the United States. Hempel himself had misgivings and was of the opinion that the true identity of the officers would come out in the long run.

The Dublin government was obviously in a very awkward situation but refused to give the necessary permission for the landing and it is obvious that they were aware of the Germans' motives from the outset. The matter assumed such importance that the German Foreign Minister himself, Joachim von Ribbentrop, became personally involved. He reminded Hempel that although the Irish were to treated in a friendly fashion they had, in fact, no right to object to the enlargement of the consular staff. It was in conformity with diplomatic usage.

Neither side would give way and the impasse continued. De Valera had authorized Walshe to say that great danger to Ireland could stem from acceding to the German request. During a personal interview that Hempel had with him, de Valera said that his country was being squeezed from both sides. and that the very basis of Irish neutrality could be undermined.

The Germans were clearly incensed by Dublin's intransigence but the Irish suspicions would prove to be well-founded. Documentary evidence of German duplicity in the affair is contained in a telegram which Ribbentrop sent to Hempel on Christmas Day 1940.[13] He said that he charged Hempel with a particular duty not to reveal the *real* mission of the new personnel – not even to his own staff. He said in conclusion that he was determined not to yield to the Irish defiance.

However, Hempel seems to have had a good sense of the delicate nature of the relations with the Irish and he finally told Ribbentrop on 30 December[14] that he thought that forcing the issue any further would only result in a hardening of the Irish attitude. At this point the attempt to enlarge the consular staff by devious means seems to have been dropped but the Germans had suffered a diplomatic reverse and were very annoyed.

A few days later, bombs began falling on Irish soil. Not surprisingly, there is nothing in the record to show that these incidents were intended as either retribution or intimidation or whether they were simply a series of unconnected events. There is, however, one item of documentary evidence which demonstrates conclusively that not all German infringements of Irish airspace were accidental at this juncture. One such incursion had a decidedly hostile intent.

On the evening of 11 January at 1720 hours BST, an He111 (identification code IT+KK) belonging to KGr 126, took off from Nantes airfield. The logbook entry of its pilot, Unteroffizier Thomas Hammerl, blandly states that it was carrying one LMB 1000kg mine 'for the Dublin area'. With the detail completed, the aircraft landed back at Nantes at 0036 hours.[15] Although LMB mines were frequently used against land targets, the probability is that this one was laid in the sea as there is no record of any mines or bombs falling in the Dublin area that night.

If Hammerl's mission had come to light at the time, the temperature in relations between Dublin and Berlin would have dropped yet further. Even if the mine had been laid outside the three-mile territorial limit it would still have been regarded as a hostile act. Coming only a week after the New Year incidents, it would have been persuasive evidence that Germany had a very pragmatic attitude towards Irish neutrality. On the other hand, if the professional diplomats at the German Foreign Office took a sceptical view of Irish impartiality they would have felt vindicated on receiving an interesting scrap of information contained in a radio transmission.

A diplomatic telegram (Number 726) from the Wilhelmstrasse (the German Foreign Office) dated 10 November 1940 contains the following intriguing passage, said to be part of a message monitored by German naval forces:

> All orders will be issued to the troops through the 'Ir. Commdr.' (probably 'Irish commander'). On no account will they fire except on his order. All concerned have been informed.

There was no speculation in the telegram about the source of the message (presumably British) which could mean that it came as no surprise to the Germans to learn that British-Irish co-operation at an operational level was taking place.

Although all references to installing additional staff at the consulate disappeared from the diplomatic telegrams for the time being, it seems that the Germans had not given up hope of establishing a source of intelligence in Dublin. The economic war against Britain had reached a high pitch and acquiring information about British shipping movements around Ireland was a priority in German eyes. From enquiries that the German Foreign Office made early in 1941, it appears that they had hopes of getting agents into Ireland by ship through Lisbon. Hempel reported that the possibilities were virtually non-existent and that only the occasional grain ship from overseas put into an Irish port. German thoroughness in researching the subject, however, can be seen in the telegrams from consulates in places as widely scattered as Lisbon, Madrid, Montevideo and Buenos Aires.

In a telegram dated 4 February 1941[16] from Lisbon signed 'Huene' (the German ambassador) it was stated that no freighter had left Lisbon for Ireland since September. The text went on to say 'confidentially' that there were two possibilities of illegal transportation to Ireland *which had been tested with success*: (1) through 'Middleman' Abwehr Brest (German Military Intelligence at Brest) and (2) by 'warship arranged with the German Navy.' Why Lisbon should have been in possession of such sensitive information about espionage operations in Ireland is not explained but its accuracy can be verified in German naval operations records. These disclose that at the end of 1940 there had already been at least two landings of agents on the Irish coast from U-boats as well as one attempted landing of saboteurs.

SPIES AND SABOTEURS

Shortly after the outbreak of war, Germany's military intelligence organisation, the Abwehr, asked the German Navy if it would be possible to land
saboteurs on the coast of Ireland. An entry in the war diary of the Naval War
Staff (Skl) dated 2 October 1939 recorded that the question was answered in
the affirmative. The Abwehr was advised to contact the Commander-in-Chief
Submarines (BdU) at the appropriate time to arrange the details.[1] Thus began
a series of enterprises which are in the best traditions of the world of
espionage but which achieved virtually nothing of any value to the German
war effort.

A comprehensive account of the various ventures undertaken comes from
the pen of Enno Stephan in his book *Spies in Ireland*, first published in 1961.
The author had the advantage of interviewing many of the principal figures
involved in the immediate post-war years but freely admits that his task was
made difficult by the intrigues that characterize the profession of spying. He
had to cope with a tangled web of lies and half-truths, compounded in some
cases by the deliberate falsification of official documents, often as a result of
inter-departmental rivalry. Although the German Navy was forbidden to
reveal details, its war diaries at least describe the background to three
operations which took place in the year under review.

In January 1940, following the Skl's agreeing to co-operate, Abwehr II,
which was the Abwehr organization's branch responsible for sabotage, sanc-
tioned the dispatch of two agents by U-boat. One of them was a colourful
character called Ernst Weber-Drohl who had worked in Ireland in the 1920s
as a circus strong man under the professional name of 'Atlas the Strong.'
Among other things, his task was to deliver messages and a large sum of
money to the IRA. He was to be accompanied by a radio operator with a
transmitter for sending information obtained back to Germany.

In keeping with the contradictory evidence usually associated with espionage, Stephan asserts that only Weber-Drohl himself actually made the trip
and that the radio operator, who was a civilian volunteer, refused to go at the
last moment. The war diary of the Skl, however, reproduces an operational
order addressed to the commander of *U-37*, Korvettenkapitän Werner Hart-

mann, providing for the embarkation of two agents at the naval base of Wilhelmshaven.[2] The operational order is very specific about the details of how the landing was to be made and makes interesting reading. It was headed 'For officers only' and referred repeatedly to the necessity for secrecy. As far as the crew was concerned, the strange passengers were journalists engaged on an assignment. Only when the boat was clear of the Heligoland Bight was the crew to be told about the mission. They were forbidden to discuss the matter among themselves or with any person outside the boat. Each sailor was to give an unconditional pledge of secrecy and receive a written notification of his obligation. It was pointed out that failure to comply would be an offence punishable by the death penalty.

The landing would take place in one of three specified areas and each area would have two alternative locations. The U-boat commander had the discretion to select one of the two locations in a particular area having regard to the weather conditions and navigational constraints. The locations were (1) Killala Bay or Clew Bay, both off the coast of Co. Mayo and code-named *Karl* and *Caesar* respectively (2) Dingle Bay or Brandon Bay in Co. Kerry, code-named *Dora* and *Bruno* respectively and (3) Dungarvan Bay in County Waterford or the neighbouring coast, code-named *Gustav* and *Nordpol* respectively. It was necessary that the landing be effected in the vicinity of a railway line and after completion the U-boat was to transmit the code-name of the place followed by the date, for example, *Karl 25* would mean that the landing had taken place on Killala Bay on thetwenty-fifth day of the month. The agents were to row ashore in a Luftwaffe rubber dinghy specially supplied for the purpose. They were *not* to be accompanied by any member of the submarine's crew and once again the requirement for the utmost secrecy was repeated. It was highly significant that the operational order stated that no advance arrangement had been made with any persons in Ireland.

The number of agents to came ashore remains obscure. According to Stephan, Weber-Drohl was alone and that he lost the radio he was carrying when the dinghy capsized. There must be some doubt about this version since it asserts that Weber-Drohl was accompanied in the dinghy by a crew member but in view of the peremptory tone of the order it is unlikely that the U-boat commander would have deviated from his instructions. If only one agent was to travel instead of two as originally intended, the Skl war diary would have been expected to contain some reference to it. None is recorded, however.

The U-boat's own war diary[3] does not disclose the number of persons to be disembarked but it states that the landing was effected in Donegal Bay on 8 February 1940.[3] Although Donegal Bay was not named as a location in the operational order, the U-boat commander, looking at a chart of the area, may have regarded Killala Bay and Sligo Bay as geographically part of the larger

Donegal Bay. Here again, it is most unlikely that he would have deviated from his orders without specific authority. Notwithstanding that, however, the commander's right to protect the safety of his vessel and the crew would have superseded all other considerations.

Nothing very much is known about Weber-Drohl's activities in Ireland but they seem to have been relatively innocuous. Apparently he delivered the money and messages to the IRA as required but he was constantly under police surveillance. After being allowed to remain at liberty for about a year he was arrested and interned.

With its limited objectives the mission of Ernst Weber-Drohl was presumably regarded as a success by the Abwehr but it was even more important to install a radio transmitter. Accordingly, four months later, another U-boat slipped into Irish territorial waters to land an agent. Walter Simon was 58 years old and had spent most of his working life at sea. He spoke excellent English and was recruited by the Abwehr before the war and had been to England on three different occasions on spying missions. In June 1940 he was told that his next assignment would take him to Ireland. A radio transmitter was supplied on which he was to furnish daily weather reports which were urgently required by the Luftwaffe. In addition, he was to log the movements of British convoys. Contact with the IRA was strictly forbidden.

The U-boat detailed for this operation was *U-38* commanded by Korvettenkapitän Heinrich Liebe.[4] The operational order issued was identical in its material details to that issued to *U-37* for the earlier mission. It contained the same categorical instructions about preserving secrecy and gave the captain the choice of the same landing places.

The entry in the war diary of the Skl recording the operational order is dated 5 June 1940 but there is no indication of exactly when the submarine left Wilhelmshaven. The landing was to take place in the course of a war cruise and after it was completed *U-38* would proceed to the North West Approaches for normal operations.

The submarine's war diary gives no information as to where or when Simon went ashore but it seems likely that it was in Dingle Bay on the night of 12/13 June. He had assumed the alias of Karl Anderson and carried a British passport in that name. After landing in a rubber dinghy he buried his radio transmitter for later collection. According to Stephan's account of Simon's mission, one of his tasks was to establish contacts in Dublin who would furnish him with information about the movement of convoys through the North Channel. The entire enterprise came to a very premature conclusion, however. Simon got no further than Tralee railway station where he was observed by detectives boarding a train and later apprehended in Dublin.

After depositing Simon on the shore at Dingle, *U-38* went on to complete a very destructive operational patrol, sinking two ships from convoy HX 48,

12 Admiral Doenitz congratulating Korvettenkapitän Werner Hartmann, the commander of *U-37*, on his return from the successful operational cruise during which Ernst Weber-Drohl was landed at Donegal Bay

13 *U-38* arriving back at Wilhelmshaven on 1 July 1940 from the patrol during which Walter Simon was landed in Ireland

homeward bound from Halifax and four other ships elsewhere, before arriving back at Wilhelmshaven on 1 July.[5]

The Skl war diary contains an entry dated 15 June in which reference is made to an order having been made on that date for the transportation to an unknown destination of 'a particularly important man' in *U-26*. No further information was given and the U-boat's war diary makes no mention of any such operation. There was at this time a German agent called Willi Preets alias Paddy Mitchell who was arrested by Irish police in Dublin some time after June 1940 but the circumstances of his arrival in Ireland seem never to have been revealed.

So far, the Germans were having a lack of success in their desire to establish a radio link with Ireland. Another attempt was soon put in train. On 5 May 1940 Dr Hermann Goertz, easily the most able German agent to operate in Eire during the war, parachuted into County Meath from an He111.[6] He had an eventful and frustrating stay in the country — much of it spent in captivity — but in the final analysis he achieved little in the context of the Abwehr's objectives. Unlike the previous agents who landed by U-boat, he was expressly charged with creating a working relationship with the IRA and fostering political instability in Northern Ireland accompanied by acts of sabotage. Also unlike his predecessors, he was a commissioned officer acting under orders from the Army High Command (OKH) and not the Abwehr.

Much of Goertz's activities is shrouded in mystery but the instructions he was given for setting up a reliable radio link were unambiguous. In a statement he made before his death,[7] he referred to a secret radio transmitter in Northern Ireland called 'Rathlin' from which the OKW was said to have received messages.[8] He had no personal involvement with the station nor was he aware of whether it was supposed to be located on Rathlin Island but he knew that the German Navy made use of it. The Irish security service apparently treated this claim with scepticism. A radio transmitter on Rathlin Island would have been in an unequalled position for sending information about the movement of convoys, that is, in the unlikely event of its escaping immediate detection.

A great deal of the bungling associated with German espionage in Ireland could be traced to rivalry between the different agencies responsible for it. The Abwehr had directed the activities of Weber-Drohl, Simon and Preetz. The OKW was responsible for the Goertz mission; now the Foreign Office became involved.

Early in 1940, the German Foreign Office began to take an interest in Sean Russell, who was then Chief of Staff of the IRA.[9] He had been in America at the outbreak of war and the Foreign Office saw an opportunity to cause Britain some embarrassment. Russell accepted an invitation to go to Germany direct from America and arrived there via Genoa on 5 May 1940.

Another militant Republican, Frank Ryan, was also recruited. He had served in the International Brigade in the Spanish Civil War and had narrowly avoided execution when he was captured by Franco's forces. The Germans secured his release from prison and brought him to Germany where he and Russell were given intensive training in sabotage. The Foreign Office was apparently impressed with both men and formed the opinion that Russell in particular was a very determined individual and could give the British a lot of trouble in Northern Ireland. However, the Germans gave no firm undertaking to supply arms to the IRA. They had no guarantee that any arms they sent would not be used in Eire and they had no desire to antagonize the government there. The main aim was to establish a radio link.

The U-boat detailed to carry the two subversives to Ireland was the *U-65* commanded by Kapitänleutnant Hans-Gerrit von Stockhausen and they embarked at Wilhelmshaven on 7 August.[10] The submarine left port the following day and headed out across the North Sea. A radio message on the 9th reported its position as 'mid-North Sea'. After rounding the North of Scotland, it radioed on the 12th that it was about to enter the operational area. Neither the U-boat's nor the Skl's war diary discloses the intended location of the landing of the two passengers. All that can be said with any certainty is that it was to be somewhere on the west coast. The U-boat was now in waters which were extremely dangerous for British shipping at that time. On the fourteenth *U-65* must have passed close to the spot where her sister ship, the *U-59*, under the command of Kapitänleutnant Matz was sinking the steamer *Betty* (2339 tons, Hunt Steamship Corp.), 35 miles from Tory Island, as she neared the end of a voyage from Saigon to Liverpool with a cargo of rice. Shortly afterwards, the *U-65* reported 'in operational area'. It was then that she transmitted the dramatic message which was reproduced in the Skl war diary in the following terms:

> August 14: *U-65* reports the death on board of General Russell who was to have been landed on the Irish coast. The discharge of the special assignment is therefore abrogated with regret.

For some unexplained reason, Ryan did not proceed with the planned landing. *U-65*'s orders were to proceed with her operational cruise but the boat sustained damage from heavy seas on the sixteenth which necessitated her return to port. She was ordered to proceed to Lorient and arrived there on 19 August. Ryan returned to Germany where he remained until his death on 10 June 1944.

There are many questions about the circumstances of Sean Russell's death which will never be answered. *U-65* was sunk with all hands (but with a different commander) in the North Atlantic on 15 May 1943. Von Stockhausen had died in a car accident in Berlin a few months earlier. In his book,

14 *U-65* seen entering Lorient harbour soon after the abortive attempt to
land Sean Russell and Frank Ryan in Ireland

Enno Stephan said that when von Stockhausen's report and that of the medical orderly who had attended Russell before he died was reviewed by doctors, they were of the opinion that the cause of death was a burst gastric ulcer. He was said to have been buried at sea not far from the Irish coast.

Over the next two or three years several ambitious schemes were hatched by the Abwehr in order to try and exploit Ireland's geographical position and her neutral status but none met with any success. This was due, in large measure, to the diligence of an Irish security organisation which had long experience in dealing with subversive elements. A combination of this and sheer ineptitude on the part of the agents and their superiors stifled most of the German espionage efforts before they had begun.

The aborted mission involving Russell and Ryan had apparently been intended as an attempt to co-ordinate German strategy with an IRA campaign in Northern Ireland aimed at the British forces. But the reality was that the massive British military presence there at the time meant that no guerrilla campaign which the IRA could have mounted would have made any real impact on the course of the war.

Berlin was not having much success in getting effective agents into Ireland either by the direct method or in the guise of consular officials. They next made enquiries about civil air services to Ireland presumably, with the same aim in mind. Here too, the prospects were not encouraging. A telegram to Hempel on 2 February 1941 from Berlin pointed out that Wendell Willkie, the Republican candidate in the recent US presidential election, had obtained permission to fly into Ireland for a meeting with de Valera. How, it was asked, did he get this permission when German requests were refused? Hempel replied that there was an agreement between Britain and Ireland that one aircraft from each country could fly to the other each day.[11] Obviously, this was no help either.

Eire's relations with both Britain and Germany were extremely delicate at this stage. A small country, geographically located in the middle of a theatre of war, her room for manoeuvre was severely limited. There was a need for fine judgment in making day-to-day decisions. This was evident in dealing with the thorny question of the radio transmitter in the German consulate.

In November 1940, General Walter Warlimont, a staff planning officer with the High Command of the Armed Forces (OKW) in Berlin had spoken of the possibility of sending German meteorologists to Ireland. They would be useful in reporting on the approach of Atlantic weather systems and help to offset the advantage enjoyed by the British in this regard. What he seems to have had in mind was the installation of trained meteorologists in the legation and not undercover agents like Walter Simon or Willi Preetz. While the proposal apparently came to nothing, it emerged some months later that a radio within the consulate had, in fact, been used for sending weather reports.

The Irish government became very agitated at any suggestion that the consulate was being used for transmitting information of a military nature. Sending weather reports would have come within this definition. It would have contravened all diplomatic convention and the British would not have tolerated it. It could, for example, have been used as a cover for giving Berlin intelligence about shipping movements round the Irish coast. A telegram which Hempel sent to State Secretary Baron Ernst von Weizsäcker at the Foreign Office via Washington on 12 August 1941 provides clear evidence that there was a transmitter in the consulate and that it had already been used for sending weather reports:

> After Walshe (Irish Minister for External Affairs) had warned me twice about the secret transmitter, de Valera returned to the matter today. In what was a careful, pointedly friendly, but at the same time very serious fashion, he repeated the request that radio traffic be halted except for those wholly rare cases of the utmost importance.
>
> It is now plainly a question of whether continuing weather reports is so important that we will, if necessary, put up with its very serious political consequences. For my part, I must strongly recommend the immediate cessation of weather reports.[12]

Hempel's advice is typical of the traditional approach of the professional diplomat which he adopted during his service at the Dublin consulate – in sharp contrast to that of his political masters.

The vexed question of the transmitter nevertheless remained throughout much of 1941 and was the cause of a great deal of worry to the Irish government. The following extract from a secret memo to de Valera from one of his senior civil servants later depicts in graphic language how serious the problem had been and highlights the ever watchful and uncompromising attitude of the British:

> I spoke to the German minister today (date unknown) about his transmitter. I acknowledged that, as far as we knew, he had not been using it for a long time but I strongly emphasised that so long as there was a wireless transmitter in the German legation, it constituted a positive danger to our neutrality ...
>
> The British Representative was constantly reminding us of the dangerous possibility of the German Minister using his wireless for such a purpose (passing military information). Indeed, hardly a week passed when we did not receive such a warning. I could tell him quite frankly and in the most friendly way that the presence of a wireless transmitter in the German Legation was giving us more worry in our relations with the British and American governments than any other factor in our many-sided dealings with these two governments.[13]

A memo to the Foreign Ministry in Berlin from the OKW on 20 January 1941 is another example of the persistence with which the Germans pursued the aim of getting agents into Ireland in the guise of consular staff. The OKW offered to land the necessary personnel by U-boat on certain conditions: The persons concerned would have to have diplomatic passports with Irish visas and would land at an Irish port.[14] These were seen as necessary requirements so that their activities would not be impeded at the outset by any lack of diplomatic standing. The German Foreign Office did not take up the offer.

Further evidence that the Germans had not given up the idea appears in diplomatic correspondence between Berlin and Hempel in February. Ribbentrop wanted to know if staff at German consulates abroad (he seemed to have the United States in mind) could be transferred to Dublin by ordinary passenger steamer. Hempel's assistant, Henning Thomsen, reported that two American shipping companies operated a service from New York to Liverpool through Dublin under the Panamanian flag but that pro-British authorities in New York and the Canadians at Halifax, Nova Scotia would make the transportation of diplomatic employees virtually impossible. Besides, the ships had to pass through British naval control in Scotland or Northern Ireland (he may have been referring here to the Examination Service facility at Bangor). This line of enquiry was also dropped but the Germans made a final attempt to achieve their aim by suggesting bringing in the bogus diplomats by air from Lisbon. On 18 February, Hempel reported that he had asked Frederick Boland at the Department of External Affairs about rumours that civil aircraft flying between England and Lisbon were making stops in Ireland. Seemingly, the Germans were exploring the possibility that such flights could be used to connect with the Pan American World Airways clipper service between Lisbon and New York. Boland denied that this was, in fact, happening.[15] This appears to have, at last, put an end to discussion about the movement of consular officials and the impression gained from the whole affair is that Irish intransigence had triumphed.

In declining the OKW's offer to convey diplomats to Ireland by submarine, the Foreign Office may have taken account of how sensitive the Irish government would be to the arrival of German personnel by U-boat. The British would have taken a very serious view of it. To the Irish, the violation of their territorial waters or airspace was now a constantly nagging problem. Each of the belligerents was watching for any sign that the other was deriving any advantage from the special circumstances created by Ireland's neutrality. Evidently, Dr Hempel had been asked by Berlin to investigate reports that British warships had been patrolling close to the Irish shoreline. He had replied to say that 'a reliable observer' had certainly seen British warships offshore but nevertheless outside the three-mile limit. At the same time the

German Navy's Skl also confirmed that there was no evidence that British vessels were freely using Irish coastal waters.[16]

On the other hand, an allegation that U-boats were being refuelled at points on the west coast provoked an angry response from the Dublin government. One such charge originated in an article in the *Daily Express* newspaper, in which a Co. Down MP at Westminster, the Reverend James Little, stated that he had it on the authority of credible witnesses that 'U-boats could get everything they wanted in west coast harbours'. Implicit in this was the accusation that the Irish government was, at worst, aiding and abetting or, at the very least, condoning such acts. The Foreign Office in Berlin, in a message dated 17 January 1941 to the Commander-in-Chief of the German Navy (Ob.d.M),[17] quoted from an article in the 'Chicago Daily News' in which de Valera had refuted the Reverend Little's allegation in detail. He was presumably using an American newspaper as a means of stating the Irish case because the United States government was taking a very pro-British stance at this time and, moreover, her own merchant seamen were at risk in the North Atlantic. In the Chicago article de Valera claimed that the entire Irish coast was kept under observation day and night from fixed points, as well as from military and marine patrols. He went on to point out that fuel oil was in very short supply in Ireland and strictly rationed. Furthermore, it was distributed exclusively by British and American oil companies who would be expected to know the destination of their deliveries.

This was a subject which occupied Churchill a great deal in the winter of 1940/41 and he was continually enquiring from the First Sea Lord as to whether he had any confirmed reports that this was happening. Quite apart from de Valera's strenuous denial of the allegation, Hempel advised Berlin that the British naval attaché in Dublin – himself a submariner – had dismissed the idea that U-boats could be refuelled in remote Irish bays as not technically feasible.

However improbable the revictualling of U-boats was, there was nevertheless evidence that they sought shelter or perhaps recharged their batteries at isolated points on the west coast from time to time. Such incidents could have provided the basis for the Reverend Little's accusation. For example, on the preceding 3 August, FOIC Belfast recorded in his war diary that the Head Constable of the RUC at Beleek had seen a U-boat lying on the surface a mile off Rossnowlagh in Co. Donegal.[18] (This was a good example of covert surveillance work carried out in wartime by the police.) Another entry stated that the master of the *Annaghmore* (573 tons, John Kelly Ltd), had reported a U-boat lying at the mouth of the Shannon Estuary on that same day, 3 August.

Occupying a pivotal position in the conflict, Ireland had become the focus of world attention as its government strove to reconcile the diametrically opposed pressures being exerted by the belligerents and – to a lesser degree– by elements within the country itself. For one turbulent year, the waters and airspace round and over the British Isles was the most vital theatre of operations in the war and Ireland's neutrality did not fit easily into the scheme of things.

What was surely conduct incompatible with neutrality at this time had nothing to do with the Irish government, however. On 21 January 1941 the Foreign Ministry in Berlin informed the Ob.d.M that 'a source who repeatedly gave reliable information' had seen sailors of the United States Navy unloading depth charges in the port of Londonderry and laying cable across the River Foyle.[19] It is probable that this incident was only one of many and, although it must have been witnessed by a large number of people in the city it naturally received no publicity. American public opinion would probably not have approved of it at that moment but it is another example of President Roosevelt's covert moves which, if continued, must eventually bring the United States into the war. In the German view, it was another demonstration of Rooseveldt's 'warmongering'. Five months later, the United States all but discarded the neutral facade at sea when its warships began openly to escort British convoys part of the way across the Atlantic.

8

LONDONDERRY, WESTERN OUTPOST

The short, dark days at the turn of the year brought cold and miserable weather. Icy winds and snow showers lashed the North Channel as the endless procession of convoys rounded Rathlin Island. The atrocious conditions in the North West Approaches brought some brief respite to anxious sailors maintaining a constant watch for submarines and aircraft but the menacing trend in the war at sea was set to continue.

The last recorded success for I/KG40 in 1940 was an attack on the *Trevarrack* (5270 tons, Hain Steamship Co.), north of the entrance to Lough Foyle on 29 December. The ship was a straggler from the slow convoy SLS 58 and in spite of low cloud and poor visibility she was spotted by a Condor at 1025 hours. Its commander was Oberleutnant Paul Gömmer who had taken off from Bordeaux at 0448 hours on an armed reconnaissance and meteorological flight with four SC250kg bombs. Gömmer made a low-level attack from the stern and dropped two bombs both of which hit the ship. One penetrated the engine room and exploded. The vessel immediately developed a heavy list and was judged by the Condor's crew to be a total loss. This assessment seems to have been shared by the ship's master as she was abandoned. The destroyers *Highlander* and *Harvester* were soon in attendance and took the survivors on board. There is some doubt as to whether the vessel actually sank for a ship bearing the same name was subsequently reported sunk by *U-46* on 8 June 1941 en route to Canada.

Gömmer himself was again engaged in sorties against shipping on 3 and 15 January but on 5 February he and four of his crew met the same fate as so many of their KG 40 comrades in the Battle of the Atlantic.

On the morning of 5 February, an aircraft was heard flying low in bad visibility in the vicinity of Cashelfean Mountain, about five miles from Durrus, Co. Cork. A witness said that its engines appeared to be 'missing' and shortly afterwards, at 0925 hours, the aircraft hit the side of the mountain at a height of 850 feet. There was a house close to the crash site and a lady named Miss Mary Nugent ran to the scene. Although there was danger of fire or explosion, she immediately went into the wrecked fuselage and dragged clear one of the crew, Feldwebel Hohaus, whom she saw was still

15 The Condor which crashed on Castlefean mountain, Co. Cork

alive. All the other five occupants of the aircraft, including meteorologist Erhard Herrstrom, were killed and are buried in the German Military Cemetery at Glencree, Co. Wicklow. The German government subsequently awarded Miss Nugent the German Life Saving, Medal for, as the citation testified, acting with great courage and in complete disregard for her own safety.[1]

When the Condors were placed under German naval command on 6 January 1941, the tactical role of I/KG 40 immediately underwent a change. The aircraft would now range far out into the Atlantic to the limit of their endurance in search of convoys. This would be their prime objective. Thus began the partnership between the Condors and the U-boats that became one of the legends of the Battle of the Atlantic. A VHF radio system for communication between aircraft and U-boats, christened *Möve* or seagull, was developed. The aircraft could both 'home' boats to a target by giving them bearings or use voice transmission. Sometimes the functions were reversed and the Condors were led to a convoy by the U-boats if an underwater attack was for some reason not possible.

A further measure was the introduction of a floating radio beacon called *Schwann* or swan. When dropped by parachute in a known position relative to a convoy, it could be used by other aircraft or U-boats as an aid to locate their targets.

These technical innovations took time to develop to full operational efficiency, however, and for the first half of 1941 the degree of co-operation between German air and sea units did not come up to expectations. Poor communications led to a lack of co-ordination and locating convoys continued to depend on a measure of luck. In addition, the Germans were suffering from a further impediment of which they were not, in fact, aware. By making use of *Ultra* (the information obtained from deciphering German codes) the British were able to change the routing of a convoy after its position had been reported to Doenitz's headquarters.

In spite of the early disappointments in working with the U-boats and the often appalling winter weather, the Condors of I/KG 40 achieved remarkable success in the first few months of 1941. A British naval intelligence report for the period disclosed that in January and February, the unit, operating with only 15 serviceable aircraft at any one time, sank 47 ships and damaged a further 17, the majority to the north and west of Ireland.[2] The surviving KG 40 unit records covering these sinkings provide confirmation of Britain's predicament at this time.

Bad weather prevented anti-shipping operations on several days in January but on the 10th a Condor under the command of Oberleutnant Franz Burmeister was shot down by the mate of the ocean-going tug *Seaman* manning a Lewis gun while it was making a low-level attack 320 kilometres north-west of Malin Head. Burmeister and two of the crew were rescued but three others died. It was Burmeister who had on 9 November made an unsuccessful attack on the *Empress of Japan*, a sister ship of the ill-fated *Empress of Britain*.

On the 21st, Condors sank two vessels off the Donegal coast. At 1120 hours, one attacked the *Temple Mead* (4427 tons, Lambert Brothers), on passage from Rosario on the River Plate with grain. The name of the Condor's commander is not recorded but he made the attack from a height of 100 metres. Two SC250 bombs hit the vessel amidships and two fell about ten metres from the hull. It quickly sank with the loss of 14 of its crew. An hour later, a second Condor sank the ocean-going tug *Englishman* (487 tons), about 100 kilometres north of Malin Head.

Two days later, two Condors took off from Bordeaux at daybreak to intercept shipping reported west of Ireland. At 1100 hours, one of them sighted the freighter *Langlegorse* (4524 tons, Medomsley Steamship Co.) 260 kilometres west of Westport on a course of 060 degrees. She was homeward bound from Durban with an undisclosed cargo. The Condor made a low pass over the ship, dropping two SC250 bombs, both of which fell amidships. There was a violent explosion and the vessel broke up and sank within 8 minutes. The crew were seen taking to the boats but, in fact, 36 of them were lost. About an hour later, at 1155 hours, the same aircraft found the Belfast-owned *Lurigethan* (3564 tons, G. Heyn & Sons) en route from Port Sudan to Hull in a position 480 kilometres north-west of Westport. The Condor attacked it with three bombs, one of which fell close to the stern. After reconnoitring the area for other shipping, the Condor returned and found the ship in a sinking condition. It made another attack with its remaining bomb which fell close to the starboard hull. The ship sank and 16 of the crew lost their lives. The Condor's crew in its report mentioned that the defensive fire from the ship's machine-guns was heavy. Two RAF Hudsons and a Sunderland flying-boat were also sighted in the area but no fire was exchanged. The second Condor also made contact. At 1215 hours it attacked the *Mostyn* (1859 tons, Martin, Mostyn & Co.) on the way from Lisbon to Port Talbot with pit wood when it was about 500 kilometres north-west of Westport. One bomb fell amidships and the other close by the bow. The Condor's crew reported that the ship had developed a list before they left the scene. The ship, in fact, sank but the fate of the crew is not recorded.

The Condor crews now shared with the men of RAF Coastal Command long hours in freezing conditions over an inhospitable ocean. When engaged in a purely reconnaissance role and carrying no bomb load, they were able to penetrate the Atlantic to a distance of 1750 kilometres, bringing them to the shores of Iceland and the Azores.

Its meagre resources rarely enabled I/KG 40 to launch an attack with more

16 A Condor crew at the end of an Atlantic patrol

than a single aircraft at any one time but on 10 February 1941, Fritz Fliegel led a flight of five Condors in a sortie to attack a large convoy to the west of the Bay of Biscay which was homeward bound from Gibraltar. It was a notable — if not unique — occasion for five of these rare aircraft to operate together in a single operation. All made low-level attacks and in spite of concentrated fire from all the ships and the escorts none sustained serious damage. Apart from Fliegel, the other aircraft commanders were Oberleutnants Adam, Schlosser and Jope (the identity of the fifth is not recorded) and they destroyed a total of five ships between them. They were the *Britannic* (2490 tons, W.H. Cockerline & Co.), *Jura* (1759 tons, Glen & Co.), *Dagmar* (1, 2471 tons, ex-Danish flag), and the Norwegian *Tejo*. All sank almost immediately. The fifth, the *Varna* (514 tons, Glen & Co.) was badly damaged and sank in bad weather on 16 February. The Condors claimed to have damaged at least three other ships. This convoy suffered particularly badly and two further ships, the *Courland* (1525 tons, Currie Line) and the *Estrellano* (1,983 tons, Ellerman Lines) were sunk by *U-37*, now under the command of Kapitän-leutnant Clausen. The following day, Clausen sank another Currie Line vessel, the *Brandenburg* (1473 tons), bound for Leith from Vila Real. Coinci-dentally, at the same time, yet another Currie Line ship, the *Iceland* (1236 tons, was being sunk by the German heavy cruiser *Admiral Hipper*, further to the west, near the Azores. It brought to an end two very bad days for Allied shipping.

In spite of the awesome reputation I/KG 40 was gaining in the Battle of the Atlantic, the reality was that the demands imposed on it by its new role as adjunct of the U-boats were too onerous. If Doenitz had hoped that the information about convoys gathered by the Condors would irreversibly tip the balance in his favour he was soon disappointed. Seldom were there more than a few of them operational. This elementary fact must have escaped the attention of the OKW, however, for the war diary of the ObdM for 14 February contains the almost incredible piece of information that the Führer had agreed to a request for the transfer of Fw200 Condors to the Mediterra-nean 'provided the naval operations staff agreed'.[3] Doenitz' reaction to this suggestion can be imagined but it serves to illustrate the OKW's (and Hitler's) ignorance of the indispensable role that these aeroplanes and their crews were playing in the Battle of the Atlantic. The idea of depriving the German Navy, which was by far the most effective arm of the Wehrmacht at that particular time, of one of its most valuable weapons was ludicrous and would have been greeted with disbelief by the staff at the British Admiralty.

There is a story that one morning Doenitz arrived at his headquarters and asked how many Condors would be available that day. When told that there was one, he shrugged his shoulders in a gesture of resignation and walked away.[4] He was utterly convinced that with enough U-boats and accurate information about the position of convoys, he could bring about Britain's defeat. In the winter of 1940/41, it was a close-run thing but that prize slipped from his grasp.

There were days in January when the Admiralty staff in London must have contemplated the latest sinkings on their wall charts with feelings of near-despair. The U-boats and Condors seemed to be vying with each other in a litany of disaster in the North West Approaches. In a period of little more than 24 hours and within 250 miles of Malin Head, three large vessels were sunk with dreadful loss of life. On the 16th, the cargo liner *Zealandic* (10,578 tons, Shaw Savill) on the way from Liverpool to Australia was sunk by *U-106* commanded by Kapitänleutnant Hessler with the loss of all 73 on board. Later the same day Hessler found and sank the passenger liner *Oropesa* (12,118 tons, Pacific Steam Navigation Co), homeward bound to the UK from East African ports. A total of 106 passengers and crew lost their lives. A little further north on the following day, *U-96* under the command of Kapitänleutnant Lehmann-Willenbrock sank the splendid *Almeda Star* (14,935 tons, Blue Star Line), bound for the River Plate from Liverpool with 194 passengers on board. All the passengers along with the crew of 166 perished.[5]

By the standards of fifty years later, these were by no means large ships but in the time of the Second World War they were very significant vessels indeed.

As the nightmarish month ended, four ships from one convoy were lost on the twenty-ninth as it was making for the entrance to the North Channel on the final stage of its voyage. The *U-93* commanded by Kapitänleutnant Korth sank the *King Robert* (5886 tons, Scottish SS Co.), and the tanker *W. B. Walker* (10,468 tons, Oriental Tankers Ltd) both bound for the Bristol Channel. At the same time as this was happening, Korth's colleague, Kapitänleutnant Kuppisch in *U-94*, was sinking the *West Wales* (4354 tons, Gibbs & Co.) and the *Rushpool* (5125 tons, R. Ropner & Co.), a sister ship of the *Troutpool*, mined in Belfast Lough six months earlier.

A little further south, about 90 kilometres west of Achill Island, a Condor, possibly operating in conjunction with *U-93* and *U-94*, made a low-level attack on the *Pandion* (1994 tons, British & Continental SS Co.) which was on her way to Portugal from the Tyne. The ship sustained considerable damage and ran aground in Lough Swilly the following day, breaking in two. The Condor concerned then apparently had a highly unusual encounter with an RAF Sunderland flying-boat. A fire fight developed between the two giant aircraft. Both sustained damage and Anton Winter, a young Leutnant who was acting as one of the Condor's radio operators, was shot in the head and died on the way back to Bordeaux. The Condor's crew reported that smoke had been seen coming from the Sunderland after the engagement and that two RAF twin-engined fighters were seen approaching. No contact with them took place.

Taking advantage of improved weather on 28 January, four Condors were sent out over an area due west of the North Channel in a search for targets. One of them was commanded by Edmund Daser (now promoted to Hauptmann) who took off from Stavanger at 0433 hours BST. Between 1010 and 1025 hours, when he was 220 kilometres north-west of Malin Head he sighted a convoy steaming towards the North Channel. He attacked a 4500-ton freighter at mast-height and saw two of his SC250 bombs hit the ship between the deck and the waterline. Neither exploded. One other bomb did explode hitting the hull just above the waterline. He then made an attack on another vessel but this time the remaining bombs failed to leave the bomb-racks and he had to abort the mission.

Three other Condors took off from Bordeaux before dawn. Fritz Fliegel was airborne at 0428 hours. He flew north up the east coast of Ireland to search the North Channel. At 1125 hours, after a protracted search, he came upon a convoy consisting of twelve ships steaming in a westerly direction at a position 80 kilometres north of Lough Foyle. They were accompanied by eight warships. He attacked three of the cargo vessels and saw one of the bombs fall under the hull. On account of very heavy defensive fire from the escorts, the effect was not observed. Oberleutnant Schlosser had more success than either Daser or Fliegel. At 1100 hours, he attacked the *Grelrosa*, (4574 tons, Cardigan Shipping Co), homeward bound from New York, and saw two bombs fall close to the hull. The vessel was seen to develop a heavy list and almost immediately there was a heavy explosion – presumed to be the boiler exploding. No further observations could be made as the Condor was running low on fuel. The ship, in fact, sank with the loss of five of her crew. The remaining Condor, under the command of Oberleutnant Robsien, located no targets during his mission.[6]

The report covering all four sorties stated that the defensive fire encountered, both from anti-aircraft guns and machine guns, was heavy. This opposition would stiffen in the coming months, something that would be felt by the U-boat men too. Among the developments that would threaten their existence was the Royal Navy's progress in perfecting the method of fixing a submarine's position by taking bearings from its radio transmissions the so-called *Huff-Duff* * system.

The war diaries of individual U-boats operating in the North West Approaches were now containing more and more entries recording emergency dives to escape the attentions of RAF Coastal Command aircraft. This trend would continue to the point where U-boats would often find it impossible to travel at all on the surface in daylight.

Other factors were influencing the course of events in the North West

*Derived from 'High Frequency Direction Finder' (HF/DF)

Approaches. The Admiralty's need to route traffic through the North Channel enabled the U-boats to narrow down their area of search for targets but by the same token their pursuers had a reciprocal advantage in that they were based close to the operational area. It was in this context that the port of Londonderry and the airfields in the surrounding area assumed unrivalled importance. An accident of geography had placed them at the threshold of the battle at a fateful moment.

By the spring of 1941, the first signs of a serious challenge to Doenitz's fleet had begun to emerge. The round-the-clock working in British shipyards (conspicuous among them Harland & Wolff's) was breaking all records in warship construction. Sixty Flower-class corvettes. the sturdy little ships which were to be at the forefront of the anti-submarine operations for the next few years, were scheduled for completion by the end of February.[7] This achievement was accompanied by improved convoy management and underwater detection methods. In the air, too, RAF Coastal Command was demonstrating its ability to harry the U-boats along the eastern stretches of the convoy routes when the miserable weather permitted.

These early, if modest, successes can in large measure be traced to operations from Londonderry and the Foyle Estuary which became the base for an ever-increasing number of warships. Even before hostilities commenced, it had been obvious that the Royal Navy would need a base as far west as possible. Britain's historic anchorages at Cobh, Berehaven and Lough Swilly, which she had retained by virtue of the treaty concluded with the newly-formed Dublin government in December 1921, were ceded to Eire in April 1938. There were no proximate substitutes for the loss of the two first-named ports but in the north the Foyle Estuary was a natural successor to Lough Swilly. In light of the unexpected deterioration in Britain's circumstances which set in after the fall of Norway in April 1940 the Royal Navy gratefully availed itself of the use of it.

The benefits accruing quickly became apparent. Escorts were able to accompany convoys that much farther west and also give incoming convoys a similar amount of added protection.

As to the waters of the lough itself, the potential for a dispute in international law existed which could have had serious consequences on a practical level. The respective rights of the two states over these waters which came into being on partition were not clearly defined by the Boundary Commission set up by the British government but in the event legalities were quietly ignored.

Plans to create all the services associated with a major naval base were implemented. New berthing spaces were created and maintenance and repair installations established, including the refuelling facilities which were to prove so indispensable to Allied navies for the duration of the war. The entire project was tackled energetically and throughout 1941 the number of escort groups using the base increased to the point where it assumed a pre-eminent position in the Battle of the Atlantic. The thousands of shipwrecked seamen landed at the port was grim evidence of this importance.

The base at Londonderry had as its first Naval Officer in Charge Captain Philip Ruck-Keane who was responsible to the Flag Officer in Charge at Belfast. In a report dated 3 May 1941 he spelt out another advantage which the base had in addition to its westernmost dimension: Its relative invulnerability to air attack.[8]

The point was apropos and one which Doenitz was already painfully aware of. The Luftwaffe had no trouble in reaching British naval bases in southern England but Londonderry's comparative isolation was something that more directly jeopardized the safety of his boats.

Elsewhere in his report, Ruck-Keane predicted:

The Battle of the Atlantic is the crux of the war and even if the battle is won in the near future it will certainly be a hard struggle until the end of the war. Londonderry will therefore remain of the highest importance throughout the war.

The accuracy of this prediction can be seen in the fact that a total of twenty-seven escort vessels, including anti-submarine trawlers, were already based there as of 1 January 1941.[9]

The use of air power in an anti-submarine role had been well recognized before the war and when hostilities began aircraft were utilized not only to supplement the surface units but to constitute an effective offensive weapon in their own right. The area adjacent to Lough Foyle provided excellent sites for these maritime operations. At Limavady, development had taken on added urgency in the summer of 1940 and at the turn of the year Whitleys of No. 502 (Ulster) Squadron began flying anti-submarine operations from the base. Construction at Eglinton and Ballykelly also commenced in 1940, the latter destined to provide Coastal Command with another of its renowned bases. Luftwaffe aerial photographs of Ballykelly and Eglinton, both taken on 28 April 1941, show the stage reached in construction and have detailed annotations giving accurate estimates of the dimensions of buildings in course of erection. They are an indication of German concern at what was going on there and, at the same time, of their inability to do anything about it. Coastal Command's advantage in having its bases left unmolested is in stark contrast to, for example, I/KG/40's parlous tenure of Bordeaux-Merignac which was regularly attacked by RAF bombers.

After the entry of the United States into the war, the status of the Foyle base as a major terminal for Allied naval operations was progressively consolidated but it was never more important than it was in the formative days

of 1940/41. Winston Churchill, writing after the war, said that the shipping
losses became most grave during the twelve months from July 1940 to July
1941 '*when we could claim that the British Battle of the Atlantic was won*'.[10] The
ships and aircraft from Londonderry and the north-west carved their own
niche in the history of that momentous time.

9

BRINK OF CHAOS

Ever since the fall of France, Eire had been faced with a dual threat of invasion. In the North, the British Army had formulated a plan to march south either to oppose a German landing or forestall one. Ideally, it would only do so if invited by the Irish government. The other, equally pervasive, threat was posed by the German forces massed on the French coast for *Operation Sealion*, the planned invasion of Britain. German records of the period contain speculation about whether the Wehrmacht might receive such an invitation from de Valera.

The telegrams passing between Berlin and the Dublin legation in the winter of 1940/41 show that the German Foreign Office was very anxious to discover what the Irish government's reaction would be in the event of military action by either of the belligerents.[1]

Some idea of the tentative nature of the diplomatic contacts taking place can be seen in Telegram No. 726 of 10 November 1940 in which Hempel said that he was meeting de Valera on the fourteenth and requested guidance as to what he should offer in the way of assistance in the event of a British attack. He referred to de Valera's 'suspicious nature' and cautioned against any suggestion that Germany might take the first step. He recalled that on 19 June the Taoiseach had said that, if attacked, Ireland would fight on the side of the country 'which was not the first attacker'.[2] Although it was not mentioned in the telegram, the Germans were well aware that de Valera had said on more than one occasion that Ireland would not allow Irish soil to be used for mounting an attack on Britain.[3] The combined effect of these statements was to rule Ireland out as a convenient stepping-stone in *Operation Sealion*.

The Irish government's deliberations centred on the question of which belligerent was likely to make the first move. This would determine the material help that she could expect but the German records are very specific about the logistical help that Germany would give if the British took the initiative and invaded. It took the form of an offer to supply British weapons captured at Dunkirk. The Foreign Office in Berlin had apparently raised the possibility of direct contact with certain officers in the Irish army about the matter but Hempel emphatically advised against it in favour of employing the usual diplomatic channels. It subsequently emerged that the available weapons included 46 field guns, 1000 anti-tank projectors, 550 machine guns and 10,000 rifles.[4]

A vague reference to another source of arms was mentioned in a telegram from Hempel on 1 November when he said that he had heard 'in confidence' from Frederick Boland, Secretary at the Department of External Affairs, that the Italian firm of Caprioni representing Edgar Brandt & Co. of Paris had suggested to the Irish legation there that a German promise of arms for Ireland made 'before the war or before the fall of France' would be honoured.

The German decision to grant Eire limited help in the shape of arms shipments if requested was made at the very highest level. An entry dated 19 November in the war diary of the staff of the important National Defence Section of the OKW, presided over by Hitler, reads:

> It may be possible in the winter months for individual blockade runners to bring weapons and munitions into Irish harbours and bays as long as no hostilities between England and Ireland exist and the Irish cooperate.
>
> The Führer agrees with this assessment of the situation and states that any support for Ireland would only arise when it was requested. It should first be ascertained by the German legation in Dublin whether de Valera wants help, for example, by means of additions to his armaments and munitions through captured English weapons delivered by steamers travelling singly.[5]

Military action beyond the supply of arms was clearly not contemplated in the existing circumstances and the same war diary entry also deals with the reasons for this policy:

> With regard to support for Ireland against England, the sending of an expeditionary corps and the occupation of the island would not be possible in view of the enemy's superior naval forces, the unfavourable geographical circumstances and the impossibility of bringing in reinforcements. Without the supply of rations, arms and ammunition, troops landed in Ireland would sooner or later be annihilated by an enemy whose continued reinforcement could not be prevented.

The influence of naval chief Admiral Raeder was to be seen behind the OKW's sober assessment. He had had grave reservations about the feasibility of *Operation Sealion*, which involved a comparatively short sea crossing, and the idea of dispatching a seaborne expedition to Ireland was for him unthinkable. The mauling his fleet had sustained in the invasion of Norway (nine destroyers were sunk in Narvik Fjord in a single action) had been a salutary reminder of British sea power.

Hitler's agreement to the OKW proposal for giving Ireland material help only is consistent with the judgment of him made by the distinguished military historian Ronald Lewin in his book *Hitler's Mistakes*. He sees Hitler as a man torn by doubt and uncertainty in the planning of *Operation Sealion* and it is open to question whether he ever really intended to invade Britain at all. Whether this is true or not, Raeder's opinion held sway.

An airborne assault on any part of Ireland was also out of the question for the reasons given and any plans submitted after 19 November 1940 had no chance of being implemented. A case in point was an ambitious plan for an airborne landing in Northern Ireland said to have been evolved by Generalleutnant Kurt Student, the commander of the parachute corps – widely regarded as Germany's finest troops. While this plan was apparently not seriously considered at the highest level, the vulnerability of an airborne force without the early arrival of ground reinforcements was demonstrated when Student led 11,000 of his men in an invasion of Crete six months later. Although Crete fell to the Germans, the cost was unacceptably high. More than a half of this elite force was killed or wounded and the undertaking proved to be the last major German airborne operation of the war.

Some accounts of Student's plan for Northern Ireland mention a figure of 20000 parachute and airborne troops. Apart from the problem of how they would be supplied and reinforced, it is difficult to see how they were going to be transported in the first place. The standard Luftwaffe troop-carrier in service was the Junkers Ju52, a slow three-engined aircraft which could not carry more than 18 fully-equipped soldiers. It had a cruising speed of only 200 km/h (124 mph) and would in any case barely have the range to fly to and from the intended landing area (Crete was a mere 100 kilometres from the Greek mainland) and if any part of the operation had to be carried out in daylight the force would be decimated by RAF fighters long before they reached Northern Ireland. In the airborne invasion of Holland in May 1940, two-thirds of the 430 Ju52s initially employed were destroyed or damaged beyond repair which is an indication of their vulnerability.

Another question which occupied German thinking at this time was the action, if any, that could be taken if Britain seized the ports which it had occupied until 1938 when it formally relinquished its rights to them. All three, Berehaven, Cobh and Lough Swilly, would have been of the utmost value to the Royal Navy at this critical time and the denial of them was the cause of much resentment in Britain.

Hempel made a few characteristically shrewd observations on the possibility of a British move in this connection. He pointed out that Berehaven and Cobh would be within range of German bombers and – more importantly – predicted the adverse effect for Britain that seizing them would have on American public opinion.[6] These factors, he thought, would nullify any advantage that the British might gain. He advised Berlin that he had had a conversation with the Irish Minister for External Affairs, Joseph Walshe, on the subject and that Walshe had said that talk about German help had been fuelled by Churchill's speech in the House of Commons on 6 November when he made no attempt to hide his smouldering resentment when referring to the ports. However, Walshe was of the opinion that the speech, along with ill-disposed comments in the British press, meant not so much an imminent attack as an attempt to deflect British public attention from the heavy shipping losses.

Reviewing the options from his office in the OKW, the German planning officer General Walter Warlimont, like Hempel, also used temperate language when looking at the problem as a military strategist. He saw no realistic possibilities other than bringing to bear a greater concentration of U-boats round the coasts of Ireland coupled with air attacks on such of the Irish ports as Britain should occupy. He, too, ruled out an airborne landing.

The German Foreign Office seems to have had no doubt that de Valera dominated the political scene in Ireland and orchestrated the policy of neutrality. His attitude towards Britain at this critical stage was considered to be very important in the context of possible German action. Accordingly, a personal assessment of the Taoiseach by a well-informed but unnamed Irish individual was commissioned by the *Sicherheitsdienst* (*SD*), the security service directly controlled by the Nazi Party. There is no explanation as to why this task should have been undertaken by the *SD* rather than by the Abwehr but it suggests that the *SD* may have had agents operating in Ireland in addition to – and possibly unknown to – the military intelligence organisation. This would have been in keeping with the suspicion with which the *SD* regarded the Abwehr whose chief, the aristocratic Admiral Wilhelm Franz Canaris, was eventually executed by the SS in the last days of the war.

The assessment of de Valera is dated 5 February 1941[7] and was obviously written by someone who probably knew de Valera as well as it was possible for anyone to know that enigmatic man. The author was very likely a politician or diplomat and his appraisal had critical undertones in places. It pointed out that the universal view of de Valera was that of an uncompromising champion of nationalism. In reality, it went on, he was continually making concessions to England which were either economic or political. The public excused the former because they did not understand them and they were unaware of the latter because of the strict press censorship.

As far as the policy of neutrality was concerned, the writer emphasized that the Irish population was overwhelmingly in favour of it and that no government in the country could alter that policy and survive. Nevertheless, some of the opinions expressed, like the following, probably confirmed German suspicions about de Valera's impartiality:

When I assert that de Valera would like to help England to win in spite of his unwillingness to sacrifice Ireland and his own position for the purpose, I base my opinion on several factors ... de Valera himself has made no secret of the fact that he hopes for an England victory ... his political friends and followers among the clergy are all convinced supporters of the English cause ... the few clergy who are not sympathetic to England are those whom he has already fought but at the same time all without exception are for maintaining neutrality ... he has not tried to work with the Republicans (presumably the IRA was meant) ... their leaders remain in prison and the arrests continue ... as recently reported the Ulster nationalists like Cahir Healy and the other nationalist elements have refused to attend the (party) conference of the governing party ...

The profile stresses over and over again the absence, at least for the duration of the emergency, of any real political opposition to de Valera and his policy of neutrality. He would continue to preside over the government of the country in an autocratic fashion and make all the important decisions himself.

The impression that the Germans would derive from all this was that de Valera's interpretation of the rules relating to neutrality would rarely ever result in any advantage to them. This was one of the consequences of Irish neutrality about which public opinion in Great Britain and Northern Ireland neither knew nor made allowances for. There was a tendency there towards over-simplification of the problems and de Valera's policy was seen – quite unfairly – to be driven by long-standing feelings of bitterness and vindictiveness. But emotions were running high and rational explanations for what was happening in Ireland were at a premium.

With the possible exception of the denial of the Irish ports to British warships, no aspect of Anglo-Irish relations seems to have engendered more feeling than the difficulties which resulted from the lack of an adequate Irish merchant fleet. The Irish reliance on British shipping and the protection of the Royal Navy was something that received regular attention in the British press. The more fervid of the critics chose to ignore the practical complexities. To them, food and fuel consumed in Eire was stained with the blood of British seamen.

The dearth of Irish ocean-going vessels thus became a burning issue for the Dublin government in the early months of 1941. The telegrams passing between Berlin and the Dublin Consulate show that the Germans were following these developments very closely. These exchanges also indicate that Dr Hempel and his staff must have had a reliable source of information. Their knowledge of the Irish government's difficulties and the steps it was considering was detailed and accurate.

It is not clear why Berlin was showing so much interest in the subject but in a series of three telegrams dated 16, 18 and 23 January,[8] Hempel gave a summary of the problems that Irish ships had encountered since the outbreak of war. He pointed out the delays in the arrival of supplies that were experienced due to the operation by the British of the *Navicert* system. Hempel also listed Irish ships sunk by mines since the beginning of 1940.

In February, the Irish government took steps to try and resolve the critical matter of a lack of ships. A new company, Irish Shipping, was formed and negotiations begun for the purchase of ships. Here again, the Germans seem to have been well-informed. On 5 March, a telegram to Berlin signed by 'Martins' reported that, in addition to the ships being purchased, five freighters (named as *Bakersfield, Egremont, Jacob Ruppert, West Pocasset* and *West Campgan*) would be chartered for trade between New York and Ireland under the Panamanian flag. The telegram claimed to have information that financing would be undertaken by the firm of 'Halohan Brothers'.

The information being sent to Berlin by the Dublin Consulate at this time included reports of surveillance at the Dublin docks – another example of the lengths to which the Germans would go to learn about shipping movements in and out of Ireland. A telegram dated 20 March stated that on a typical day five vessels, each of about 1000 tons engaged in the Irish coastal trade and two trading with England entered or left Dublin. Foreign ships lying there on the date in question included two Greek steamers being repaired, two Panamanian freighters and one Jugoslav.

Another possible explanation for the close German interest in shipping movements in and out of Ireland was that the Foreign Office in Berlin wanted to exploit abroad what was a highly-charged atmosphere by emphasizing the effect of restrictive measures taken by Britain allegedly aimed at preventing a neutral country from carrying on normal trade.

There would be many ups and downs in wartime relations between the British and Irish governments – some very serious and bitter – but the winter of 1940/41 probably marked the low point. In British eyes, the terrible shipping losses had been bound up with Irish neutrality but with the coming of summer emotions began to subside. The invasion of the Soviet Union caught world attention and although the U-boat menace would intensify yet further the focus of the war at sea began to shift. The North West Approaches were becoming more and more dangerous for the U-boats and as Doenitz took delivery of more of the larger ocean-going boats he sent them further west into the Atlantic away from Ireland. But what the U-boat men had called 'the happy time' was at an end.

BRIEF ENCOUNTER

By the end of 1940, the ravages of war had already laid waste large areas of Britain's industrial cities and killed more than 23,000 civilians. In contrast, Belfast passed the hours of darkness in a state of prolonged uneasiness but nevertheless remained unscathed. The eerie silence on moonlit nights, when conditions were favourable for attack, gave rise to questions about the enemy's apparent indifference. Many speculative theories were advanced about this, including the suggestion that in some way German restraint was in deference to Eire's claim of sovereignty over the North. But this was not a plausible explanation. It would have been absurd for the Germans to treat Northern Ireland as *de facto* neutral territory while it was being used by Britain for some of its most important strategic bases in fighting the Battle of the Atlantic.

De Valera's views on partition were well known to the Germans but there is nothing to show that he ever made any specific representations to them to refrain from bombing Belfast. However, he came very close to it when he cleverly pointed to German forbearance and at the same time drew an inference from it that suited his purpose. In telegram No. 787 to Berlin dated 5 December 1940, in which Dr Hempel dealt with possible armed intervention in Ireland, he said that neither de Valera nor any of his officials had ever mentioned that the question of German help in the event of a British invasion was linked to the question of 'getting back' the Six Counties. He said that this scenario was one that appealed to what he called 'nationalist circles', however. The telegram ended:

> It is to be noted that I heard reliably that de Valera commented favourably on the absence to date of German air attacks on Northern Ireland and he is said to interpret this as an indication that we regard it as territory which rightly belongs to the Irish state and is only retained by force.

It is ironic that within weeks of this telegram relations between the two countries would be soured by the consular staff affair and that de Valera would be more concerned with bombs falling on territory south of the border.

A more frequently heard explanation for Belfast's immunity was the belief that the city lay beyond the range of German bombers but this was ill-founded. The public did not have the technical knowledge to evaluate the facts but any lingering doubts that the authorities may have had were dispelled on the night of 13/14 March when a large force of bombers passed up the Irish Sea to launch the first major. attack on Glasgow. It was now clear that distance, in itself, was no impediment in the case of Belfast.

A much more cogent reason for Belfast's favourable treatment so far was logistical. The Luftwaffe had more targets than it could deal with, both in terms of priorities and the scale of its resources. More then 50 years on, an examination of the war diary of the OKW throws some light on the reasoning behind the selection of targets. In a Directive (*Weisung Nr.9*) issued 29 November 1940[1] the General Staff had established that London, Liverpool and Manchester were the three most important transhipment ports in Great Britain but it goes on to name seven others including Newcastle-upon-Tyne, Swansea and Cardiff, through which, it was thought, 58 per cent of all imports passed. It is only when the Directive lists twelve secondary ports handling traffic involving specific goods that Belfast is first mentioned.

The logic of concentrating attacks on the entry points for essential supplies and materials appears to have eventually been recognized by Hitler himself. A document entitled 'Criteria for a new directive in the prosecution of the war against the English economy'[2] was stated to have been issued at the Führers headquarters on 13 January 1941. This began by stating that, contrary to an earlier belief held by the High Command, the greatest effect of the war against Britain was being achieved by attacks on merchant ships by sea and air forces. (No doubt, Doenitz received this pronouncement with a mixture of grim satisfaction and annoyance. It was a belated vindication of everything that he had been saying since before the war.) In future, it would therefore be necessary to concentrate attacks to a greater extent on targets 'whose destruction lies in the same direction as is brought about by the sea war'. Consequently, the document concluded, serious food shortages in Britain could be expected. and only in this way could a decisive result be achieved in the foreseeable future.[3]

The Directive identified the following three objectives in order of importance: (1) the destruction of the most prominent import harbours along with their ancillary installations and the ships lying there (2) the heaviest possible mining of the approaches to those harbours, combined with an intensification of attacks on coastal convoys and (3) the systematic destruction of Britain's aircraft industry. There then followed a very significant sentence which gave a hint of Hitler's plans for the near future. 'Although for some months in the course of the year, the bulk of the Luftwaffe will be deployed in other theatres of war, these three tasks must be pursued with the remaining forces in the battle against Britain'. This clearly referred to the planned invasion of the

Balkans and the Soviet Union. One passage, with which Doenitz would also have agreed, stated that 'the destruction of 35,000 tons of enemy cargo shipping is more important for deciding the course of the war than the sinking of an enemy battleship'. It was stipulated that subsidiary targets would only be attacked when weather conditions and other factors prevented attacks on the three categories named.

The document, which was important in that it revealed what Hitler saw as practicable in the remaining months of the aerial assault against Britain, also contained some advice to the Luftwaffe which — coming from him — is surprising:

> On the other hand, no result which has any relevance to the outcome of the war is to be expected from systematic terror attacks against residential areas or on army lorries and coastal fortifications.

The use of the word 'systematic' may be significant in that the right to carry out selective attacks aimed at terrorizing the civilian population was reserved. Hitler was particularly incensed by RAF raids on Berlin which he maintained were purely indiscriminate and he frequently ordered attacks against British cities in retaliation. There is reason to believe that the Luftwaffe leadership saw the futility of these retaliatory attacks and often exercised moderation in interpreting their orders.

An analysis of the attacks launched during February and March show that the newly-defined strategy was adopted. Bad weather often curtailed operations but on those nights when bombing did take place there was a marked concentration on ports. For eight consecutive nights beginning on 8/9 March, for example, a series of major attacks were launched against places such as London, Liverpool, Glasgow and Clydeside, Bristol, Portsmouth and Southampton. The port installations at Glasgow and Clydeside were bombed by large formations on two successive nights.

By the end of March the German night bombing campaign had been in progress for approximately six months. Although the losses resulting from British defensive measures had been modest, the Luftwaffe had become debilitated by other factors. It had originally been conceived and equipped as a tactical arm in support of ground forces pursuing the *Blitzkrieg* concept but the unexpected prolongation of the war after the fall of France called for a radically different *modus operandi*.[4]

The bomber formations deployed against Britain were organized in Luftflotten or air fleets. Luftflotte 2, commanded by General Field Marshal Albert Kesselring, occupied bases in the Low Countries and France north of the River Seine. The units comprising Luftflotte 3, commanded by General Field Marshal Hugo Sperrle, were based south of the Seine. The numerically small Luftflotte 5 operated from Norway and Denmark but was mainly

engaged in maritime operations. Within the Luftflotte structure, the largest
bomber unit was the Kampfgeschwader, made up, at this stage of the war, of
three operational Gruppen or groups. Each group had a nominal establishment of thirty aircraft with the addition of a staff flight of four aircraft.
However, by the spring of 1941 a Gruppe's technical officer would have
considered himself very fortunate to be able to put up more than half of these
numbers. One logistical source states that, at 1 October 1940, the Luftwaffe
possessed 898 bombers[5] but it is probable that the number actually available
for operational flying on nights of maximum effort never exceeded 600.
Where the records state that a greater number than this was deployed, it is
very likely taking account of the fact that some aircraft were able to fly two
or even three sorties in the same night, for example, against targets in
Southern England.

Contrary to what the embattled citizens of Britain might have thought at
the time, the Luftwaffe was far from omnipotent. The war diary and other
documentary records of Erhard Milch, its wartime Inspector-General and
sometime acting Commander-in-Chief,[6] are a chronicle of ineptitude and
misjudgment. War had broken out much sooner than had been expected.
Hitler had not calculated that Britain and France would declare war when
Poland was attacked and while German aircraft production was not geared
up to reach full capacity until 1942 or 1943.[7] Goering and Hitler together are
accused by Milch of abandoning plans in 1937 for the construction of a fleet
of four-engined bombers such as the RAF and US Air Force would later
employ to devastating effect over Germany. The result of this lack of foresight
was that after its decisive defeat in the daylight Battle of Britain the Luftwaffe
was launched into a strategic bombing campaign at night for which it was
neither equipped nor trained. At the outbreak of war its bomber force relied
on three types of twin-engined aircraft, the Heinkel He111, the Junkers Ju88
and the Dornier Do17. The last-named was phased out after the Battle of
Britain and only participated marginally in the night campaign. For that task,
the burden fell on the He111 and Ju88. Both excellent aeroplanes, their
limitations nevertheless became apparent very quickly. With a full load of fuel
and bombs, neither was able to maintain level flight on losing an engine and
many missions had to aborted for this reason. In attacking targets which were
more than 700 kilometres distant, fuel considerations could become critical.
A reasonable time over the target area had to be provided for and if the aircraft
became lost, which was common, the aircraft commander could be faced with
difficult decisions.

Among the German aircrew of the time, morale seems to have been
generally good without being particularly high. Their experiences in the
daylight Battle of Britain had had a chastening effect. Dissatisfaction with
equipment was widespread, particularly when it seemed to bomber crews

17 A striking photograph of an He111 pictured at dusk on the way to a target
in the British Isles

that even elementary foresight had been lacking in forward planning. For example, bombers attacking targets in the London area during the daylight battles had been left unprotected at vital moments when the single-engined fighters escorting them did not have enough fuel to stay and see the mission completed. There was incredulity when it was discovered that bombers and fighters could not communicate with each other because their respective radio sets were not compatible.

For the bomber crews flying in the night campaign, it was probably the absence of reliable radio navigation and target-finding aids that concerned them most. All were equipped with the *Knickebein* system, which was an adaptation of the *Lorenz* VHF blind-landing system developed by German engineers before the war. However, British scientists soon devised effective counter measures which involved superimposing spurious signals on the *Knickebein* beam, causing a pilot listening to them to steer a wrong course. More sophisticated radio navigation aids, the *X-Verfahren* and *Y-Verfahren*, were developed and installed in He111s belonging to two specialist units. They had early successes but, like *Knickebein*, their effectiveness was eventually undermined by counter measures. In addition, they suffered from the usual range limitations to which VHF transmissions are subject.

The extent of the disquiet among German aircrew about the lack of these aids is illustrated by an incident in the winter of 1940/41 which the Luftwaffe leadership regarded as blatant insubordination, if not near-mutiny. The occasion was recalled in a book written after the war by Werner Baumbach, perhaps the most famous of all German bomber pilots.[8] When Field Marshal Milch paid an inspection visit to Baumbach's unit, Kampfgeschwader 30 (KG 30) in Holland, officers and men who had been continuously engaged in demanding night missions were sharply critical of the lack of adequate target-finding equipment and of various operational features of the Ju88. The complaints, coming from a unit which had suffered heavy casualties, seemed reasonable but a serious view was taken of the affair. The Gruppe was disbanded and several of the officers demoted and dispersed among other units. Milch displayed a marked lack of sympathy for these genuine grievances and is said to have facetiously reported to Goering that 'the Gruppe feared the Ju88 but not the enemy'.

Early in 1941, RAF intelligence became aware that several Luftwaffe bomber units stationed in France and the Low Countries had been withdrawn. An explanation for these moves came on 6 April when Hitler's armies invaded Jugoslavia and Greece. This was to herald no respite for the beleaguered British, however, and as if to emphasize that fact, Goering ordered a maximum effort for the following night. It was to mark the beginning of a sustained series of attacks, timed to take place at and around the period of the full moon, which would occur on 11 April. It was given the code-name

Moonlight Sonata and on the afternoon of Monday 7 April every serviceable German aircraft that could carry bombs was put on stand-by. In addition to the units normally engaged, Luftflotte 5 units in Norway interrupted their anti-shipping operations to send aircraft down to Danish airfields to join in the assault. Even reconnaissance units had to contribute their meagre resources and turn their aircraft into conventional bombers.

At Gilze-Rijen airfield, 10 kilometres west of Tilburg in southern Holland, Feldwebel Peter Stahl of II Gruppe Kampfgeschwader 30 (II/KG 30), equipped with the Ju88A-5, waited to hear his assigned target for the night. At 1800 hours local time, the pre-flight briefing took place at which it was announced that the Gruppe's target was Greenock at the mouth of the Clyde. The attack was to be part of a massive bombardment of port and industrial installations all along the Clyde estuary. The estimates of the total number of aircraft employed in the Luftwaffe operations that night vary but it was well in excess of 500.

Stahl and his crew of three corporals were veterans of the night campaign and had flown on many of the major operations throughout the winter. He himself was a prolific diarist and used the entries as material for a book he wrote after the war entitled *Bomber pilot: From the Artic to the Sahara.*[9] His graphic account of the night bombing campaign is, in fact, unique as no other serving flyer in the Luftwaffe appears to have published his recollections of this phase of the war in such detail.

The flight to Greenock and back was calculated to take six hours and was, in fact, the longest that Stahl had yet undertaken. In order to carry the maximum fuel load of 3600 litres, the bomb load would have to be limited to 1500 kg. The weather forecast for the mission issued at 1800 hours predicted varying cloud amounts for the North Sea crossing. On reaching the east coast of England the cloud cover locally would be in the region of 7/10ths to 8/10ths but on reaching the Scottish lowlands it would improve to between 2/10ths and 4/10ths with horizontal visibility of 25 to 30 kilometres at 1600 metres altitude and 50 kilometres above that. Similar conditions could be expected at the target with light haze under 1600 metres and between 2/10ths and 4/10ths of thin cloud.[10]

After the customary tension-filled wait for take-off, Stahl's heavily-laden Junkers was airborne at 2035 hours and set course direct to Greenock. They left the Dutch coast overhead The Hague and climbed laboriously to 3200 metres. The Automatic Direction Finder (ADF) was tuned to one of the beacons on the coast behind them to obtain a bearing that would provide a check on the forecast wind aloft. This revealed that it was a good deal stronger than predicted and that the aircraft was drifting left of track. It was the first of several errors detected in the weather forecast.

There was still no sight of the surface as they crossed the North Sea and

Hans Gross, the navigator, estimated by dead reckoning the time for crossing the English coast in the vicinity of Flamborough Head in Yorkshire. There was no sign of the forecast break in the overcast on crossing the coast but the glow from the searchlights at Newcastle seen through the clouds was confirmation that the aircraft was on course. Soon afterwards, the target area was easily identified by the exploding anti-aircraft shells ahead. Stahl climbed to 4200 metres, which was his allotted bombing level, and flew into the centre of the barrage. He then discovered that, far from the forecast 2/10ths, the cloud cover was total and it was obvious that visual bombing would be impossible. After a few minutes deliberation, Stahl asked Gross to estimate when they would be over the centre of the target area. When it was reached, the bombs were released.

It is almost certain that Stahl would have been given at least one alternate target in his pre-flight briefing but his account of the mission makes no mention of one, although it is possible that he was aware from radio transmissions that he would encounter similar conditions over the rest of Scotland and Northern England. The 10/10ths cloud cover over the Clyde valley had been completely unexpected and near-chaos prevailed throughout the entire attacking force. The Luftflotte 3 records state that of 213 Luftflotte 3 bombers that set out for the Clyde only 97 arrived over the target[11] and dropped their bombs by dead reckoning.

The following day, the commander of Luftflotte 2. Field Marshal Kesselring sent a message to all his units by teleprinter from his headquarters in Brussels. He did not conceal his disappointment at the night's events or mince his words:

8 April 1941

I express to the units my recognition that last night they deployed the greatest possible number of aircraft against the enemy ... However, I must describe last night's operation as a failure ... So as to avoid an erroneous weather forecast in future, the Luftflotte will arrange a wide-ranging weather reconnaissance for the evening in question. In addition I must raise a question about the individual aircraft which flew through the entire target area without finding one of the alternate targets that were prescribed for the full moon period. Above all, the bombing of an inconsequential town, village or searchlight emplacement without proper sight of the ground is indefensible and is for the future forbidden. I call on crews for a more closely co-ordinated approach. I find that a sufficiently keen sense of leadership is lacking at a senior level of command. This demands that during night attacks of this nature a responsible individual of command rank is either involved or causes appropriate orders to be issued to aircraft commanders. A prerequisite for this is that individual crews make lucid combat reports promptly and organize the monitoring of wireless messages.

I also require that in future all favourable weather opportunities be fully utilized by maintaining the utmost state of operational readiness.[12]

Signed: Kesselring

General Field Marshal

This was trenchant criticism indeed and left no one in any doubt as to where the shortcomings lay. Kesselring had managed to focus the attention of his subordinates on two areas of difficulty, namely, weather forecasting and an effective command structure. The scope for improving weather forecasting in wartime was limited but the flying crews would have agreed with the Field Marshal about some of their superiors, especially those who showed a disinclination to fly on missions themselves. On the other hand, the absence of any generalized criticism of the crews was understandable. Kesselring was well aware that after six months of night operations without a break many of his men had reached the point of exhaustion.

There was, however, at least one of Kesselring's officers who could not be criticized for his actions on the night of 7/8 April. Siegfried Röthke was a 25-year-old Oberleutnant from Angermünde near Berlin who had seemed destined for a career in sculpturing before being called up for service with the Luftwaffe in 1939. Attached to I/KG 4 at Soesterberg, the resourcefulness and determination he was to show had fateful consequences for the city of Belfast that night.

All the aircraft commanders of Röthke's group were commissioned officers and were ranked among the best in the entire bomber force. The two 1,000kg LMB parachute mines Röthke would carry on his He111H-5, in common with the smaller 500kg LMA version, had been adapted for attacks on land targets. A conventional impact detonator replaced the magnetically or acoustically- activated detonator employed against ships. The use of the parachute meant that the mine struck the ground with little force. There was no penetration of the surface and maximum blast damage occurred to the surrounding area. The mines were slung externally under the aircraft's fuselage and the aerodynamic drag thereby induced, especially with full fuel tanks, made the take-off potentially very hazardous. Consequently, only experienced pilots were cleared to carry mines in this way.

Dumbarton was the target assigned to I/KG 4 for the mass attack on the Clyde.[13] The order was issued at 1630 hours and 16 Heinkels were declared serviceable, one of them being nominated reserve aircraft. Each of the 15 aircraft making the attack was to carry two mines and 4200 litres of fuel, which was, in fact, the Heinkel's capacity. Liverpool was designated the first alternate

18 Oberleutnant Siegfried Röthke, one of the first German airmen to bomb Belfast

target and Newcastle the second. The attack was to be made from below 3000 metres altitude and was timed to start at 0405 and end at 0435 hours. There would therefore be a two-minute horizontal separation between aircraft over the target. The navigation officer for the night's operation was Oberleutnant Kalckreuth who briefed the crews on the route to the target and the geographical features to look out for. First to take-off at 0040 hours local time (one hour in advance of British Summer Time) was the Gruppe commander, Hauptmann Klaus Nöske. The remaining 14 aircraft followed at two-minute intervals. Fourth in line, Röthke with the call-sign *Anton Hans*, was airborne at 0046.

Leaving the Dutch coast overhead the *Katrin* light beacon, all the Heinkels commenced their climb to a cruising level of 3500 metres or above. By the route they were taking, they would cross the English coast north of Blyth in Northumberland and then proceed to the northern shore of the Firth of Forth, approaching Dumbarton from a north-easterly direction. Röthke's navigator, Feldwebel Joachim Fehde, was able to take bearings from the powerful radio transmitters at Bremen and Hilversum on his ADF during the North Sea crossing. On reaching the English coast, however, both were no longer usable due to night fading and static. As had been the case with Stahl, the weather forecast was now seen to be disastrously wrong. The ground was not visible from this point onwards and navigation for the remainder of the approach would have to be carried out by dead reckoning.

The Glasgow Corporation Reservoir was to be used as a reference point from which aircraft would proceed to their targets but when he came overhead the city at approximately 0215 hours BST it was immediately obvious to Röthke that a visual attack was impossible. He set course for Liverpool, his first alternate target, without delay. On monitoring the brief weather reports transmitted by aircraft already in the vicinity of Liverpool, however, he discovered that conditions there were not much better than at Glasgow. It was at this stage, flying south over Ayrshire, that Röthke noticed that the sky away to the west was much clearer than anything he had seen since taking-off. It was then that he decided to attack Belfast.

Although Belfast had not been specifically named as an alternate target for the night's operation, Röthke was able to take advantage of a discretion given to some of the more experienced aircraft commanders. The practice of nominating what were known as *Sonderbesatzungen*, or special crews, had been introduced to relieve aircraft commanders of the responsibility of rigidly following a set pattern even though it was obvious that there was a more promising alternative. Röthke clearly fell into this category of officer.

The records of the RAF Wireless Intelligence Service, or 'Y' Service, for this particular night give some indication of the chaos that developed throughout the German bomber formations. The wireless-telegraphy monitoring unit at Cheadle in Staffordshire had difficulty in logging the large number of aircraft calling their control stations to request radio direction finding (RDF) assistance. This could help pilots who were unsure of their positions to obtain a bearing from the station. The 'Y' Service records show that the frequencies were saturated with messages from aircraft over the Scottish Lowlands and the Irish Sea reporting that they had been unable to find their targets.[14] Twenty-four aircraft from KG 4 alone called Soesterberg Control, many of them trying to get bearings to guide them back to base in the miserable weather conditions. This gives some idea of the confusion which can be directly traced to an inaccurate weather forecast. The same records also reveal that on this same night the Irish Observer Corps was relaying information to the 'Y' Service about aircraft movements in Irish airspace. Three separate movements over the border area between Co. Cavan and Co. Tyrone were transmitted.[15]

Fifty years after the event, Röthke himself was unable to remember all the details of his attack on Belfast (four more years of operational flying still lay ahead of him) but much valuable information about it is contained in a special dispatch dated 14 April 1943 compiled by his friend, Gefreiter Doctor Gerhard Donner, a war correspondent attached to KG 4 on the Eastern Front.[16] The dispatch was sent to Berlin on the occasion of the completion of Röthke's 400th operational flight and gave particulars of his distinguished service record.[17] Of the missions he had completed, 101 (including minelaying sorties) had been flown against targets in Britain, most of them in the course of the night campaign. It was an impressive record for which he was awarded the Knight's Cross.

From an attacker's standpoint, the weather conditions at Belfast were ideal. No meteorological report from RAF Sydenham is available for the hours of darkness but RAF Aldergrove at 0200 hours BST reported that only 1/10th of the sky was obscured by stratocumulus cloud at 2,500 feet. There was 10/10ths cover at 20,000 feet but this was well above the level from which any attack would come. The surface wind was a gentle three knots from the south-east (125 degrees/03 kts), well suited to the dropping of parachute mines.[18]

Shortly after 0300 hours Röthke came in sight of the city. A huge fire was burning on the north-west side of the harbour complex. This was undoubtedly the fire at McCue Dick's timber yard in Duncrue Street, started by an earlier attacker. It was described in the I/KG 4 unit war diary as consisting of 16 to 20 small fires coalescing in one large conflagration and extending over an area of 200 x 50 metres 'on the north side of target 835'. (All the principal targets in the United Kingdom were classified in a catalogue and given a number. Target 835 was the number allocated to the Harland & Wolff shipyard).

Approaching from the north-east, Röthke prepared for the bombing run with Fehde taking up the bomb-aimer's position in the nose of the aircraft. It was at this moment that a terse message was received from Soesterberg by Morse code instructing aircraft *Anton Hans* to bomb Chatham as an alternate target. Donner's dispatch contained the cryptic remark that 'it was too late, Röthke was committed to bomb Belfast.'

The approach to the bomb release point was to be made by the *Schleichflug* method, which involved a gradual descent with the engines throttled back. The procedure was to make an initial run over the target, starting a timed descent and a wide turn calculated to bring the aircraft back over the target at a predetermined altitude. The direction of the bombing run is not known but Fehde would have had little difficulty in estimating the wind velocity from the behaviour of the smoke from the fires.

An aircraft making a *Schleichflug* approach was particularly vulnerable to light anti-aircraft fire and it is interesting to note that, in his report, Röthke states that at Belfast 'the light and heavy flak, some of it from ships, was very well-aimed'. Aside from its accuracy, however, he did not make any comment on the volume of the anti-aircraft fire overall. This was the subject of considerable criticism in the city after the raid.

The Heinkel continued its descent until it came over the boundary of the target area at a height of 1900 metres. This level was selected because, on the initial pass over the city, the crew had counted 15 barrage balloons flying at 1600 metres. From this altitude every detail of the harbour complex was shown up with stark clarity. Both mines were released in quick succession. The parachutes would open at about 1,000 metres above the ground and, given the negligible surface wind, the mines could be expected to fall well within the target area. The time was 0322 hours BST.

Röthke's report of the attack made on his return to Soesterberg stated that both mines were seen to detonate, one in the south-west of Target 835 and the other in the south-east. Accompanying the latter explosion was a vivid flash followed by a huge fire that could be seen for 20 minutes after leaving the target area.

From the time of the attack and the description of the seat of the explosions there can be little doubt that they were those that occurred at Rank's flour mill adjacent to Pollock Dock and at the aircraft construction shed at Harland & Wolff's although it would have been more accurate to describe the latter as being in the centre rather than in the south-east of Target 835.

It was, in fact, the final attack of the night and on leaving the target area, Röthke set course direct for Soesterberg where, according to I Gruppe's mission report, *Anton Hans* landed at 0709 hours local time, six hours and 23 minutes after take-off. Röthke would twice return to attack Belfast in the final weeks of the night campaign. He survived the war to become a successful sculptor working in plastics but Gerhard Donner and Röthke's three crew members who made the unplanned flight to Belfast that night, including Feldwebel Fehde, did not. All were killed in action on the Russian front. Writing of that first attack almost 50 years later, Röthke regretted that the people of Belfast should have reason to associate him with such an unhappy event.[19]

The large-scale destruction of military records ordered by Josef Goebbels in the final days of the war makes research into Luftwaffe operations difficult and it is impossible to state with certainty how many aircraft, in fact, took part in that first air raid on Belfast. The FOIC Belfast in a report to the Admiralty on 8 April, stated that seven distinct attacks were made, the first at 0004 hours and the last at 0320 hours. Five separate wireless (radar) plots were obtained over the lough and eight over the coast between Bangor and Downpatrick. However, not all of these may have actually attacked the city. The FOIC said that all the aircraft were thought to be of the He111 type.

What German records there are add little to this information and only one other Luftwaffe unit participating in this first attack can be identified. An imprecise operations report in the files of Luftflotte 3 reveals that a single He111 of III/KG 26, 'because of the weather situation' dropped one SC 500kg high-explosive bomb and 432 BIEl incendiaries on Belfast 'between 2150 BST and 0224 BST from a height of between 1200 metres and 3500 metres'. There was said to have been visual contact with the ground and two large fires burning in harbour installations were observed.[20] This aircraft was one of a specialist pathfinder group which was based at Poix, near Amiens but on this occasion it was probably operating in a conventional role. The unit seems to have come in for particular attention from the 'Y' Service which logged 16 different call-signs used by its aircraft. It is likely that the remaining aircraft which bombed Belfast came from various units and had Clyde and Liverpool as their primary targets. Whether they had been specifically assigned Belfast as an alternate target or whether aircraft commanders had exercised discretionary authority in the same way as Röthke is not known. Whatever the explanation, the intentions which the German military planners had for the city would soon become clear.

The much-criticized defences claimed one success in this initial attack. A Hurricane of 245 Squadron from Aldergrove, flown by the unit's commanding officer Squadron-Leader J.W. Simpson, reported intercepting two He111s at 7000 feet east of Downpatrick. One of them blew up and disintegrated when it was hit by the Hurricane's fire.[20] No wreckage or bodies were apparently recovered and it is not possible to identify the aircraft or its unit from the Luftwaffe's loss reports for that night.

TARGET 'ETAPPE'

The crucial importance of the northern half of the Irish Sea to Britain was plain for all to see and no amount of deception could conceal the daily stream of shipping through it in both directions. The great convoy terminals at Liverpool and the Clyde as well as the Bristol Channel and Bangor Bay were, in effect, in full view of the enemy and it was only his lack of resources that prevented direct air attacks on the ships lying there. Attacks had to be confined to the adjacent ports at night.

Subject to weather conditions, German reconnaissance aircraft maintained constant surveillance over the area. One of the Luftwaffe units charged with the task at this time was based at Paris/Buc airfield. In April 1941, Wekusta 51 had an establishment of seven He111H-3s and its principal function was that of weather reconnaissance. It was, however, employed in a dual capacity, often assisting the hard-pressed conventional reconnaissance squadrons. When engaged in meteorological work, a uniformed member of the German Meteorological Service was carried and he made the observations on which weather forecasts were based. A camera was part of the equipment and at least one of the crew members was trained in aerial photography.

It is at this time that the code-name *Etappe* appears in Luftwaffe records for the first time. All the principal cities in Britain were given a code-name and these usually had a bearing on the city's reputation or its significance in German eyes. The much-bombed Liverpool was *Speisekammer*, or larder, in recognition of the port's importance as a point of entry for food supplies. The steel-producing city of Sheffield was aptly called *Schmelztiegel*, or crucible. Belfast was known as *Etappe*. In the context in which it was used, the German word means a stage or staging post in lines of communication and this description clearly fitted the entrance to Belfast Lough with its busy anchorages. Frequently, Belfast was also the first port of call for warships and cargo vessels requiring assistance after attack by U-boats or aircraft. It therefore bore all the characteristics of a staging post in addition to its other wartime activities and a successful attack on it would have produced a disruptive effect.

In the week following the near-debacle of 7/8 April, several heavy night attacks took place in England. Birmingham was bombed on two successive nights by more than 200 aircraft and suffered severe damage and casualties. But despite this dogged persistence on the part of the German leadership, the rank and file of the Luftwaffe were well aware that a change of policy would have to be made in the near future. The shrinking hours of darkness that came with spring meant that distant targets could no longer be attacked without part of the flight, either at the beginning or end of it, taking place in daylight. No one in the Luftwaffe seriously believed that those responsible for decision-making were going to again expose the bombers to the perils of daylight combat over England. The Battle of Britain had been a painful experience. Moreover, the RAF's fighter strength had not only been restored; it had expanded. This was not the case with the German bomber force. The comparative figures for aircraft production show a startling deficiency on the German side. For the whole of 1940, the Luftwaffe received only 2852 new bombers, that is, an average of 237 per month.[1] If the daylight attacks were resumed and bomber losses occurred at the same rate as in the preceding summer and autumn, the Luftwaffe bomber fleet would be reduced to impotence. In contrast, Britain was producing an average of almost 900 non-fighter aircraft (most of them bombers) per month.[2] It was not until 1942 that German aircraft production and armaments in general began to achieve more realistic levels. Added to this, the Luftwaffe was still far from solving the problem posed by the lack of long-range fighter protection for its bombers. Without it failure was again assured if daylight operations were resumed. Unknown to the anxious German bomber crews, however, any energy expended in wondering how to deal with RAF Fighter Command in the immediate future was wasted. Hitler had long since solved that problem by deciding to turn his back on it and attack the Soviet Union instead.

In the meantime, the daily routine remained the same for the German aircrews. Targets were selected from the familiar catalogue of industrial and commercial centres and reconnaissance sorties flown. At least once in every two or three days a He111 of Wekusta 51 left Paris/Buc and flew west to the air base at Brest-Langveoc in Brittany where it would take on enough fuel to sustain a flight of approximately six hours. The log of a typical flight shows that after take-off from Brest, the Heinkel would climb on a north-westerly heading to skirt the Scilly Isles before turning north on to a course which would take it up the Irish Sea by way of the St George's Channel.[3] Weather observations were made at various levels over the whole length of the area to be covered, which might stretch as far north as the Hebrides. Shipping movements or unusual activity would be recorded and a report sent to air intelligence on return. Shipping in and around Belfast Lough would invariably figure prominently in the reports. The flights tended to be of long duration and fuel often ran low, in which case the aircraft returned to Brest or Caen rather than fly back direct to Paris.

One such flight did not complete its mission. On Easter Sunday, one of Wekusta 51's Heinkels, under the command of Oberfeldwebel Willi Decker, was intercepted and attacked over the St George's Channel by two Spitfires of 152 Squadron. It crashed into the sea and all five crew members, including meteorologist Georg Gründel, died.[4]

That night, there was a low level of enemy air activity over Britain but this did nothing to dispel the uneasiness that pervaded Belfast the next day. Publicly, there was no speculation about the meaning of the indecisive raid of a week earlier but, privately, people had a sense of foreboding. The normal Easter programme of outdoor events had a wartime look about it but the day was bright though cool.

Beginning around noon, several observations were made north and south of the Irish border which would be shown to have an ominous significance for the city. At 1228 hours, Irish Defence Command reported an aircraft entering Irish airspace at Fethard on the coast of Co. Wexford. It flew north-west to Campile before turning on to a north-easterly heading which took it past Enniscorthy. It reached Drogheda at 1308 hours and crossed the border near Newry at 1315. Its course at that time would have taken it over Belfast and at the speed at which it was travelling, the city would have been reached shortly before 1330 hours.[5] This is consistent with observations made from the ground. It was sighted by troops manning 102 HAA's U3 site in the Castlereagh hills on the south-east side of the city. It was positively identified as an He111, flying at an estimated 22,500 feet, and each of the battery's four 3.7-inch guns fired one round at it.[6] The fact that the aircraft was clearly visible at this altitude indicates that aerial photography was possible.

Thirty minutes later, at 1345 hours, an aircraft was plotted entering Irish air space in a southerly direction between Newry and Dundalk.[7] It is reasonable to assume that it was the same aircraft and that its mission had been reconnaissance and/or aerial photography over Belfast. It flew south to Athaboy before turning south, passing Enniscorthy at 1417 hours and finally leaving Irish air space at Forlorn Point at 1426. It is not possible to confirm from the fragmentary records of Wekusta 51 that the Heinkel in question was from that unit but the almost daily sorties flown by its aircraft in the Irish Sea area before and after the incident points in that direction. The loss of a colleague the previous day over the open sea may well have tempted an aircraft commander to disregard standing orders and choose the safety of Irish airspace. In any event, it seems certain that the Luftwaffe now had some up-to-date photographs of Belfast and the surrounding area.

The significance of that flight over Belfast on Easter Monday can be seen in the German records for the following day, 15 April. At the Luftwaffe's tactical headquarters (oddly named *Robinson I*) *Etappe* was for the first time named as the primary target in a bombing operation. Several units normally based in Northern France had been moved into forward airfields with the aim of bringing targets in the northern part of the British Isles more easily within range. This was particularly important for the Junkers Ju88 and two units equipped with the type, KG 76 and KG 77, had temporarily vacated their bases near Paris and taken up residence in Dutch airfields for the April full moon operations.[8] It becomes clear at this juncture that Belfast was now included in the list of primary and secondary targets selected for that period.

Weather forecasts for all bombing missions were vitally important. The one that was circulated throughout the units on the afternoon of 15 April was to have dire consequences for Belfast. It predicted that:

> over the English mainland and at the target there will be cirrostratus cloud cover of probably not more than 7/10ths with lower accumulations of 5/10ths of cumuliform (heap) cloud between 600 and 1800 metres.[9]

Cirrostratus cloud (Cs) is a veil of thin cloud at heights in excess of around 16,000 feet, or just over 4875 metres. This would be above the level from which bombing normally took place and consequently would present no problems. However, the important thing to be deduced from this forecast was that, with only half of the sky obscured by low level cloud, bomb-aimers could expect to have a reasonable sight of the targets.

This forecast, in terms of cloud amounts, was very wide of the mark. Over Northern England cloud was much thicker than expected. making it impossible for some crews even to find the Isle of Man. Again, what the leading crews who succeeded in locating Belfast encountered was very different from the forecast. They reported cloud cover ranging from 8/10ths to 10/10ths, (that is, total cover) at altitudes well below their assigned bombing levels.

The conditions described by the leading aircraft are borne out by the official records of the Meteorological Office. The last observations at Sydenham airfield, made before the raid started, took place at 1900 hours BST and recorded 8/10ths cumulus (Cu) and cumulonimbus (CuCb) at 1800 feet after recent rain.[10] The observations at Aldergrove airfield are even more pertinent. At 2300 hours BST – that is, after the air raid warning had sounded but before the attack had commenced – the cloud cover was given as 9/10ths stratocumulus (Sc) at 2200 feet, again after recent rain. At a time when the spearhead of the attacking force was approaching the city, these conditions were destined to radically influence the course of the raid. Three hours later, at 0200 hours, when the raid was in progress, Aldergrove was continuing to make observations. The cloud amount was then unchanged at 9/10ths but the base had come down to 2000 feet. That made it impossible for many navigators to find the city let alone individual targets. Others were only able to do so with the greatest of difficulty.

In Belfast, the 'Red' alert was posted and the sirens sounded at 2240 hours (some RAF and military sources say 2235 hours) but there appears to be a lack of precise information about the length of the interval that elapsed before the first bombs fell. Some accounts suggest that the interval was a long one and there may be several explanations for this.

Every evening, strenuous efforts were made by the intelligence agencies in Britain to try and discover the enemy's targets for that night. This work is described by Professor R.V. Jones, one of those intimately involved, in his book *Most Secret War*. The success achieved in decyphering German communications using the *Enigma* cypher system had proved to be invaluable in anticipating the enemy's intentions. In addition to information obtained from intelligence sources, the bombers' movements after take-off often enabled the defence services to narrow down the range of possible objectives. In the case of a distant target, such as Belfast, a relatively early warning might be possible. On this particular occasion, an explanation for the uncertainty about the time bombing started may be that aircraft were over the city for some time but were having difficulty in identifying ground features. The presence of flares and the sound of anti-aircraft fire could have created the impression that bombing had actually commenced.

There is documentary evidence of the difficulties that the early arrivals experienced in distinguishing ground features and targets through the occasional breaks in the cloud cover. The report of the raid contained in the war diary of one of the units involved, I/KG 53 states:

Target *Etappe*: 8/10ths to 10/10ths cloud cover: In spite of a sometimes very long search, bombing was only possible by some aircraft, that is, those which identified the target beyond doubt.[11]

Some idea of the scale of the problem can be gleaned from the number of diversions recorded. Many aircraft commanders had obviously followed the instructions contained in the pre-flight briefings, a specimen of which appears in the records of KG 4:

If the target *Etappe* cannot be clearly identified with sight of the ground, alternate targets are to be attacked having regard to the conditions prevailing at each.[12]

It is safe to say that many lives in Belfast were spared in the course of the night by the large number of diversions which took place.

Although the files in the German archives belonging to the higher echelons of command do not state the exact time when the attack started, some surviving records from individual Luftflotte 3 units provide valuable information. A smaller number of Luftflotte 2 unit records are also helpful.

The first aircraft from Luftflotte 3 to drop bombs – as opposed to flares – were drawn from I and III Gruppen of KG 76.[13] The first of these Ju88A-5s had taken off from their temporary base at Leeuwarden on the northern coast of Holland around 2100 hours BST and set course direct for Belfast. Each was carrying four SC 250kg and two SC 50kg high explosive bombs. In addition, they each carried around two hundred 1kg incendiaries. This was calculated to be the maximum bomb load that a Ju88 could deliver while, at the same time, carrying enough fuel for approximately seven hours flying. The balance between bomb load and fuel was a delicate one and due allowance had to be made for the time taken in climbing to the cruising level and, very importantly, possible delay in finding the target or diverting to an alternate. If additional fuel was required, reserve tanks were installed in the forward bomb compartment and the bomb load reduced. If, on the other hand, flying time of not more than six hours was estimated, a 500kg bomb load could be substituted for fuel.

The recommended course to be taken by the KG 76 Junkers was calculated to take them across the North of England and the northern tip of the Isle of Man before commencing the final approach to the target area. The island had acquired a strategic importance for the night's operation which is illustrated by a reference in the unit history of KG 55, another of the participating formations. This discloses that no less a person than Reichsmarshall Goering himself directed that Belfast was only to be attacked when the Isle of Man had first been positively identified. The imperative tone of the order is emphasized by the requirement that 'all (aircraft) commanders must sign for this instruction!' The inclusion of an exclamation mark by the unit historian suggests that this was an unusual stipulation.[14] Although Irish neutrality is not mentioned in the context, it is clear from several references in unit records that this lay behind the Reichmarshall's personal intervention. At the same time, it provides no help in explaining the bombing south of the border a few months earlier.

Provided that the leading Junkers of KG 76 could satisfy the visual requirement at the Isle of Man, they would continue towards Belfast in the hope that the forecast 5/10ths cloud cover over the target would materialize. For navigation, they were now relying completely on fleeting glimpses of the surface seen through breaks in the undercast. Radio navigation aids at this distance were virtually non-existent. Although the *Knickebein* system had proved to be almost worthless, the Luftwaffe continued to factor it into operational planning. For the Easter Tuesday attack on Belfast, three *Knicke-bein* beams, Kn 3, Kn 7 and Kn 9, were available for use. Kn 3, transmitting from Julianadorp on the Dutch coast, was oriented on the southern tip of the

19 A Ju88 taxying in preparation for a night take-off in the winter of 1940/41

Mull of Galloway, some 65 kilometres east of the target. Kn 7 and Kn 9, located on the French coast near Dieppe and Cherbourg respectively, were oriented so as to intersect over Target 835, Harland and Wolff's shipyard. This perseverance with a discredited system was, as Professor Jones pointed out in his book, puzzling. The German pilots themselves were aware of the effectiveness of British jamming and, in any event, the reception of usable VHF signals for navigation at a range of almost 800 kilometres was highly unlikely. According to Jones, a story current at the time was that no one in the Luftwaffe wanted to take on the unenviable task of telling Goering that *Knickebain* was no longer of any real use. It is clear from the accounts given by airmen who took part that it played no role in target-finding for the attack on Belfast. Various reports state that use was made of cross bearings from powerful broadcasting stations, such as Stavanger, Hilversum and Brest.[15] These stations could be tuned on an aircraft's ADF (radio compass) but the transmissions were susceptible to atmospheric interference and suffered particularly from 'night fading'. It is also suggested that Luftwaffe aircraft sometimes made use of the old Radio Eireann station, broadcasting from Athlone on 531 metres, but it went off the air at 2300 hours and probably no use was made of it.

Apart from Goering's warning, there is much emphasis elsewhere in the German files on the need to respect Irish neutrality on this occasion. For example, aircraft approaching Belfast from the north of England were forbidden to fly south of the Isle of Man. One entry in the pre-flight briefing for a unit coming from Holland states that 'particular attention is to be paid to possible violations of neutrality. Bombing is to be with positive sight of the ground and on the approach there can, in no case, be any deviation south of the beam'.[16] The 'beam' referred to was the *Knickebein* beam and even though its signals were not being received, the instruction, in effect, meant that those particular aircraft were not to fly south of the southern tip of the Mull of Galloway. The KG 4 operations file contains the following passage on the same subject: 'Due to the danger of a violation of neutrality, only good crews are to be employed and, of these, the best are to lead'. This illustrates that bombing Belfast was considered to be a demanding undertaking.

It is not known at what time the leading KG 76 Junkers came overhead the city but doubtless the aircraft commanders spent some time in trying to identify what ground features they were able to see. A standard procedure had been prescribed whereby all aircraft would approach the city from a north-easterly direction. This was an elementary precaution to ensure that there was no risk of collision between aircraft approaching from different directions. Accordingly, all would first proceed to a position on the coast in the vicinity of Larne. Provided there is vertical visibility, a coastline can be discerned from the air even on the darkest of nights but the prevailing cloud cover of 8/10ths to 10/10ths would have made orientation very difficult.

The official German record states that five Junkers from I and III/KG 76 dropped their bombs from heights ranging from 3000 metres to 3900 metres in a period of 11 minutes between 0005 hours and 0016 hours BST. These may well have been the first bombs to fall. The report further states that bombing was carried out by means of 'sight of the ground and dead-reckoning'. There is nothing to indicate which of these means predominated but the ambivalence points to uncertainty. In view of the emphatic orders that all bombing was to be strictly visual, no aircraft commander was going to omit the word 'visual' from his debriefing report. In any event, an occasional glimpse of the ground meant that it was not too difficult to satisfy the condition and although vertical visibility was undoubtedly very intermittent, the report of these first five Junkers claimed that hits and an ensuing fire were observed in the northern and southern part of the shipyard. However, if the cloud made bomb-aiming difficult it would also have made observing the effect difficult and such claims would have to be viewed with some scepticism.

No comprehensive target map illustrating all the individual targets appears to have survived but pre-flight briefings and mission reports indicate that the target area was divided into two parts extending across the harbour complex. The portion west of, and excluding, the shipyard was designated 'a' and code-named *Anton*. The area comprising the shipyard and everything to the east of it was target area 'b', code-named *Bruno*. The outer limits of the entire target area are not delineated.

Individual targets assigned to units or even single aircraft were drawn from the Luftwaffe's target catalogue 'GB' and each bore a number. Examples of those selected for the Easter Tuesday raid were: 835 (Harland and Wolff's), 7413 (Short and Harland's aircraft factory), 35162 (harbour installations), 5049 (harbour power station) and 2126 (the oil storage tanks at Airport Road). Each target included in the catalogue was the subject of a separate *Zielstamm-karte*, which listed detailed information. Although one existed for every target considered of any consequence, there is nothing in the available records to show how many were selected for attack on Easter Tuesday.

The desultory nature of the raid on 7/8 April had ill-prepared the people of Belfast for a major attack. The intermittent sound of engines heard at the outset developed into a continuous and ominous rumble after midnight as more and more aircraft reached the target area. At 0015 hours, the first of 10 He111Ps of III/KG 55 dropped two SC 250kg high-explosive bombs, one of them with a delayed-action fuse, together with eight SC 50kg high-explosives and an unknown number of incendiaries after a flight of approximately two and a half hours from Caen in Normandy. The unit to which it belonged had its base at Villacoublay on the southern outskirts of Paris but for the attack on Belfast it was to use the airfield at Caen as a forward base so as to maximize the range of its Heinkels.[17]

The order to bomb the unfamiliar target *Etappe* was issued at Villacoublay in the early afternoon of the fifteenth. Fourteen of the group's aircraft were serviceable for the operation and they began leaving for Caen at around 1500 hours local time. They landed about an hour later and began the refuelling and other pre-flight preparations. The crews received the weather forecast for the route and the target area. The general warning against proceeding to Belfast without first establishing visual contact with the Isle of Man was issued.

The leading aircraft of the Gruppe took off from Caen at 2250 hours local time and headed for Cap Barfleur on the Cherbourg peninsula. In accordance with standard Luftwaffe practice, aircraft commanders were given a wide discretion in choosing the route to the target. The unit navigation officer would acquaint them with the options available and remind them of the constraints imposed by fuel consumption, weather conditions and the potential danger from night fighters and ground defences.

Aircraft commanders who elected to take the direct route from Cap Barfleur to the Isle of Man would be flying through very dangerous airspace. The effectiveness of RAF night fighters was steadily increasing and the trend was expected to continue with the advent of better weather. More and more fighters were being equipped with Airborne Interception Radar (AI) which worked in conjunction with Ground Control Interception (GCI) stations to pose a serious threat to the bombers. The most famous of the RAF night fighter pilots of the time, Squadron-Leader (as he then was) John ('Cat's Eyes') Cunningham was known to the Luftwaffe to be very active in the central Southern England area. The Operations Records Book of Cunningham's squadron, No. 604, based at Middle Wallop, show that he was operating in the area on Easter Tuesday in his twin-engined Beaufighter, under the control of Exminster and Sopley GCI stations. The records of RAF's 10 Group state that altogether 71 night fighters flew patrols in the group area that night and give an indication of the hazards facing the bombers on the way to Belfast.[18]

One of III/KG 55's Heinkels bound for Belfast may have evaded the night fighters but nevertheless failed to reach its target. It was under the command of Unteroffizier Walter Kölz, who was on his sixth operational flight against targets in Britain. His intended course lay to the west of Bristol but what was probably a minor navigational error brought the aircraft within range of the city's anti-aircraft guns. Kölz's original handwritten report of what happened is held at the German Military Archives:[19]

On 15 April 1941, I took off on a bombing mission to Belfast. My altitude was 4500 metres. North-west of Bristol, the aeroplane was hit by anti-aircraft fire in the port engine which started to burn. I immediately gave the order to jettison bombs. This order was probably not understood by the observer in the commotion because, after I had regained control, I called the radio operator and got no answer. It then became clear to me that I was alone in the aircraft. I then pulled the emergency bomb-release. After a few minutes, the fire in the engine stopped. I then made the decision to try to get back to base on my own – which I succeeded in doing without radio bearings and on one engine. Shortly before reaching the airfield, I lost the left landing wheel which had been damaged in the explosion. The landing took place on one wheel, which also broke off during the landing roll.

The explanation for the crew's action was that they had misheard Kölz' order in the noise. In spite of the factual tone of his report and the fact that the incident was the subject of some. hilarity in his unit, it was recognized that Kölz had displayed airmanship of a high order. The commander of V Fliegerkorps, to which KG 55 belonged, had witnessed the Heinkel's return and was impressed. He promoted Kölz to sergeant and recommended him for the Iron Cross (First Class). The three crew members who had baled out landed safely and were taken prisoner.

Several of III/KG 55's aircraft elected to take the Irish Sea route and fly as close as possible to the coast of Eire. According to the records of the Irish Air Defence Command,[20] a number of aircraft must have adopted this course. Between 1139 hours BST on the fifteenth and 0239 hours on the sixteenth, 22 aircraft, presumed to be German, were plotted at various positions along the coast. With the exception of one aircraft, it was not alleged that there had been any violation of Irish airspace. The implication is that they remained outside the three-mile limit and were using the coastline for navigational purposes. In one case, the continuous plot recorded gives a good representation of an aeroplane that is lost. It crossed the coast south of Wicklow Head at 0200 hours and flew north-west to Naas before turning north. It passed abeam Dundalk at 0239 hours and continued towards Newry. Altogether, it circled three different positions for several minutes, presumably trying to establish its position.

Three of the III/KG 55 Heinkels that took off from Caen did not, in fact, attack Belfast and bombed Liverpool, the alternate target,instead. They may have been unable to establish visual contact at either the Isle of Man or Belfast itself. The unpredictable gaps in the cloud cover produced contrasting results. One crew confirmed having seen the Isle of Man clearly from 4,000 metres while others encountered 10/10ths cover for much of latter stages of the flight. The Gruppe operations report for the ten aircraft which actually commenced their attack at 15 minutes after midnight states that bombing was carried out 'mostly by visual means'. Here again, the deliberate ambivalence is present. While the ratio of 'blind' to 'visual' bomb releases is obviously unknown, the chronicle of events as seen from the ground suggests that a large number of the bombs carried by these aircraft may have fallen on north and west Belfast.

All the accounts of the early minutes of the raid which emanate from civilian sources, including civil defence agencies, agree that the northern area of the city, west of the shoreline of Belfast Lough bore the brunt of the initial attack. That there was a significant proportion of incendiaries among the early bomb loads dropped seems to be borne out by the entries in the Operations Record Book (ORB) of the RAF's No. 968 Balloon Squadron.[21] The crews manning the waterborne sites were well placed to observe the effect of the first bombs. The relevant ORB entries state that 'the tactics seemed to be to bomb the main areas of fire, corresponding to the northern shore of Belfast Lough'.

It seems safe to say that the action of the leading crews in dropping incendiaries well west of the intended targets in the harbour complex had a disastrous sequel for that part of the city. The crews of following aircraft, straining for some visual reference, would have been quick to assume that the fires were burning in the target area and aim their bombs accordingly. Undoubtedly, civilian lives were lost because of a lack of preparedness on the part of the authorities but much of the city's misfortune stemmed from the fact that the early German arrivals wrongly identified the target area. This, in turn, can be traced to weather conditions which were not anticipated in the forecast. The combined effect of these negative factors made a telling contribution to the unhappy story of Belfast and the 'Blitz'.

GLIMPSES OF THE GROUND

In the immediate aftermath of the Easter Tuesday raid, there was a tendency for the public to put the heavy loss of life down to deliberate terror tactics on the part of the enemy. This was an understandable reaction at the time and the authorities made no attempt to correct it. The Germans would not have denied that a side effect intended in all their night bombing attacks at this time was a weakening of the civilian will to resist. This was equally valid on the British side.

In the course of time, however, an objective analysis has shown that the bombers' primary targets in Belfast were not residential areas. Nevertheless, the reason why so many bombs fell in these areas – particularly in the north of the city – gave rise to speculation which has remained and is, in itself, of historical interest. The fragmentary Luftwaffe records are, in themselves, no great help but when they are supplemented by meteorological records and the personal recollections of former German airmen who participated some conclusions may be drawn.

Walther Baron von Siber (after the war he discontinued the use of the title 'Baron' and chose to be known simply as Walther Siber) was a young Leutnant attached to I Gruppe of Kampfgeschwader 53 (I/KG 53). During the night campaign of 1940/41, his Gruppe, equipped with the He111H-5 variant, was based at Vitry-en-Artois, an airfield in Northern France east of Cambrai. By the spring of 1941 he was already an experienced pilot having taken part in the Battle of Britain and many of the large-scale night operations.

On 15 April, I/KG 53 was ordered to stand-by for what was described as a major attack on *Etappe*. Because of his experience, Siber was detailed to act as a *Beleuchter*. The task of a *Beleuchter* (the German airmen themselves translated the word as 'lamplighter') was to mark the target as accurately as possible by laying a carpet of incendiaries for the guidance of following aircraft. It called for above-average skill in navigation and airmanship.

Siber's recollections of the period include a description of the preparations for the attacks during the April full moon period.[1] On 5 April Field Marshal Kesselring paid a visit to Monchy-le-Preux, a small village close to Vitry airfield, and listened to a lecture given by Siber's staffel (squadron)

20 Leutnant Baron Walther von Siber at the controls of his He111

commander, Hauptmann Werner Hörenz. Sand pits were used, in which models of targets earmarked for possible attack in the full moon period, including Belfast, were constructed for the benefit of the *Beleuchter* crews and others with special assignments. Siber was personally acquainted with Kesselring and the lecture was recalled when both men met at Karnten in Austria after the war. Siber is, in fact, mentioned in Kesselring's autobiography *Soldier to the last day*, which was published before his death in 1960.

Twenty-two aircraft of I/KG 53 were declared serviceable for the operation against Belfast. The Gruppe had consistently been able to put a larger number of aircraft into the air than any other group engaged in night operations – something for which Kesselring had expressed his appreciation. This attack was regarded as more than usually demanding. The geographical location of the target meant that the attacking force would have to fly across Northern England in both directions and consequently face exposure to night fighters for prolonged periods. While Siber took the view that every operation was inevitably hazardous, he found the strain of long night flights over hostile territory gruelling. Newcastle and Hull were the alternate targets named. Both were looked on as comparatively easy targets, since they were adjacent to the relative safety of the airspace over the North Sea.

After a lapse of 50 years, Siber was unable to remember his flight to Belfast in any great detail but with the aid of a map and extracts from his unit's war diary, he was able to reconstruct an outline of his part in the night's operation. His Heinkel was airborne at Vitry some time shortly after 2130 hours BST. Its bomb load consisted of one BSB incendiary bomb container with 720 one-kilogram bombs and 16 BSK containers with fragmentation bombs. In addition to Siber, it carried a crew of four. The navigator/observer was Feldwebel Johann Fischer and the flight-engineer Oberfeldwebel Herbert Meister. Feldwebel Ernst Wylezol and Unteroffizier Alfried Schurff were the radio-operator and air-gunner respectively.

After take-off, the Heinkel flew north, leaving the Belgian coast at Ostend. It continued on the same heading across the North Sea to remain clear of the coast of East Anglia before changing course to cross the Yorkshire coast north of Hull. Siber recalled utilizing bearings from the Deutschlandsender radio station at Emden to steer a course for the northern tip of the Isle of Man.

The Heinkel negotiated the airspace over the north of England without incident although the crew saw gun flashes from the Leeds anti-aircraft defences in the distance. Werner Hörenz, who had played such a prominent role in preparing for the mission, was not so lucky. His Heinkel crashed near Leeds but Hörenz and his three crew members baled out and were taken prisoner.[2] The circumstances of the crash are not clear. One cause suggested was mechanical failure but Hörenz himself, who died in 1966, believed that he had been hit by fire from a night fighter.[3]

21 Field Marshal Albert Kesselring

After leaving the north-western coast of England near Barrow-in-Furness, the Isle of Man was identified and the flight continued towards Belfast. On studying a map of Northern Ireland, Siber remembered passing to the east of Newtownards before heading for the northern side of Belfast Lough where he would turn on to the final approach for the target. According to the unit war diary, it was approximately 0045 hours. By this stage, the cloud cover was virtually unbroken and finding the turning point by visual means would be very difficult but Siber remembered that he was able to get an idea of the distance from the target by taking cross bearings from the broadcast stations at Brest and Stavanger.

German bomber units had a standard procedure for bombing in conditions of marginal or zero visibility. Once the target was thought to have been identified, the aircraft would overfly that position and commence a timed procedure on instruments during which the bomb-aimer would make his calculations. The course flown would be held for two minutes, after which the aircraft would make a turn (known as a 'rate one' turn) of 210 degrees to the left or right. Provided any necessary allowance for wind effect was made, this was calculated to bring the aircraft back over the bomb release point at a known time.

It was this '210 degree procedure' that Siber decided to adopt. His account of this phase of the attack reads:

> Although almost total cloud cover lay over the target area, the mainland, water and bay (Belfast Lough) could be seen through the available breaks in the clouds. We dropped the bomb load along the coastal strip on the shipbuilding installations. Attacking aircraft preceding me had also laid so-called 'incendiary carpets' so that the city and the shoreline could be recognized. During the time I was over the target, the anti-aircraft fire – as far as I can remember – was not heavy, neither was I aware of any night fighters.

Where Siber's bombs actually fell will never be known but it is notable that the operations report for his Gruppe makes no claim that the shipyards were actually seen to have been hit by any of the bombs. This is not surprising since the momentary breaks in the cloud were probably not sufficient to allow the effect to be observed. The extent of the difficulty which this unit experienced as a result of the weather conditions can be gauged from the fact that, of the twenty-two aircraft which set out for Belfast, only seven succeeded in attacking it. Of the remainder, four attacked Hull and nine Newcastle. The target of the one remaining aircraft (excluding Hörenz's) is unknown.

It was one of the duties of a *Beleuchter* aircraft to break radio silence and transmit a brief report of weather conditions at the target and Siber's transmission may have prompted some of the diversions. In any event, Belfast was thus spared something in the region of 25 metric tonnes of high-explosive and incendiary bombs.

The first bombs were estimated to have fallen on the city about an hour before Siber's attack, many of them in the vicinity of the reservoirs and waterworks lying to the west of the city's Cavehill Road. Official acknowledgment of this is contained in an entry in the operations journal of 102 HAA:

> Flares dropped by early raiders illuminated the waterworks and reservoirs and many bombs were dropped in this area.[4]

The belief that these landmarks in the north of the city fatally deceived the first German bomb-aimers into thinking that they were part of the harbour complex has become part of Belfast's wartime folklore. It is a view that is indeed borne out by the facts.

All aircraft were to approach the target area from the north-east. None of the original target charts carried on the raid have survived for inspection in the German archives. These would have indicated the final turning point as well as the true and magnetic compass headings for the approach to the target. It seems probable, however, that the final turn was planned to take place somewhere on the stretch of coast between Whitehead and Larne. Crews of the RAF's No. 77 Wing, manning a radar station further up the coast at Glenarm, observed aircraft turning on the Maiden's Rocks, about six miles north-east of Larne,[5] but there is no evidence that this was a prescribed turning point.

With the limited sight of the ground which existed, it was important to locate the turning point and to fly the correct compass heading to the target. An error in one or both could result in failure to find it. For example a deviation of a few degrees to the right of the required track could have brought an aircraft over the north of the city instead of the harbour. At this crucial stage of the flight, bomber crews would have been trying to identify ground features through the breaks in the overcast. This can be seen in all the available crew and unit reports. In these conditions, it is very possible that a few of the early attackers strayed to the right of the approach track causing their bomb-aimers to mistake the reservoirs on the Cavehill Road for the outer reaches of the harbour basin. An artificially-enclosed body of water seen momentarily by the light of flares could well have led a bomb-aimer to believe that he had arrived at the target. In such case, he might also have assumed that the adjacent built-up areas were shipbuilding or dock installations. Fires started here by *Beleuchter* aircraft at this early stage would have had a decisive effect on the course of the raid. Failure to identify and mark the targets at the outset could easily lead to failure of the entire operation. Bomb-aimers in following aircraft would have assumed that the *Beleuchters* had done their job properly and proceeded to aim at the fires.

The last of the seven Heinkels of I/KG 53 to successfully locate the target.

dropped its bombs at 0145 hours. Between them, these aircraft had dropped seven SC1000kg high-explosive bombs and a total of 3456 BIEI incendiaries. By all accounts, they had encountered little in the way of opposition. The Gruppe operations report sent to Luftflotte 2 headquarters noted that 'the flak over Belfast was variable in aim and intensity'. Several barrage balloons had been observed but there was no mention of any smoke screen.[6]

Siber himself took the most direct route back to Vitry-en-Artois where he landed shortly before 0500 hours local time. He was not to return to Belfast. On the night of the heavy raid of 4/5 May, he bombed Barrow-in-Furness but, by then, the war was almost over for him. A week later, on 11 May, while he was engaged in what was virtually the last great attack of the night campaign, his Heinkel was hit by ground fire over London and burst into flames. Two of the crew, Meister and Schurff, were killed instantly. Feldwebel Wylezol was mortally wounded and unable to crawl towards the escape hatch. The navigator, Johann Fischer made desperate efforts to save him but eventually he was ordered by Siber to bale out. After Fischer had gone, the aircraft went into a spin and Siber was just able to struggle through the hatch over the pilot's seat before losing consciousness. He must have pulled the rip-cord as he did so because, when he came to, a detachment of the Home Guard was standing over him. He spent most of the rest of the war in a prisoner of war camp in Canada.

In Belfast, eye witnesses and others close to events on the ground on that Easter Tuesday night seem to agree that there was a marked intensification of the attack after one o'clock. Up to that point, around forty He111s and Ju88s, drawn from KG 55, KG 76 and KG 77 are known to have unloaded their bombs over the city. For the most part, the high-explosives were of the 500 kg, or lighter, calibre, although five SC1000kg bombs and one very large SC1800kg are recorded. The last-mentioned bomb was carried by an He111P-4 of I/KG 55, based at Dreux, near Paris. Christened *Satan* by the Germans, it was one of the largest pieces of ordnance in the Luftwaffe's armoury and could cause widespread devastation.

It is significant that the escalation which occurred after 0100 hours coincided with the arrival over the city of the first of the Heinkels of I/KG 4 from Soesterberg. This unit, which could justifiably claim the status of an elite formation, would deliver a bigger bomb load per aircraft than any other unit taking part in the raid.

At Soesterberg, the preliminary order for the night's operation was issued at 1615 hours. The force available consisted of a staff flight of two aircraft (commanded by Gruppe staff officers) together with six aircraft from the 1st Staffel and nine from the 3rd. One of the aircraft of the staff flight was piloted by the Gruppe commander Hauptmann Klaus Nöske, who would also act as a *Beleuchter*. One aircraft from each of the two staffels was also nominated as a *Beleuchter*. Each would carry sixteen BSK incendiary containers with a total of 576 one-kilogram incendiaries. A decision on the composition of the remainder of the bomb loads to be carried by the *Beleuchters* was postponed until shortly before take-off. In the case of the staffel aircraft, each would carry two LMB 1000kg parachute mines. The distance to be flown combined with the weight of two mines slung externally under the fuselage and full fuel tanks demanded maximum commitment and left little margin for error either in aircraft handling or navigation.

The dearth of official records covering many Luftwaffe operations in the Second World War stems from a general order for the destruction of documents issued by Nazi Germany's propaganda minister, Joseph Goebbels, in the closing days of the war. In view of this handicap, it is fortunate that I/KG 4's war diary relating to its part in the attacks on Belfast has survived. It contains unusually detailed information of an operational nature and is invaluable in any attempt to reconstruct the events.[7]

The order confirming the operation against *Etappe* was received by the Gruppe from Luftflotte 2 headquarters in Brussels at 1830 hours. Alternate targets named in order of importance were Dumbarton, Barrow-in-Furness, Preston and Liverpool. A sister Gruppe, III/KG 4, which was based at Leuwarden in the north of Holland, would attack Newcastle with 16 aircraft.

The three *Beleuchters* of I Gruppe, each loaded with an LMB mine in addition to the incendiaries, were ordered to light the targets at 2350, 0020 and 0050 hours BST respectively. The first was commanded by Hauptmann Nöske and the time of the task assigned to him meant that he would have been over the city at a very early stage of the raid. However, there was a delay in the departure of all aircraft from Soesterberg because of a power failure and Nöske's actual take-off time is not recorded.

The navigation officer for the raid, Oberleutnant Kurt Zecher, briefed the crews on the choice of routes and the available navigation aids. Once the Dutch coast had been cleared, the flight to Belfast was to be made above 3500 metres and the attack itself at below 3000 metres. At 3000 metres altitude, the en route forecast of wind velocity was 290 degrees at 50 km/h for the first half of the outbound flight and 300 degrees at 50 km/h for the second half. This meant that aircraft would be flying into a head wind and their speed over the ground would be reduced to approximately 275 km/h with a corresponding increase for the return flight. The prohibition against flying south of the Isle of Man and the order to bomb by visual means only were reiterated. At Belfast, target area *Anton*, covering the western side of the harbour complex, was assigned to the two aircraft of the staff flight along with six from 1st Staffel and area *Bruno*, covering the eastern side, to seven aircraft from 3rd Staffel. The effect of these dispositions would have been to give Nöske and one other *Beleuchter* the task of illuminating area *Anton*, that is, up to, and including, the western shore of Belfast Lough.

The Gruppe's war diary records that sixteen Heinkels were found to be operational and that they started to take off at 2138 hours BST. The mines weighing 2000 kg, along with more than 4000 litres of fuel made take-off a critical manoeuvre and all of the runway was needed to get the aircraft into the air at a speed of 150 km/h. When airborne, they set course for one or other of the specified radio or light beacons on the coast, passing over the city of Amsterdam on the way. They were restricted to a height of 700 metres until reaching the coast, after which they would start the slow laborious climb to their cruising level of 3500 metres or above. The last aircraft was airborne at 2212 hours BST.

Once over the North Sea, the *Knickebein* Kn3 beam from Julianadorp, which was oriented on the Mull of Galloway, was intercepted and utilized for navigation as long as possible. Normally, it could not be relied upon after crossing the English coast but, until then, it was useful in getting established on track and ascertaining wind drift.

By 2350 hours, fifteen of the group's sixteen aircraft had reached various stages of the flight to Belfast. One had had to turn back because of trouble with the propellor pitch mechanism and landed at Soesterberg at 2358 hours. The time originally planned for the group's attack was 0050 hours but this would not be met because of the delay in take-off. All radio operators listened out for the weather report from Belfast which was to be transmitted by the *Beleuchters*. On learning the marginal conditions prevailing there, individual aircraft commanders would have begun to prepare for the possibility of attacking one of the alternates. The pre-flight briefing provided that aircraft should be prepared to receive instructions by radio to proceed to an alternate target. In the absence of any such instructions, however, the aircraft commanders of I/KG 4, all of whom were highly-experienced commissioned officers, had a discretion to take whatever action they thought appropriate.

By midnight, any doubt that Belfast was the Luftwaffe's principal target for the night had disappeared. The RAF's 12 Group, whose area covered the coast of Yorkshire, advised that after midnight there was a significant movement of enemy aircraft through the area in a westerly direction.[8] When these developments were linked with early reports of bombs being dropped on Belfast, the 'Y' Service was in a position to confirm that the city was, in fact, the main target for the night. It is noteworthy that 12 Group's ORB states that, in spite of the large enemy force deployed, no night fighter interceptions were claimed in the Group's area. This was possibly due, at least in part, to the cloudy conditions which did not favour interception.

The leading aircraft of I/KG 4's mine-carrying Heinkels approached Belfast shortly before 0100 hours. The unit's war diary puts the time of the first attack at 0111 hours and the last at 0150. In these 39 minutes, eleven aircraft dropped a total of 20 LMB mines. Of these, it was estimated that five did not explode and probably fell into the harbour basin. There seems little doubt that many of the fifteen mines which did explode fell in the north of the city, within a short distance of the lough shore. This is borne out by the recollections of eye witnesses recounted in Brian Barton's book, *The Blitz; Belfast in the War Years*. Any attempt to match the sequence of events in the city with the incomplete Luftwaffe records immediately runs into difficulties. While the latter are usually accurate in relation to the time at which events occurred, there was an understandable lack of precision among people on the ground. However, an exception is provided by records of St Ninian's Parish Church on Whitewell Road in the north of the city.[9] One entry reads: 'Shortly after 0120 two parachute bombs landed – one in Barbour Street and one in front of 74 Whitewell Road.' Both locations lie close to the lough shore and the time of the occurrence coincides with the time of I/KG 4's attack. Combined with the fact that the mines fell on the fringe of target area *Anton*, which was assigned to the unit, there is a strong presumption that they came from one of its aircraft.

It is impossible to say with any certainty how many mines actually fell in the target areas, *Anton* and *Bruno*. From all the evidence, probably very few. On the German side, the bulletin issued by I/KG 4 after crew debriefing could not disguise the inconclusive result of the operation:

> Due to the prevailing 9/10ths cloud cover, the effect was not clearly observed. The attack took place visually through gaps in the clouds in conjunction with *Beleuchters*. On the basis of the aiming points, all bombs fell in target areas *Anton* and *Bruno*.[10]

The final ambiguous sentence of the report sums up the uncertainty experienced by all the crews. There is no positive claim that any of the mines were seen to explode in the target areas; merely that the aiming points had been identified. Luftwaffe pre-flight briefings were thorough and the boundaries of the target areas would have been clearly demarcated with detailed annotations about industrial installations and other features. It was an unsatisfactory result and the staff of I/KG 4 clearly regarded the attack as abortive. When the Air Staff at Luftwaffe headquarters had evaluated all the mission reports, Belfast would remain near the top of the list of future targets.

The airmen themselves would have been quick to point out that the unexpectedly poor weather conditions had necessitated an abnormally long search for the target. As a result, pilots would have been anxiously watching their fuel gauges and target identification was hurried and suffered accordingly. As one German pilot had said on another occasion, it was inevitable that the siting of densely-packed rows of workers' houses close to factories and mills, which was a feature of the Industrial Revolution in Britain, contributed to the heavy civilian casualties during the whole of the night campaign.

While these factors may carry some weight, the attackers would have conceded that the parachute bomb (or mine) did not lend itself to accuracy. The vagaries of the wind over its entire descent influenced its point of impact and it could be some distance away from the aiming point.

Not all the LMB mines dropped on Belfast during the Easter Tuesday raid were carried by I/KG 4. However, in all the other known cases, only a single mine was carried. Unteroffizier Thomas Hammerl of I/KG 28 (formerly KGr 126), who had carried a mine to the Dublin area in January, also took part in the Easter Tuesday raid.[11] The number of aircraft his unit had been able to put up that night is not known but the 'Y' Service logged transmissions from six, one of which reported having made an attack at 0210 hours adding that 'the target was burning fiercly'.

Hammerl was a member of the crew of Oberfeldwebel Albert Engel (in the Luftwaffe, the pilot was not necessarily the aircraft commander). The other crew members were Gefreiter Wolfgang Schüller and Gefreiter Rudolf Mattern. All had flown together on a large number of mining sorties in the Irish Sea throughout the winter. On 15 April, Engel's mission was to attack Belfast with one LMB parachute mine. When employed in anti-shipping or mining sorties in the Irish Sea, aircraft from Nantes often used the airfield at Brest-Langveoc as a forward operations base, depending on the payload and the distance to be flown. As a bomb load of only 1,000 kg was to carried on this occasion, the round trip of approximately 1,850 kilometres could be made without an intermediate landing.

Engel's Heinkel, identification code IT + EK, took off at 2245 hours BST and headed due north towards the coast of Brittany at St Brieux. It passed to the west of the Channel Islands and over the western part of Cornwall so as to come within reach of the coast of Co. Wexford. The coastline was followed north and the target reached at about 0200 hours. The attack was made at 0215 hours but no details of where it was claimed the mine had fallen were given. By all accounts, it seems to have been an uneventful operation and the Heinkel landed back at Nantes at 0515 hours BST. This was to prove to be the last mission that Engel and his crew would complete. The following night, 16/17 April, they were shot down by a night fighter south of London. Engel and Hammerl baled out and were taken prisoner but Schüller and Mattern were killed.[12]

Further evidence of the intensification of the attack after 0100 hours is provided by Luftflotte 3 records of units carrying more conventional bomb loads. Between 0055 and 0158 hours, 16 He111s of I and II Gruppen of KG/27, coming from from bases at Brest and Dinard dropped 8 SC 500kg,

33 SC 250kg (including three with time fuses) and 94 SC 50kg bombs along with 2304 BIEI incendiaries. The bombing was said to be either 'visual' or 'partly visual'. Numerous fires and heavy explosions were observed but not the effect. An unspecified number of hits in the harbour complex were claimed.

Substantially the same kind of report was filed by 10 Ju88A-5s of I, II and III Gruppen of KG 54 operating from airfields north of Paris and dropping three SC 500kg, and thirty-four SC 250kg. bombs but no incendiaries. All fell between 0115 hours and 0200 hours. Hits were claimed in or near the harbour complex but again, the effect was not observed.

The picture emerging from these combat reports is that by 0200 hours the city had already sustained a very heavy attack. Its plight could have been a good deal worse, however. The records show that many of the attackers were still failing to find and bomb the primary target and were diverting to the alternates. For example, in the case of the KG 27 and KG 54 aircraft mentioned, while a total of 26 aircraft attacked Belfast, another 15 bombed Liverpool as an alternate.

The crews over the city at this intermediate stage of the raid were doubtless surprised at the almost total absence of anti-aircraft fire. The 102 HAA reported that at 0155 hours, GOR (Gun Operations Room) communications broke down. Contact was eventually re-established by W/T (Wireless Telegraphy).[13] The breakdown had been caused by bomb damage to the telephone exchange and from this time on, the city's already meagre defences were virtually impotent.

The composite report on the night's mission issued by Luftflotte 3 described the fire from the heavy batteries as 'very badly aimed'. In contrast, the medium calibre fire was said to be 'well-aimed'.[14] The crews of I/KG 53 judged the anti-aircraft fire to be 'variable in aim and intensity'.

Barrage balloons were reported flying at heights varying from 1500 metres to 2000 metres but do not seem to have been particularly troublesome. This is not to say that balloons were not taken seriously and throughout the winter there had been instances of aircraft having been destroyed or damaged by collision with the cables. Leutnant Robert Bubaszu, the commander of an He111 belonging to Transportgeschwader 30, based at Nantes, carried an LMB mine in the Easter Tuesday raid. He had good reason to be apprehensive about barrage balloons. On 13 January, during a raid on Liverpool, his aircraft collided with a balloon cable which ripped off the aileron and part of one wing.[15] His crew must have considered themselves very lucky indeed to have survived that experience. In an attempt to counter this hazard, the Luftwaffe had fitted an *Abweiser* to some of its Heinkels. This was an alloy frame fitted to the leading edges of both wings. The frame sloped back from a point at the nose of the aircraft to the wing tips. If contact was made with a cable, it would be diverted to either wing tip where a small explosive charge was located. When this exploded, it was hoped that the cable would snap. The idea was not a success, however. The frame was cumbersome and had an adverse aerodynamic effect. It had been found that if the aircraft lost an engine, or suffered a serious reduction in power, it could not maintain level flight.

Crews over the city at or later than 0200 hours reported that a large number of fires were burning and that, in some instances, they had developed into conflagrations. Luftwaffe intelligence officers were very interested in receiving detailed descriptions of fires. They were at pains to exclude the possibility that crews had been deceived by decoy fires.

This preoccupation with British deception methods stemmed from a raid on Liverpool on the night of 30 August when the Luftwaffe spent several hours bombing an area of open countryside in North Wales where extensive fires were seen to be burning. Originally code-named *Crashdecks*, the idea of igniting rows of baskets containing combustible material near urban areas had developed into a sophisticated system, renamed *Starfish*. It was recognized that there was no point in using the fires on bright moonlit nights when the deception would soon be discovered. Conditions were more favourable when vertical visibility was marginal.

Although there appears to be no evidence in British source documents that *Starfish* fires were ever used in the attacks on Belfast, a crew from I/KG 4 filed the following report on returning from the Easter Tuesday raid:

> Several expanses of fire were seen near Belfast. It is possible that some of these were decoy fires. In particular, there seemed to be such installations, partly feigning incendiary bombs, laid out on the north-west side of Strangford Lough.[16]

A possible explanation for this observation was that these fires were caused by incendiary bombs which had fallen on and around Scrabo Hill, adjacent to Newtownards airfield shortly before 0100 hours. The airfield itself had been attacked with high-explosives and incendiaries, resulting in casualties among the military detachment providing airfield defence.[17]

The Luftwaffe went to considerable trouble to alert flying personnel to the enemy's deception measures. Maps were prepared showing locations throughout Britain where decoy fires and other artificial installations existed or were thought to exist. Belfast was included in the series. A sketch map, entitled 'Decoy installations ascertained by flying units from Luftflotten 2, 3 and 5 in the period January to April 1941', depicts five locations round the city where such sites were thought to be. Two of them suggest decoy fires, one on the north side of Belfast Lough and the other on the south. The first was believed to be in open countryside to the north of Carrickfergus. The second is indicated in the Holywood hills, south-east of Belfast. There were three locations where unspecified deception measures were thought to exist. One was immediately to the north of the city and the other two to the south-east within a radius of 30 kilometres of the harbour targets.

It is difficult to see how the Luftwaffe could have ascertained the existence of suspect sites other than by means of aerial photography – or possibly intelligence. Prior to Easter Tuesday, the only occasion on which decoy fires could have been lit during a raid was on the night of 7/8 April and there is nothing to suggest that this happened.

It is not known whether the German reconnaissance aircraft that had overflown the city the previous day had detected the presence of the aircraft carrier HMS *Furious* lying at Victoria Wharf. The ship's twelve 4-inch anti-aircraft guns could have made a valuable contribution to the city's defences but the breakdown in landline communications or other difficulty in aiming apparently prevented this. A report of the night's events by the ship's second-in-command, Commander M.B. Laing, sent to the Admiralty, provides some more information:

> While moored at Victoria Wharf, a raid took place on the town and docks. Bombing mainly from 4,000 to 10,000 feet. There was low cloud and a light south-westerly breeze.
>
> The number or type of aircraft unknown but numbers considerable. Moon two-thirds full rose about 0100 hours but mostly obscured by cloud. No aircraft observed.
>
> The-ship was straddled by a stick of 4 bombs, the second being 20 yards off starboard quarter and the third falling on jetty. Another stick fell ahead, the nearest being approximately 30 yards distant. The fuses appeared to be either instantaneous or fitted with long delay varying from six to 16 hours.
>
> The ship's armament organized to augment shore defences in barrage fire with direct link to GOR (Gun Operations Room). Only one barrage was fired as guns could not be brought to bear. 0.5 machine-guns opened fire on parachute flares without success.
>
> Minor damage only.[18]

From the available information it therefore emerges that the effectiveness of both the attacking force and Belfast's defences was greatly reduced by unforeseen circumstances, the former by an inaccurate weather forecast and the latter by a failure in communications.

The losses recorded by the Luftwaffe in the night's operations amounted to four aircraft (in addition to that of Unteroffizier Kölz which was destroyed in an emergency landing) of which two at least were known to be heading for Belfast.[19] Three fell to night fighters over southern England.

At around 0200 hours, the raid entered its final phase. It is estimated that by now at least 100 bombers had unloaded their bombs over Belfast. The remainder of the force dispatched was either on the way to the city or to one of the alternates. Included in these formations were the He111Ps of III/KG 27 from their base at Brest-Langveoc, led by the Gruppe commander, Hans Henning, Baron von Beust.

Since February, von Beust's Gruppe had been heavily engaged in daylight anti-shipping operations in the Irish Sea and Bristol Channel. It had suffered severe losses due to inexperience in this type of work which probably explains why only nine aircraft could be made available for the night's operation. Von Beust himself had already more than 100 operational flights over and around the British Isles behind him, an indication of the demands made on German aircrew during this phase of the war. Unlike the RAF, the operational tour was unknown in the Luftwaffe at this time. Crews simply continued to fly at the discretion of the operational commanders or until they were killed or wounded.

After leaving Brest, von Beust's Heinkels crossed the western tip of Cornwall and then took the direct route to Belfast, flying as close as possible to the Irish coast. It is very likely that some of them were those whose progress was monitored by the Irish look-out posts (LOPs) and reported to RAF Intelligence. It seems that close to the vicinity of the Isle of Man, three of the aircraft commanders decided that conditions did not favour an attack on the primary target and turned instead for Liverpool.

The remaining five aircraft continued to Belfast and claimed to have made their attack 'visually between 0205 and 0225 hours in target area *Bruno*'. The bomb load dropped consisted of six SC 250kg, two SC 250kg (with time fuses), forty SC 50kg high explosives and 1005 BIEI incendiaries. This report stated that fires were seen to be developing to the north-west of the target area, accompanied by explosions. The use of the word 'developing' indicated a continuing deterioration on the Co. Antrim side of the lough. Other crew reports spoke of 'very heavy explosions' being observed in positions that could not be identified.

Among the last aircraft to take off for the long flight to Belfast were 12 Ju88A-5s of III/KG 1. Their base was Roye-Amy airfield, which lay to the east of the city of Amiens in Northern France. One of them was commanded by 25-year-old Leutnant Gerhard Baeker. With the aid of his original pilot's log-book entries, he was able to supply some details of his flight that night:

I was a member of III Kampfgeschwader 1 'Hindenburg' which was deployed in two night attacks on the harbour and shipyards of Belfast. We had the Ju88A-5 with armament categories B and C. Instead of the fuel tank installed in category C aircraft, the B category had 10 x 50kg bombs in racks in the forward fuselage compartment in addition to four 250kg bombs in the external racks. However, that meant that the B category had one and a half hours less endurance. As regards range, the Ju88 with armament category B (flying time six hours) could only barely reach Belfast from the base at Roye-Amy (a distance of about 800 km) under operational conditions by direct flight across England. Because the Ju88 with category C armament could make a flight of seven and a half hours, it could take a circuitous route round the west of England.

On 15 April 1941 I took off from Roye-Amy at 2355 hours (2255 BST) on a direct flight to Belfast but on passing Liverpool I had to decide, by reason of the weather conditions and because I was flying a category B aircraft, to attack my alternate target which was the harbour and dock installations at Liverpool. I landed back at base at 0450 hours.[20]

Although Baeker's account of his sortie is rather concise, it nevertheless highlights the limitations of the Ju88 as a long-range bomber and emphasizes the pressures that this put on aircraft commanders. Navigating by 'dead reckoning' over a blacked-out landscape was difficult enough without the added anxiety about fuel consumption. At Liverpool, Baeker obviously viewed the chances of identifying the Isle of Man as too uncertain to go any further and risk having to make a protracted search for the target. Three other aircraft of his Gruppe also bombed Liverpool.

Over a period of two hours ending at 0345 hours, seven aircraft from Baeker's unit dropped 28 SC 250kg bombs (4 of which had time fuses) and 160 BIEI incendiaries on Belfast. These figures indicate that, since these aircraft each carried a 1,000kg bomb load, they had armament category C, giving them an extended endurance of seven and a half hours.

The time of 0345 hours is, in fact, the last recorded attack made by a Luftflotte 3 machine in the raid. The absence of Luftflotte 2 records makes it impossible to say whether any other aircraft dropped bombs after that time. The uncertainty about when the attack actually commenced is mirrored by conflicting data about the time it ended, as opposed to when the 'all clear' was sounded. The 102 HAA war diary put it at 0322 hours,[21] 23 minutes before the Luftwaffe record. Both sources are ordinarily reliable but timing the dropping of the last bomb from a position on the ground would have been difficult in the chaotic conditions prevailing.

The indications are that these last attackers benefited from what appears to have been a temporary improvement in the cloud cover over the city. This comes out in an extract from the files of Luftflotte 3, most of whose units approached by the Irish Sea route:

From Cherbourg to the Isle of Man, almost cloudless with slight haze. Between the Isle of Man and Belfast 7/10ths to 10/10ths cloud cover. Several cloud layers with base at 1000 metres and overcast at 3500 metres above which there was thick haze up to 6000 metres. From about 0400 DGZ (0300 hours BST) cloud over Belfast fluctuated between 2/10ths and 8/10ths.[22]

The improvement referred to would have created conditions for much more accurate bombing than had earlier been the case. Any good breaks in the cloud cover would have given the attackers a further advantage. The moon had risen at 0035 hours but the overcast skies had nullified its effect at the beginning of the raid. Although in its final quarter, it would have thrown the harbour complex into sharp relief for bomb-aimers in the closing stages. As a result, a high proportion of the last bombs dropped found the intended targets. It had, however, come too late to help the Luftwaffe accomplish its aims of paralysing production throughout the harbour estate and disrupting movements at the port. By the same token, it came too late for the hundreds of civilians who had died as a result of inaccurate bombing or inadequate target identification. The irony is that, from 0300 hours onwards, probably less than 10 or 12 aircraft benefited from the clearer skies and that none of them carried bombs of a calibre heavier than 250 kg.

The clearance experienced by the rear echelon of the attacking force was evidently of short duration. No weather reports were issued by RAF Aldergrove between 0200 hours[23] and 0500 hours but the latter did not, in fact, differ materially in cloud amounts from that issued earlier at 2300 hours. It recorded 9/10ths stratocumulus at 1800 feet and 1/10th low stratus at 800 feet, conditions which all but precluded any vertical visibility.

In the final half hour of the raid, the last few Ju88s of III/KG 1 were flying unmolested over a defenceless city. One crew reported that defensive fire was non-existent and that target areas *Anton* and *Bruno* could be attacked without hindrance. Fresh fires were seen to be breaking out in Harland & Wolff's shipyard.

The following day, Luftflotte 3's commander, General Field Marshal Hugo Sperrle, issued a summary of the night's operation from his headquarters at St Cloud. Of a total of 270 bombers deployed by units under his command, 118 had attacked Belfast. A further 51, whose primary target had been Belfast, had been forced to bomb Liverpool as their secondary target.

The review went on to make this guarded assessment of the night's operation:

Because precise target orientation and identification were not possible due to unfavourable weather conditions, only a mediocre result can be reckoned with. On account of the small number of aircraft engaged, the effect was minimal.[24]

The sober tone of this analysis, which was not, of course, intended for public consumption, contrasted with the pretentious claims made by the German press and radio. These were based on the bulletins prepared by the propaganda companies which were attached to units in the field and which came under the direct control of Josef Goebbels' propaganda ministry.

One reason for the tentative nature of the Luftwaffe's appraisal was that the adverse weather conditions persisted for two or three days and prevented the taking of the aerial photographs normally used to corroborate crew reports. There is no record of any attempt being made on the sixteenth but detailed descriptions of reconnaissance sorties made by Wekusta 51 on the two succeeding days are available.

A Heinkel He111H-3, piloted by Oberfeldwebel Heidrich, left Paris/Buc airfield at 1152 hours BST on the 17th with orders to take photographs of Belfast showing the effect of the raid.[25] It made a refuelling stop at Brest-Lanveoc, taking off again at 1348 hours. It climbed on course for Belfast via the Scilly Isles, passing through thick layers of cloud all the way up to 6500 metres. On nearing the city, Heidrich descended to 1000 metres without encountering visual conditions. Photography was out of the question and he abandoned the attempt.

The following day, another Heinkel, piloted by Feldwebel-Hollerbach, took the same route, leaving Brest at 0955 hours. At no stage of the flight was there any visual contact with the surface and navigation had to be carried out by 'dead reckoning.' On coming overhead Belfast, it was found that the cloud cover was 10/10ths and once again the mission had to be aborted. This aircraft ran short of fuel after collecting meteorological data round the north coast of Ireland and had to make an emergency landing at Dinard.[26]

Although there is no record of any evaluation photographs in the German archives, some were probably taken subsequently. The evidence from these would merely have confirmed that the raid had been a failure. A large number of the designated targets were unscathed and the photographs would have shown that the shipyard, which was regarded as the prime target, had only sustained limited damage. It was consistent with the large number of crew reports that spoke of bombs being dropped 'without the effect being observed'. In many cases, this was simply tantamount to saying that they did not fall in the target area.

Although the Luftwaffe leadership might try to minimize the ineffectual outcome of operations like that against Belfast, the flying personnel had no illusions about the effect it had on them. They saw themselves required to spend six or seven hours in a hostile and dangerous environment carrying out a mission rendered futile by an inaccurate weather forecast. Complaining about weather forecasts is the perennial pursuit of fliers but there was genuine resentment about the continued absence of reliable navigational aids. There had been no effort to remedy this deficiency since the officers of KG 30 had come close to being accused of mutiny when they raised the subject six months earlier.

The truth was that night bombing, at this early stage of the war, was a very inexact science and RAF Bomber Command was having no more success in picking out targets among the densely-packed industries of the Ruhr valley. The RAF pilot who said that 'we were lost as soon as we left the airfield' may have only been guilty of a slight exaggeration.

On the question of numbers, it is impossible from the available information to state definitively how many German aircraft attacked Belfast on Easter Tuesday. In addition to the 118 from Luftflotte 3, an unknown number from the numerically smaller Luftflotte 2 – probably not more than 40 – took part, which would have put the total involved at under 160.

Although the attack was planned and launched as 'a major attack' (the Luftwaffe's description), the large number of diversions to alternate targets must have substantially reduced the effect in terms of casualties and damage. The diversions were of the order of 35 per cent of the total force deployed. In spite of this, the number of civilian deaths – more than 700 – was high, relative to the size of the attacking force. A comparison with what happened the following night when London was attacked in what was described as the heaviest raid of the night campaign is instructive. Then, more than four times the number of aircraft were employed but the civilian deaths, estimated at 1100,[27] were proportionately much lighter than in Belfast. There were two possible explanations for this: Firstly, the weather over London was good thus enabling the attackers to achieve a greater degree of accuracy in targeting dockside and industrial installations. Secondly, the painful experience gained in London over the winter months ensured a higher state of preparedness.

With the coming of daylight, fear of further attacks swept through Belfast. Although the possibility of a daylight raid was virtually non-existent, something approaching panic gripped the inhabitants when in the afternoon the sirens sounded again and explosions were heard throughout the city – probably from bombs with delayed time fuses. There was an overwhelming sense of exposure and an exodus from the city began.

Away from Belfast, the most serious incident occurred at Londonderry where 15 civilians were killed when two parachute mines, apparently dropped by the same aircraft, fell on the Derry to Buncrana Road at 0012 hours. A report made by a local ARP officer recorded that there was 'a fairly strong breeze from the north-west' and that 'it was a dark night with intermittent showers and some heavy clouds'.

There is no authenticated explanation for the attack on Londonderry nor does any German record throw any light on the subject. The naval installations would certainly have been a worthwhile target but the use of one aircraft appears to rule out any intention to make a purposeful attack. A diversionary raid made for deception purposes also seems unlikely for the same reason. There is always the possibility that an aircraft approaching Belfast from the south-east inadvertently flew past the city in the overcast conditions and that Lough Foyle, which was a further 20 minutes flying time away, had features similar to Belfast Lough when seen through breaks in the cloud.

In Britain, the official line was that civilian morale remained steadfast in face of the onslaught but behind the defiant rhetoric there were doubts as to how much more the population could take. After the war, Churchill revealed the extent of his apprehension at the course of events:

> Our outlook at this time was that London, except for its strong modern buildings, would be gradually and soon reduced to a rubble heap. I was deeply anxious about the life of the people of London, the greater part of whom stayed, slept and took a chance where they were.[28]

It was fortunate for morale that Churchill did not translate his sombre thoughts into words at the time but it was the kind of realism that most people in Britain would have recognized as the long, melancholic winter drew to a close.

BEHIND THE HEADLINES

When March began there was little in the daily reports from the troubled waters of the eastern Atlantic to suggest that Admiral Doenitz was about to suffer a serious reverse. After the slight fall in the number of ships sunk in the last two months of 1940 and in January, the sinkings rose again in February.[1] But March was to prove to be a bad month for the U-boats. Before it was out, Doenitz would have lost five of his boats and his three most celebrated captains with them, Günther Prien, Otto Kretschmer and Joachim Schepke.

Prien's *U-47* was the first to go but there is some doubt about the circumstances. The last radio contact with her took place on 7 March. On that date the destroyer *Wolverine* sank a submarine by depth charge but the noted U-boat authority Horst Bredow believes that this boat may, in fact, have been the *U-70*.[2]

St Patrick's Day proved to be a very lucky day for the Royal Navy. Both the boats commanded by the remaining members of the dangerous trio were sunk. *U-100* was rammed by the destroyer *Vanoc* and sank with only six of the crew scrambling to safety. Schepke was killed by the impact as he stood in the conning tower.[3] Less than an hour later, *U-99* was also sunk, in this case by gunfire from the *Vanoc* and a sister destroyer, the *Walker*. Three of the crew were lost but Kretschmer and the rest were taken prisoner when the boat was abandoned.[4]

If March was a bad month for the U-boats, April was far from good for I/KG 40. Four Condors were lost with 18 crewman killed or missing and six taken prisoner.[5] Viewed as a percentage of their operational strength, these were heavy losses. On 16 April, an RAF Beaufighter twin-engined fighter from No. 252 Squadron, based at Aldergrove, was patrolling about 70 miles west of Erris Head in County Mayo, when the pilot, Flight-Lieutenant W. Riley, saw a Condor flying below him in a south-westerly direction at an estimated 50 feet above the water. Riley immediately attacked and saw the Condor catch fire. Both its port engines stopped and it yawed to the left before crashing into the sea.[6] No survivors from the crew of six were observed. Its commander was Oberleutnant Hermann Richter and the pilot Oberleutnant

Heinz Daemer. According to the Luftwaffe's loss report, the aircraft had been operating to the north of Scotland and was presumably on the way back to Bordeaux when it was intercepted. This appears to be the first time that a Condor was intercepted in this way by a shore-based fighter aircraft specifically engaged in searching for Condors by means of a methodical 'grid' system.

The next day, the aircraft of Oberleutnant Kalus was lost while engaged in an attack on a convoy off the coast of Northern Scotland. Nothing more about the circumstances is known but the body of one of the radio-operators, Unteroffizier Zeller, was subsequently washed ashore in the Shetland Islands.

For a third day in succession, one of I/KG 40's aircraft failed to return from a mission. On 18 April, a Condor commanded by Oberleutnant Ernst Müller was severely damaged off the south-west coast of Ireland when it was hit by anti-aircraft fire from warships escorting convoy HG 58, homeward-bound to the UK from Gibralter. The aircraft began to lose height and Müller made for the Irish coast. He succeeded in ditching a short distance from the shore in Co. Cork between Calf Island and Goat Island. The crew took to two rubber dinghies and were picked up by an Irish vessel. All were interned in the Curragh for the duration of the war.

By the end of the month, it had become clear to Edgar Petersen, I/KG 40's commanding officer, that the losses from low-level *Steckrübe*, attacks on heavily-armed convoys was becoming unacceptably high. When approaching a ship at mast height the large aircraft presented a relatively easy target for the ship's gunners. While most of the merchant ships attacked had only machine-guns for self-defence, the almost total lack of armour-plating in the early-built Condors rendered them extremely vulnerable.

On the 29th, another of Petersen's force, this time operating out of Stavanger, was shot down by an unnamed British destroyer which was escorting a convoy near the Faeroes. All six men on board lost their lives. Some months later, the International Red Cross reported to the German authorities that the bodies of the aircraft commander, Oberleutnant Roland Schelcher, the co-pilot, Unteroffizier Josef Obergauling and air-gunner Ernst Sengbusch were recovered from the sea.

There is no doubt that the Focke-Wulf Condors were infringing Irish neutrality on an almost daily basis. Flying at a few hundred feet, they were a common sight to the residents of villages on the west and south-west coast as they used Irish landmarks on the long flight between Bordeaux and the convoy routes that converged on the North Channel. Although the benefit they derived from being able to do this should not be exaggerated, life would have been much more difficult for them if the RAF had had the bases in Eire that Churchill wanted.

Although the simmering resentment over de Valera's refusal to make the

Irish ports available often exploded in print in the British press during the winter of 1940/41, there was, in fact, a good deal of cooperation on the part of the Irish authorities that was not in keeping with neutrality and could not be revealed at the time. Some idea of the extent of this wartime collaboration became public knowledge on 1 January 1991 when state papers in the Republic of Ireland for the years 1922–60 were opened for inspection.[7]

It becomes clear from these records that virtually every movement of German submarines and aircraft that was known to the Irish authorities was transmitted to their British counterparts. This included the Condor activities along the western side of the country in addition to the movement of bombers around the east coast flying to and from targets in Britain.

As a corollary to this kind of cooperation, a blind eye was usually turned to flights by RAF aircraft through Irish airspace. Furthermore, as the war progressed, more and more Allied airmen whose aircraft had crashed in Southern Ireland were taken to the border and quietly released without formality. By the end of the war, all pretence of impartiality had vanished. In the early days, however, there seems to have been some inconsistency in the policy. While the criteria were not publicized, it seems that if an aeroplane crashed or force-landed in Eire, account was taken of whether the occurrence had followed a deliberate or accidental infringement of Irish airspace. It was nevertheless recognized that a deliberate intrusion could have been the result of an emergency. In the case of German airmen, however, no such considerations were applied. All without exception were interned.

Although the personal records relating to the German and Allied servicemen interned in the Curragh remain closed to public inspection, a telegram to Berlin from the German Consulate on 6 February 1941 provides an insight into conditions there at the time:

> In Ireland, interned flyers are housed in wooden barracks originally intended for officers. The food is good, especially since one of the internees has taken the kitchen in hand. Apart from uniforms, civilian clothing is provided and their state of health is good.
>
> The flyers are on the whole treated in a friendly fashion. However, all kinds of understandable protests have arisen which are no doubt due basically to clumsiness and lack of foresight on the part of the military authorities. These have been ironed out by the Foreign Ministry here after my strenuous objections had been sympathetically received.
>
> Post delivery is slow and some internees complain of not yet having received any news at all.[8]

This balanced account of conditions at the Curragh was typical of the measured approach that Hempel adopted towards potentially troublesome situations. A biased report containing any hint of discrimination against internees could have exacerbated the already volatile relations between the two governments.

A lawyer by profession, Hempel was a career diplomat of the pre-Nazi era. He had served in the First World War as a cavalryman and was wounded in Poland. He entered the diplomatic service in 1921 and after holding a number of junior and intermediate posts he was appointed envoy to Dublin in June 1937. His career details show that he became a member of the Nazi party on 1 July 1938 but it is likely that this was obligatory for a diplomat of his standing. He remained in Dublin until the end of the war and seems to have been universally respected and even liked. He had a reputation for integrity and fair-mindedness in his dealings. When the war ended he returned to Germany to live in the town of Stade near Hamburg. In common with all officials of his rank who were members of the Nazi party his record was investigated by an Allied tribunal in 1949 but he was completely exonerated. He died on 12 November 1972.[9]

Included in the catalogue of Anglo-Irish cooperation was a very important ad hoc arrangement which provided the RAF with direct access to the Atlantic through defined airspace over Co. Donegal.[10] This was particularly useful for Coastal Command flying boats operating from the Lough Erne bases. They were able to use a corridor running due west from Castle Archdale and Killadeas thereby avoiding a circuitous route northabout round Lough Foyle. A similar facility was available across the Inishowen Peninsula and was valuable for aircraft covering the waters immediately west of the North Channel.

For obvious reasons – not least domestic considerations – this complaisant attitude on the part of the Irish government was not made known at the time. It was, of course, no secret to the people living under the flight path of the aircraft daily making use of this convenience nor, it appears, to the Luftwaffe. An excellent aerial photograph of Killadeas taken in late 1940 is proof that the Germans took an interest in the area and it is inconceivable that they were not aware of the existence of the corridors. The Irish authorities would have been very conscious that the Germans knew of the concessions. This no doubt explains the lack of protests when the low-flying Condors ostentatiously waggled their wings to the lighthouse crews at Mizen Head and Valentia Island as they passed.[11]

There was another sphere in which clandestine collaboration – this time between Britain and the United States – was being planned and exercised in the spring of 1941. Once again, it was no secret to the Germans. During his visit to Britain, Wendell Willkie, the defeated candidate in the American presidential election in the previous November, discussed the possibility of establishing US bases in Northern Ireland. Willkie was acting as an emissary of the United States government and his role is a further example of President

22 **Eduard Hempel** (right) presenting his credentials to Eamon de Valera and
Sean T. O'Kelly (left) on his appointment as German envoy to Dublin in June 1937

Roosevelt's determination to aid Britain, almost to the point of engaging in actual hostilities. He forcefully pursued this policy while at the same time taking care to see that the American public was kept in the dark as much as possible.

The evidence that the Germans were aware of Willkie's activities is provided by a telegram sent to the German Foreign Ministry by Hempel's deputy Henning Thomsen, a few months later.[12] Dated 24 July, it disclosed that J.M. Andrews, the Northern Ireland Prime Minister, had welcomed Willkie's expressed desire to see American bases established in the province. This was, no doubt, only one of many strands of the secret Anglo-American negotiations that were taking place at different levels. Another was the work of the US Special Observer Group (SPOBS) in London, headed by Major-General James E. Chaney. This group was involved in preparing for the eventual arrival of the US Army Air Corps (as it was then called) in the British Isles. In the summer of 1941, Lieutenant-General Ira C. Eaker, who was later to command the US 8th Air Force, flew secretly to Belfast to select suitable sites for airfields in Northern Ireland.[13]

The hand of friendship and co-operation which America was extending to Britain in her hour of peril was noticeably absent south of the Irish border. There were several areas of contention between Dublin and the United States administration. One was the refusal of Washington to supply the arms and military equipment that the Irish defence forces urgently required. Another was the denial of the ports to Britain, a subject in which President Rooseveldt took a personal interest.

In March 1941, Mr Frank Aiken, who was a member of de Valera's cabinet, was sent to Washington to raise the arms issue directly with the President. The meeting, which took place at the White House, was nothing short of disastrous from an Irish standpoint. It was said that Aiken, who hailed from South Armagh, was uncompromisingly anti-British. He claimed that the weapons were needed to repel possible British aggression. This sparked off what Tim Pat Coogan, in his biography of Eamon de Valera, has described as 'a blazing face-to-face row' between the two men.[14] No arms materialized and the only result of the meeting was a good deal of bad blood.

In Aiken's estimation, the need for arms was bound up with the burning question of the ports. In April, the possibility that British forbearance *vis-à-vis* this problem would snap was very real in Eire. Troop movements north of the border did nothing to allay such fears. On the face of it, there seemed to be no pressing need to increase troop levels in Northern Ireland for purely defensive purposes at that particular time. Any threat of a German invasion (if there had ever been one) had disappeared.[15] Having broken the German codes, British Intelligence was aware of massive troop movements towards the frontier with the Soviet Union. One report stated that, in March, 2500 fully-laden German troop trains had been detected going east.

Notwithstanding this development, which promised some relief to the beleaguered British, a decision to reinforce the army presence in Northern Ireland appears to have been taken at this very time. The 5th Infantry Division was hurriedly dispatched and began disembarking at Larne on 31 March.[16] The move was completed on 16 April and to observers in the south who had access to uncensored information it was a reminder that the seizure of the ports was an option that the British still retained.

CRIMSON SKY

After the traumatic experience of Easter Tuesday the public mood in Belfast was marked by the inevitability of another attack. No one doubted that it would come and normal business had been largely paralysed. Many people contrived to spend at least the hours of darkness away from the city and in the evenings the near-deserted streets heightened the sense of foreboding.

For a brief period on the night of 26/27 April it seemed that another onslaught was imminent. The sirens sounded shortly after midnight and at 0030 hours, 102 HAA's 3.7-inch guns fired 72 rounds at a single enemy aircraft but no attack developed.[1] The batteries were in the course of being strengthened but the precise number of additional guns is not recorded. It is known, however, that four guns which had been moved from Londonderry at the end of March and that four 40mm Bofors light guns which had been sited at Larne to cover the arrival of 5th Division were re-deployed on the day after the Easter raid, two to Aldergrove airfield and one each to Victoria Barracks and Victoria Park in the city.

On the night of 16/17 April London had been battered by almost 700 bombers and again, four nights later, on the 19/20, by an even greater force. (In both attacks, a large number of the bombers made two or even three sorties). Civilian morale could not fail to be affected by this seemingly endless ordeal but if the suffering population had only but known it, their feelings of near-despair were sometimes shared by the men who were dropping the bombs.

There are few written accounts of the night bombing of Britain in the winter of 1940/41 emanating from German airmen who took part. The decisive encounters of the daylight Battle of Britain have been extensively covered by both sides but the unspectacular yet equally dangerous night operations from a German perspective have been largely neglected. The diary of Peter Stahl is a conspicuous exception.[2]

Stahl copiously recorded every sortie he flew against Britain between June 1940 and May 1941. He does so in a very objective manner but the factual language he uses nevertheless vividly conjures up the often terrifying night environment in which Allied and German airmen fought.

When he comes to the period April/May 1941. Stahl conveys a sense of the disillusionment and exhaustion experienced by the bomber crews as the night campaign neared its end. The disillusionment is reflected in the criticism of some senior officers who, although qualified pilots, never flew on a single operation themselves. He recounts how, towards the end of April, Hermann Goering had come to hear that compassionate Staffel and Gruppe commanders had, on their own initiative, been giving weary airmen unauthorized rest days. Such action was henceforth expressly forbidden.

The extent of the exhaustion is well illustrated by the description of a flight made by Stahl and his crew on 28 April. The target was Portsmouth and after taking off from Gilze-Rijen they headed south-west over Belgium and the coast of Normandy.

Flying conditions were smooth and Stahl engaged the autopilot at a height of 3000 metres. There was none of the usual trivial banter over the intercom that the crew usually engaged in to hide their anxiety and he began to feel drowsy in the warm air from the cabin heater. He fell asleep and woke with a start to find the aircraft passing through 4200 metres in a gradual climb. The other three were fast asleep too. He had been awakened by the sound of the propellers changing from coarse to fine pitch, something that happened automatically after passing through 4000 metres. They were now at a level where oxygen masks were necessary and all four needed to breathe pure oxygen for a minute or two in order to regain their senses. Stahl was horrified to find that they had been asleep for almost an hour and that the aircraft was heading for the Bay of Biscay.

A few days later, Stahl reported the incident in confidence to his staffel commander after a rest day had been cancelled and be was ordered to fly in an operation against Hull. He protested vehemently, claiming that his men had reached the end of their tether. Although the officer was sympathetic, he was powerless to rescind the order. In the briefing room before the flight, Stahl's navigator, Hans Gross, openly voiced criticism of Goering in front of the assembled crews. This was something which had never happened before. Stahl wrote that he held his breath but the silence that followed the remarks clearly indicated that they were supported by everyone present. Goering had not been forgiven for accusing German fighter pilots of cowardice in the Battle of Britain. They had no illusions about his opinion of themselves.

There are several references in Stahl's diary as to how the German airmen were viewing the course of the war at this juncture. One of his staffel commanders was the famous Werner Baumbach, who was widely respected throughout the Luftwaffe. His skill and courage were legendary but he also gained a reputation for frankness. He had been among those in KG 30 who had criticized the Luftwaffe's equipment when Milch visited the unit and his questioning of the war against Britain in general and the night campaign

23 Werner Baumbuch (right) pictured at an investiture in Berlin
with Field Marshal Erhard Milch

in particular was well-known. At times, he seemed to have gone too far but his popularity among the personnel would have made it difficult to discipline him. He survived the war and went to live in Argentina in 1948 where he was employed as a pilot. On 20 October 1953, at the age of 36, he was killed when the ex-RAF Lancaster he was flying crashed into the River Plate. Such was his fame that the Argentine government sent his body back to Germany in a naval vessel with several air force officers acting as pallbearers. Thirty thousand people were said to have lined the streets of his native Cloppenberg for the funeral.

'Fly, sleep, eat, wait'. This was how Stahl described life in a bomber station at the beginning of May 1941. With a total of 60 operational flights behind him, most of them at night, he tried to forget that many of his friends had not survived more than three or four missions. On those occasions when crews were called upon to fly two or even three missions in the same night the demands imposed on crews were severe and landing accidents in the crowded airfields were frequent.

On the afternoon of 3 May, the long-suffering city of Liverpool was named as II/KG 30's target for the night. The forecast was for clear skies and bright moonlight. Stahl wrote that the prospect filled him with dread. The western-most targets, such as Liverpool, Glasgow and Belfast meant facing long hours in dangerous airspace, patrolled by ever-increasing numbers of radar-equipped night fighters. As of 1 May, German Intelligence estimated that the RAF now had operational at least five squadrons of twin-engined Beau-fighters with AI radar. The coming full moon period was going to be a testing time for friend and foe alike.

At 0100 hours the following morning, 4 May, Double British Summer Time (DBST) became effective throughout the British Isles (except Eire). Clock time was now 2 hours in advance of Greenwich Mean time (GMT)[3] and daylight in Belfast could therefore be expected to last until 2100 hours at least.

Pressure was high over Northern France and the Low Countries as well as the British Isles during the day and the fine weather continued into the evening. At RAF Aldergrove, the surface wind was calm and a temperature of 60.2 degrees Fahrenheit was recorded at 2000 hours DBST.[4] Apart from 1/10th cumulus cloud at 3500 feet, the sky was clear. The moon was in its first quarter and 3 AA Corps headquarters in Edinburgh judged the possibility of attacks within its command area (which included Northern Ireland) to be high.

Since the objectives of the Easter Tuesday raid on Belfast had not been achieved, the Luftwaffe command apparently concluded that the target was important enough for another attempt to be made. Tactical considerations, related to the decreasing hours of darkness, required that it be made as soon as possible. To allow a margin for contingencies, a timetable for the attack would have to provide for flying time of approximately seven hours. (KG 55 had recorded airborne times of up to 6 hours 45 minutes for an attack on Glasgow.) With the approach of midsummer, this would come close to flying in daylight. With the benefit of hindsight, it can be said that a further attack on Belfast was due.

All the Luftwaffe units which had made the attack on Easter Tuesday would again be represented with the addition of a few others. The absence of complete Luftflotte 2 records once again makes it impossible to be precise about the number of aircraft which had been assigned Belfast as their primary target but it probably exceeded 200. The war diary of the OKW puts the figure which actually attacked the city at 181.[5] A few Luftflotte 2 units attacking Barrow-in-Furness, namely KG 28, KG 30 and KG 53, had been given Belfast as their alternate target but it is not known whether in fact any diversions were necessary.

The attack would, in the main, be again concentrated on the area encompassed by the harbour estate. This would, as before, be divided into sectors *Anton* and *Bruno*. Individual targets designated, in addition to the shipyard and aircraft factory, included Target 5049 (Twin Islands Power Station), Target 5677 (Rank's flour mill) and Target 2126 (the oil storage tanks at Airport Road). The constraints imposed by the dwindling hours of darkness meant that the raid would be compressed into a period of about two hours. Large numbers of aircraft would be over the target at the same time and vertical separation would be an important factor in pre-flight planning.

The operation would be characterized by the weight of incendiaries carried. De-briefing records filed at the conclusion of the mission show that units delivered anything from two to three times more incendiary bombs than was the case in the previous attack. Another prominent feature was the high proportion of LZZ 250kg bombs. These missiles were fitted with time fuses and were intended to prolong the disruptive effect of the raid. Thirty-two He111Ps from all three Gruppen of KG 27 dropped 96 250kg high explosive bombs of which 20 were of the LZZ variety.

The weather forecast distributed appeared to be favourable. Cloud amounts en route and at the target were expected to be negligible. However, the high daytime temperatures would fall quickly after sunset, creating conditions conducive to the formation of ground mist.

Shortly after the onset of darkness, the Heinkels and Junkers began departing their bases. At Leeuwarden, on the north coast of Holland, 25 Ju88A-5s of KG 76 took off at three minute intervals. One of them was commanded by Austrian-born Leutnant Dieter Lukesch. Although still only 22 years old, he already had considerable combat experience and had been mentioned in dispatches for a particularly daring night attack on an aircraft factory in Poland from a height of between five and 10 metres. Airborne at 2210 hours, Lukesch flew west to the Texel radio beacon on the coast, north of Den Helder, where he set course for the Isle of Man and started his climb to 4500 metres.[6]

Across the French border, at Roye-Amy, Gerhard Baeker prepared to make another attempt to reach Belfast. His Ju88A-5 was one of 21 aircraft from III/KG 1 declared serviceable for the night's operation. As on Easter Tuesday, Baeker would carry armament category B made up of 1500 kg of high-explosive bombs and consequently his reduced fuel capacity required that he take the most direct track to Belfast. On the face of it, the weather forecast was positive but he would wait until he reached Liverpool before making a final decision about continuing to Belfast. After being briefed about the heightened night fighter activity that could be expected, Baeker took off at 2205 hours and headed out over the Pas de Calais.[7]

On 4 May, there was intense activity at all the German bomber bases in Holland. Normally based on French airfields. KG 77 was using Amsterdam-Schiphol as a forward base in order to slightly increase the range of its Ju88s for missions like that against Belfast. As dusk fell, 24 of them were ready for take-off. The Schiphol base records disclose the seemingly irrelevant information that in the middle of these hectic preparations two Dutch airmen, named Leextrad and Voos, took off in a Fokker G1 aircraft without authority and were believed to have flown to England.

It again fell to I/KG 4 to deliver the heaviest bombs to be carried on the 4 May raid. On this occasion, the Gruppe would be represented by one aircraft flown by the Gruppe commander, Hauptmann Klaus Nöske, six from 1st Staffel and four from the 3rd Staffel. Three of the aircraft carried three BM1000kg bombs and the remainder were each loaded with two LMB parachute mines. A few of the Heinkels had been modified to carry in addition a small number of BSK containers each with sixteen 2kg incendiary bombs. The Gruppe was assigned target area *Anton*.

For the mission, I Gruppe was to be joined at Soesterberg by its sister group, III/KG 4 which had not been involved in the Easter Tuesday raid, having attacked Newcastle that night. Normally based in Leeuwarden, the Gruppe had had to vacate that airfield to provide KG 76 with a forward base for its Ju88s. The details of the bomb loads it carried are not specified but it is known that eleven aircraft were to bomb target area *Bruno* which included the shipyard and aircraft factory.

Shortly before 2300 hours, the 11 Heinkels of I Gruppe began rolling out towards the active runway at Soesterberg. The first was airborne at 2355 hours and the rest followed at three-minute intervals. Siegfried Röthke was airborne at 2310. The tyre of one aircraft burst on the take-off run and its bombs became dislodged from the racks in the ensuing skid. The take-off was successfully aborted and no casualties or serious damage occurred. The remaining 10 Heinkels laboriously climbed out over Amsterdam, whose citizens were subjected nightly to the ominous rumble of heavily-laden bombers heading towards the coast. The projected route was: Radio beacon 32 (outside Amsterdam) − Flamborough Head on the Yorkshire coast − Ramsey in the Isle of Man − Belfast.

At Vitry-en-Artois, Walther Siber learned that I/KG 53 was only to attack Belfast as an alternate target. The primary target was Barrow-in-Furness and it had been selected in an attempt to create uncertainty in the defence. Its Heinkels were to cross the Yorkshire coast at Flamborough Head and Barrow lay across the track from that position to the Isle of Man, the mandatory check point before proceeding to Belfast. However, when approaching the west coast of England, I/KG 53 would suddenly break off and launch what was hoped would be a surprise attack on the shipbuilding yards at Barrow. Only if the visibility there was unsatisfactory would the Gruppe continue to Belfast.

Some of the aircraft which would have the longest flight of the night belonged to the three Gruppen of KG 55 based south and west of Paris. Following the tactic adopted for the Easter Tuesday raid, III Gruppe first flew to Caen in Normandy to refuel and receive a final briefing. One of the Gruppe's staffels, the 7th, was commanded by Oberleutnant Joachim Herrfurth. He flew in the observer's seat in the lead aircraft and had, as his pilot, Oberfeldwebel Peter Baumgartner. The flight engineer was Oberfeldwebel Leo Neidel and the radio operator Feldwebel Georg Aigner. All were veterans of the night campaign.[8]

Herrfurth's He111P-2, which had the call-sign *Ida Richard*, took off from its base at Villacoublay at 1505 hours and landed at Caen at 1604. It had a passenger on board. He was Fritz Krause, one of a group of war correspondents who were going to report the raid for the press and radio. Krause's paper was the Nazi Party organ *Völkischer Beobachter* and, although he could be expected to exploit the propaganda dimension, Krause gives a vivid and unique description of the bombing of Belfast as seen from a German bomber. The paper's headline read:[9]

WE HIT BELFAST

The greatest transhipment port for US aid in flames

The first two paragraphs of the article not only set the scene for the operation but illustrate the strategic importance which the Germans had accorded the city:

VÖLKISCHER BEOBACHTER *1941*

Wir trafen Belfast

Der größte Umschlaghafen für die USA.-Hilfe in Flammen

Von Kriegsberichter Fritz Krause

dnb. PK., 6. Mai

Wenn Belfast, ein englischer Hafen in Nordirland, erst gestern zum zweiten Male seit Beginn des Luftkrieges gegen England angegriffen wurde, dann liegt das nicht etwa daran, daß Belfast bedeutungsloser sei als vielleicht Liverpool, Birmingham oder andere kriegswichtige Ziele, im Gegenteil! Belfast ist nicht nur erst seit den Lieferungen der USA das Einfallstor für die amerikanischen Geleitzüge geworden, sondern steht als Hafen schon immer in der ersten Reihe der englischen Wasserstraßen-Ein- und Ausgangspunkte. Darüber hinaus befinden sich in Belfast viele kriegswichtige Ziele: Die viertgrößte Reparaturwerft Englands für Kriegs- und Handelsschiffe, ein bedeutendes Flugzeugwerk, Tankanlagen, Getreidemühlen, Vorratsspeicher, Gas- und Kraftwerke, Dock- und Werftanlagen, Materiallager. Das sind einige der wichtigsten Punktziele, die uns bei der Einsatzbesprechung erst so ganz die Bedeutung unseres Auftrages erkennen ließen.

„Kameraden, ich erinnere euch nochmals an das Wort unseres Reichsmarschalls, der immer wieder von euch fordert: ,Wir wollen nicht wie die Engländer in Deutschland Häuser und Menschen zerstören, damit gewinnen wir den Krieg nicht. Es heißt, England dort zu treffen, wo es am empfindlichsten ist. Das ist seine Wirtschaft, seine Industrie und nicht zuletzt der Handel. Schiffe und Hafenanlagen sind unsere ersten Ziele!'" Mit dieser Ermahnung an seine Besatzungen schließt der Gruppenkommandeur Hauptmann W. die Einsatzbesprechung.

Ich fliege mit der Besatzung von Oberleutnant H., der über achtzig Feindflüge hat. Zwei anderen hat heute der Gruppenkommandeur nach dem Einsatz für je sechzig Feindflüge die silberne Frontflug-

schein noch nicht reicht. Die Hafenanlagen mit den kriegswichtigen Zielen sind rund 300 000 Quadratmeter groß. Sie alle in einem einzigen Angriff zu erfassen, ist ganz unmöglich, die Hälfte aber in rollenden Punktzielen so anzugreifen und zu zerstören, daß sie für den Gebrauch ausfallen, muß gelingen.

Vorn in der Kanzel liegt Oberleutnant H. Vor sich hält er die Karte. In den roten Schein seiner Taschenlampe, der über der Karte und das gebeugte Gesicht des Beobachters fließt, mischt sich von unten der Schein der Brände und der wie Trauben in der Luft hängenden Leuchtbomben. Wir fliegen auf das Ziel zu. Oberleutnant H. aber wirft die Bomben noch nicht. Erst sondiert er den Luftraum. Unter uns stehen wie dunkle Würste pralle Sperrballons über dem Schein der Brände. Nicht zwei oder drei, nein zehn bis zwanzig machen wir aus. In einer weiten Schleife fliegen wir noch einmal an. Scheinwerfer leuchten überhaupt nicht auf. Es wäre wohl auch vergebens; welche von den über dem Ziel kreisenden Flugzeugen sollten sie auch anleuchten für die Flakartillerie. Die schießt einfach Sperrwürfel in die Luft vor den Zielräumen. Wenn sie auch eine Maschine vor Ziel durch direkten Beschuß abdrängen würde, wären dafür sogleich, von einer anderen Seite kommend, vier bis fünf weitere da, die dann ungehindert ans Ziel kämen.

Wir gehen hinunter um hundert und aber hundert Meter. Schon flitzen neben uns die Leuchtgeschoßbahnen der leichten Flakartillerie vorbei. Das Feuer der schweren Flak liegt nun zu hoch. Wieder liegt der Beobachter in der Kanzel. Der Teppich über dem Zielgerät ist heruntergerollt. Die Bombenklappen werden geöffnet. Wie der Beobachter trotz heftigen Flakfeuers — eine schwere Salve muß tief liegen, denn unsere Maschine wurde mehrmals

24 *Völkischer Beobachter* headline reading 'We hit Belfast'

If Belfast, an English [*sic*] port in Northern Ireland, was only yesterday attacked for the second time since the beginning of the air war against England, it is not because Belfast is less important than, say, Liverpool, Birmingham or other targets vital to the war effort. On the contrary, Belfast has not only become the gateway for American convoys because of the shipments from the USA; it is among the foremost English maritime arrival and departure points. Furthermore, many other important targets are located in Belfast. There is England's fourth largest repair yard for warships and cargo vessels and an important aircraft factory as well as oil installations, grain mills and storage silos. There are also gasworks and power stations, docking and shipbuilding installations and warehouses. These are some of the most important individual targets which, at the pre-flight briefing, made us realize for the first time the importance of our mission.

'Comrades, I remind you yet again of the words of our Reichsmarshall, who time and again, maintains that we will not destroy houses and people like the English are doing in Germany. We will not win the war that way. Rather, will we hit England where she feels it most, that is, in her economy, industry and not least in her trade. Ships and harbour installations are our primary targets.' With this exhortation to his crews, Gruppe commander W closes the briefing. [For security reasons, the Gruppe commander's name was not given. It was, in fact, Hauptmann Heinrich Wittmer.]

As might have been expected, the *Völkischer Beobachter* was at pains to compare the RAF's methods unfavourably with those of the Luftwaffe but, aside from that, it is a fact that all the surviving German records relating to the bombing of Belfast specified only targets that would have been regarded as legitimate by any belligerent. The explanation for collateral damage and casualties lies elsewhere.

By midnight, all but a few of the bombers assigned to targets at Belfast were airborne. The forecast slack winds aloft proved to be correct and in spite of the widespread ground mist obscuring the surface in many places, navigators — in the early stages of the flight, at least — were able to find most of the check points they were looking for by the light of the moon. The almost total absence of cloud created the conditions that the night fighters wanted and every available pair of eyes in the bombers anxiously scanned the sky for the first sign of danger.

A sizeable contingent of journalists were observing the raid at close quarters. German Radio alone had six correspondents travelling in the attacking aircraft and all were given instruction in what to look out for.

Flying at a height of 4,000 metres, Dieter Lukesch had no trouble establishing his position as he crossed the coast of Yorkshire and flew on towards the Isle of Man. The sky remained clear and the moon gave enough light to enable him to make out some ground features such as rivers and towns. He had tuned his ADF to Stavanger Radio and the bearings indicated on the dial confirmed his calculations. By the time he reached the coast of Lancashire, accumulations of cloud were to be seen. As he crossed Morecambe Bay shortly after midnight, the Point of Air weather station, at the mouth of the Dee Estuary, was recording 7/10ths cloud at 5000 feet. With the falling temperature, the relative humidity had reached 70 per cent and ground mist began to form.[10] This, combined with the increasing cloud cover, was to cause unexpected problems for some aircraft for the next hour or so. A Ju88 of II/KG 76 broke radio silence at 0025 hours to report 'very misty' conditions at St David's Head on the Welsh coast.

It gradually became apparent to RAF Intelligence that another major operation was under way. 'Y' Service monitors maintained a watch on all the usual frequencies but if radio silence was observed by the bombers on their outbound journey it was impossible to obtain a D/F 'fix' on their positions and make an early prediction of the intended targets. However, on the night of 4/5 May, there were a number of instances when radio silence was broken. These and scattered radar contacts together with reports of engines overhead various positions soon indicated that the targets lay in the northern half of the British Isles. When westbound aircraft were eventually known to be continuing beyond Liverpool it was clear that the target was Belfast and a 'Red' alert was issued there at 0010 hours.

As happened on Easter Tuesday, the Irish Air Defence Command began to report intense activity along the east coast, commencing at 2335 hours local time (0035 hours DBST; Eire did not change to Double British Summer time).

Numerous incursions into Irish airspace were reported at different locations. Approximately 30 aircraft were estimated to have done this at Campile and Waterford. The official log held at the Irish archives contains a summary of these movements:

> It would appear that six flights of aircraft passed up the east coast between the hours of 2335 and 0234.
> Two aircraft, possibly more, passed through Waterford and flew in a north-easterly direction to Dublin where they proceeded north.
> It would also appear that approximately three flights returned by the coastal route branching off in a south-easterly direction between Bray and Arklow (approximately 30 planes must have participated in this flight).[11]

The chart showing the traces of the two northbound aircraft referred to suggests that they were unsure of their positions. On the other hand, the incursion by so many of the homeward-bound aircraft was scarcely accidental although it is possible that sight of the ground was obscured in places. The Phoenix Park weather station at 2200 hours had reported rapidly falling temperatures with widespread ground mist.[12]

After the sirens had sounded in Belfast, an uneasy silence prevailed for approximately 50 minutes. All gun batteries stood to at 0013 hours. As on Easter Tuesday, the aircraft-carrier *Furious* was moored at Victoria Wharf but this time her armament would make a significant contribution to the city's defence.[13] The first hostile plot appeared on radar at 0047 hours and this correlates with the German records which show that the first aircraft to make an attack was over the target at 0057 hours. All anti-aircraft guns opened fire five minutes later at 0102 hours.

Luftflotte 3 records disclose that the attack was opened by a He111P belonging to II/KG 55, based at the cathedral city of Chartres, south-west of Paris. Fourteen of the Gruppe's Heinkels, under the command of Major Dr Ernst Kühl, had embarked on the mission but only six of them were to reach Belfast. Six bombed Liverpool as an alternate target, two because they had technical faults and four because they were unable to find the primary target. Another bombed Weymouth as an alternate and one had to abort the mission because of failure of the aircraft's intercom system.

To an anxious observer on the ground in Belfast, the clear moonlit sky seemed ideal for bombing when the sirens sounded but, once again, the weather would to some degree blunt the force of the attack. It had been a fine, warm day over Ireland and north-west England but low air temperatures after dark combined with high humidity inevitably caused ground mist to form in places. A large number of the operations reports compiled by the various Luftwaffe units contained the phrase 'primary target not found'. It must be assumed that most of these decisions to divert to alternates were made in the early stages of the raid, since the fires in the city gradually grew in intensity until the enormous red glow in the sky was visible from Liverpool and the coast of North Wales. This would have more than outweighed the effect of the ground mist.

The failure of some crews to find Belfast in what were, at worst, marginal conditions was probably a reflection of the inexperience and lack of confidence on the part of some of the personnel. Moreover, a strain of elitism ran through the Luftwaffe and some units had acquired a certain preeminence in the course of time. This was true in the case of Kampfgruppe 100 (KGr100).

At the start of the bombing campaign against Britain, KGr100, led by an exceptional officer, Hauptmann Kurd Aschenbrenner, had been given the task of developing the sophisticated VHF target-finding aid *X-Verfahren* at an operational level. In the early stages of the night campaign, the system was used to good effect, particularly in the attack on Coventry on the night of

14/15 November, but its value gradually diminished in the face of British counter-measures. However, even when using conventional navigation methods, as on the night of 4/5 May, KGr100 could be expected to demonstrate superior navigational skill. It is noteworthy that of its 16 He111H-3s which set out for Belfast from Vannes in Brittany (the unit did not participate in the Easter Tuesday raid), all found and bombed the designated target area *Bruno*. They dropped 9000 metric tonnes of high explosives and 6046 BIE incendiaries on the shipyard and aircraft factory as well as installations to the east of them between 0113 and 0155 hours. The crews claimed that a high degree of accuracy was achieved.[14]

On passing abeam Liverpool at 0020 hours, Gerhard Baeker was satisfied that, in spite of some haze, conditions were good enough to carry on towards Belfast. Although he had the limited fuel capacity associated with category C armament, by restricting his engine revolutions (RPM) to 2200 per minute he could keep his fuel consumption well within limits. He reached the city at around 0115 hours and, although the attack was still in its early stages, he could see large fires already burning in the haze. The smoke from the fires was now combining with that belching from the smoke screen canisters sited throughout the city but Baeker reported that he could identify the targets relatively easily. Four other Ju88s of his Gruppe also succeeded in bombing the same targets but a further four, which had not taken the direct route to Belfast, had trouble with the visibility and attacked Liverpool instead rather than take the risk of running short of fuel. One other aircraft from the Gruppe, which had taken off five minutes after Baeker on a similar track, was shot down by a Beaufighter of 25 Squadron over Lincolnshire at 2345 hours. It was commanded by Unteroffizier Adam Becker who was killed along with two of his crew. The air-gunner, Gefreiter Rudolf Dachsel, baled out and was taken prisoner.

The times of attack recorded by the units involved are an indication of the ferocity of the initial phase of the assault lasting from 0100 to 0200 hours. Judging by the number of aircraft that were over the city at any given time during this period, it is clear that the defences were virtually overwhelmed by sheer weight of numbers. An examination of individual unit reports shows that, in the first half hour, aircraft from almost every unit in the mission had been over the target. The plan of the attack followed that of Easter Tuesday. Aircraft initially routed to the Co. Antrim coast somewhere in the vicinity of Larne or Whitehead from where they started their final approach to the target.

The large number of aeroplanes over the city at the same time made it imperative for aircraft commanders to maintain the bombing altitudes assigned to them. These ranged from 600 metres to 5800 metres and the wide divergence created almost impossible problems for the anti-aircraft gunners in choosing the fuse settings for their shells. Gun crews had also to contend with low-level attacks on their battery positions.[15] Two sites known to have been singled out were the 3.7-inch gun site U6 at Sunningdale Park in the north of the city and the Bofors site UL9 on the bank of the River Lagan close to Ravenhill Road. A few Ju88s were seen to make dive-bombing attacks (the He111 was not capable of dive-bombing). Dieter Lukesch's was one of them. As a staffel commander, he was authorized to adopt the dive-bombing method provided he was satisfied that no other attacking aircraft was endangered. He described it as follows:

> Because of the favourable weather, the flight at a height of 4000 metres presented no difficulties nor did finding the target. The attack was carried out in a dive at an angle of 70 degrees in the face of very heavy ground fire. The position of the strikes in the target area was observed but not the effect, due to the necessary defensive measures we had to take.

A high degree of accuracy was normally achieved by dive-bombing. Lukesch's target was Harland and Wolff's shipyard and the probability is that his bombs had a telling effect. The collective mission report of his unit, KG 76, spoke of the last crews to arrive over the target at about 0200 hours finding 'large fires spread out (over the target area) especially in the region of Harland and Wolff's and the harbour installations'.

It was 2250 hours as Joachim Herrfurth's He111P-4 *Ida Richard* took off from Caen and set course for Belfast via the radio beacon at Cap Barfleur on the Cherbourg peninsula. Radio operator Georg Aigner monitored the H/F frequency 4480 kc/s on which the staff of KG 55 maintained contact by morse code with individual aircraft from its headquarters in the Chateau Montecelin at Villacoublay. Unknown to Aigner, the frequency was also being monitored by the RAF's No. 61 Wireless Unit (61WU) at Cheadle, near Stafford.[16] During the course of the night, this unit logged 28 transmissions between KG 55 aircraft and their headquarters, many of them from aircraft on their way home from Belfast when the need for radio silence was no longer so imperative.

The He111, with its large Plexiglas cockpit, afforded excellent all round visibility and Fritz Krause was able to see all aspects of a bombing operation at close quarters. Carrying war correspondents or other noncombatant passengers was not, in fact, popular with the Luftwaffe crews. They were regarded as excess weight without adding anything to the effectiveness of the mission. Krause was soon to find out that he was, at the very least, expected to put his eyes to the best possible use:

> I was flying with the crew of Oberleutnant H (Herrfurth) who has completed more than 80 missions. After today's flight, the Gruppe commander

will be able to bestow the silver clasp for 60 operational flights on two of the others. They are all old bomber men who know the ropes. They have the necessary experience but they know as well the harsh reality of battle, especially of night attacks.

Over the intercom, Oblt H is continually shouting at us to watch out for other aircraft. From the middle of the (English) channel on, it is a ceaseless look-out for enemy fighters. This is more nerve-racking than flak or worse than being sought by a searchlight. We can't look in another direction for even a second, for the fraction of a second that it takes to see or not to see the enemy can mean the difference between life and death.

There behind us! An aircraft. A rapid deflection and he loses us. Another sighting and another encounter but again we succeed in shaking him off. We don't want to get into a fight unless it is absolutely necessary. The load we are taking to Belfast is a valuable one.

After midnight, we approach the target.* There it is below, burning in many different places. The dazzling light of the fire bombs is seething over an area of nearly a square kilometre of the harbour. The vivid, red glare from the huge fires reflects on the layer of haze which lies over the target to a depth of several thousand metres. That is where we have to go. The flames point the way for us. Although our eyes had been threatening to close from the strain of keeping a look-out for enemy fighters, now they are wide open again to see the unique spectacle being staged there below.

The light of the moon is reflected in the water over which we make our approach and enables us to make out the outlines of the harbour installations. These installations, with their targets so important for the war, occupy around 300000 square metres. To include them all in a single attack is quite impossible. Success must lie in so attacking and destroying the half of them by pinpoint bombing so that they cease to be of any use. Oblt H. lies in the nose of the cockpit, holding a chart in front of him. The light from the fires below and the flares hanging in the air like clusters of burning grapes merges in the glow of his pocket lamp and spills over his face. We are coming over the target but H doesn't release the bombs yet. First, he scans the sky around us. The bulging barrage balloons underneath us hover like dark sausages against the light of the flames. Not two or three but ten to twenty we can make out. We make a wide orbit and approach again. There is no sign at all of searchlights. It would probably have been fruitless for them to choose which of the aircraft circling the target to illuminate for the AA gunners who are simply throwing up a curtain of shrapnel over the target area. If they wanted to drive away an

* The Luftwaffe records and the crew's logbooks indicate that Herrfurth's aircraft did not make its attack until after 0105 hours.

aircraft from the target by direct fire, there would be four or five others coming unimpeded from another direction at the same time.

We are going down. Hundreds and hundreds of metres. Already the luminous tracks of tracer rounds from the light flak streak past close to us. The fire from the heavy flak is too high now. The observer (Herrfurth) is again lying in the the nose. The cover is rolled back from the bomb-sight and the bomb-bay doors opened. In spite of the intense flak fire - a heavy salvo must have been close as our aircraft shook several times - the observer is quite calm and concerns himself solely with the target. The thought occurs to me that this (the scene below) could be a work in bronze created by the best of German artists. We have probably been over the target area for a quarter of an hour. Seldom have we seen such a sight. Huge shipbuilding sheds and docks are already burning. Hit at the beginning of the attack, some of them are already burnt out and have collapsed, still smouldering. But nearby, enormous fires are developing from the patterns of bursting incendiary bombs. We drop our bombs of both light and medium calibre alongside the existing fires. We are simply creating new ones as do the other aircraft. Soon, while we circle the target, a sea of flame opens up there below us. In the middle of all this, we see bombs of the heaviest calibre crashing into storehouses, docks and shipyards, ripping them apart. Gasometers explode and fuel tanks are torn open with enormous flashes reaching upwards. Burning ships are lying in the Victoria and Musgrave Channels. One explosion follows another. Incendiaries, detonations and bursting flak shells. Dazzling tracer trails and blazing fires. All surpassing each other and interacting in a brilliant spectacle.

Belfast, now the most important transhipment port for deliveries of war materials from the USA, may not be totally destroyed but it has been dealt a severe blow. The first attack on the city was a serious blow for this gateway on the north-west side of Great Britain. However, today's attack surpassed it, favoured by good weather and also by the resolution of our bomber crews, which is daily growing and benefiting from experience.

Krause may have given rein to all his journalistic instincts in writing the article but people on the receiving end would not have quarrelled with its underlying veracity. Although there was worse to come, it is clear from his description that the first half hour or so of the raid (*Ida Richard* probably left the target area around 0145 hours) was ferocious.

As a staffel commander and very experienced officer, Herrfurth had a discretion to make a low-level attack. Accordingly, he made his bombing run over the harbour at a height of 800 metres, aiming his bombs at target area *Anton* west of the Victoria Channel. Georg Aigner had left his radio set and manned the upper gun-turret (known as the *B-Stand*) and Leo Neidel, the flight engineer, took the *C-Stand* in the underbelly of the fuselage. Both opened fire on light anti-aircraft gun sites identified adjacent to the harbour, one of which was possibly the Bofors gun site on the roof of the Custom House, close to Donegall Quay.

On leaving the area, Herrfurth elected to make the return flight across Northern England and down the east coast, where he calculated there would be less night fighter activity. Fuel consumption had been satisfactory and he ordered Baumgartner to miss out Caen and fly direct to their base at Villacoublay, where they landed at 0425 hours.

The unremitting stream of Hellls and Ju88s that dumped their bomb-loads into the spreading conflagration was followed at 0155 hours by the first of the mine-carriers of KG 4. Ten aircraft from I Gruppe were to make their attack between 0155 and 0225, followed immediately by eleven from III Gruppe. One from I Gruppe developed a fault in the propeller pitch control and diverted to make an attack on military installations at Scarborough.

Siegfried Röthke was flying one of the leading aircraft. He first saw the deep red glare of the sky over Belfast when he was at least 200 kilometres away. There was no longer any need to identify the Isle of Man check point. His Gruppe had been allocated target area *Anton* and the attack was to be made from below 3500 metres. By this time, the whole of the target area resembled a cauldron and, in spite of the refractive effect of the haze, individual target identification presented little difficulty as the burning installations threw the whole harbour basin into stark relief against the dark outline of the lough.

While the composition of the bomb loads carried by III Gruppe, which had been assigned area *Bruno* is not recorded but if it was similar to I Gruppe's, then a total of nearly 40 tonnes of high-explosives was dropped into the harbour complex or the surrounding area. The destructive effect of these large missiles falling into burning buildings and other installations was devastating and made a huge contribution to the success of the raid.

The report sent by I Gruppe to Luftflotte 2 headquarters in Brussels after the attack categorically states that all but two of its BM1000 bombs and LMB parachute mines had fallen into area *Anton* which would have accounted for much of the damage to Pollock Dock and the LM&S Railway Station at York Road. This assessment is borne out by the report of the Belfast Harbour Commissioners[17] which summarized the damage caused in all the raids on the city. It states that 'much damage was caused to the Commissioners' property, mostly to sheds throughout the Co. Antrim side of the harbour'. It went on to say that about 90 per cent of the total damage to the Commissioners' property occurred in this raid. The other two bombs or mines of I Gruppe's ordnance missed and fell into the adjoining area *Bruno* which encompassed targets such as the Musgrave Channel, the Airport Road oil storage tanks and aircraft factory.

In addition to the widespread damage to buildings and installations, the Harbour Commissioners' report detailed the damage sustained by ships within its complex. The *Fair Head* (1719 tons, G. Heyn & Sons) with a cargo of government stores was sunk at Dufferin Dock East* and declared a total loss. The *Cape Breton* (5970 tons) with a cargo of timber from British Columbia was sunk in Dufferin Dock West but was refloated on 14 May and later sailed from the port. The *Frederika Lensen* (4283 tons), which was being refitted in Musgrave Channel, developed a list as a result of damage sustained but was repaired and later sailed from the port. Although it is not possible to correlate the vessels named in the Commissioners' summary with those described in a claim quoted on German radio, the latter version is (somewhat unusually) not extravagant. On 10 May, the Finnish Service of Königsberg Radio (Finland was now an ally of Germany) stated that reconnaissance aircraft flying over Belfast after the raid of 4/5 May took photographs which showed that hits were scored on three ships in Belfast, a tanker of about 10,000 tons and two merchant ships of approximately 8000 tons and 7000 tons respectively. No mention was made of vessels not lying within the shipyard itself. The reconnaissance flight referred to in the radio report was very likely that which took place on 6 May by a Luftflotte 3 aircraft. One of the photographs it took clearly shows the extent of the destruction throughout the harbour estate, including damage to ships under construction on the slipways in the Musgrave Channel.

In spite of the claims by the German crews to have bombed the designated targets, it is almost superfluous to record that many bombs also fell a considerable distance away – at a cost of many civilian lives. This could be ascribed to a variety of unknown causes but the Lofte tachometric bomb-sight then used by the Luftwaffe for horizontal bombing required a straight and level run of approximately 40 seconds before the bombs were released. A course deviation or human error on the part of the bomb-aimer could account for strikes far from the aiming points.

It is reasonable to assume that some of the bombers were deflected by anti-aircraft fire as they made their bombing runs. Although the sky was virtually 'saturated' with aircraft at times, the city's thinly-spread batteries put up a creditable performance on this occasion, firing 3128 heavy rounds of 3.7-inch ammunition along with 54 rounds of 3-inch and 319 40mm Bofors shells. The comparatively small number of Bofors rounds fired is probably explained by the fact that most of the attackers were flying at heights in excess

---

* The Dufferin Docks, which were subsequently filled in, lay between Pollock Dock and the Victoria Channel.

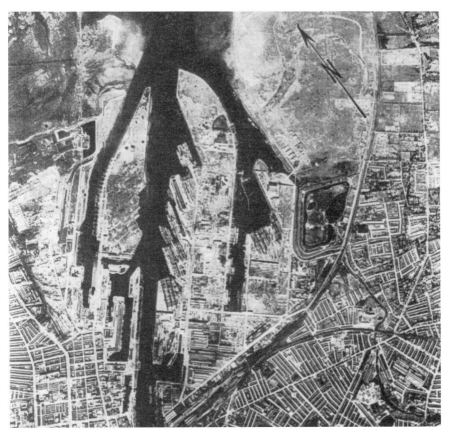

25 Luftwaffe aerial photograph of Belfast harbour complex taken on 6 May 1941.
The effects of the incendiary bombs can be clearly seen.

of 3000 metres, that is, almost 10000 feet. Although this was not outside the absolute range of the Bofors it became ineffective at these levels. Considering that the raid was compressed into a period of little more than two hours, the rate of fire by the heavy guns was very respectable contrasting with the earlier raid when 1418 3.7-inch rounds were fired over a period almost twice as long. The Luftwaffe's judgment of the defence was in no way dismissive. The Luftflotte 3 Operations Report described the AA fire as 'moderate to heavy with some of it well-aimed'.

The German propaganda organs supplied their own version of events. A news broadcast on Deutschlandsender the following day[18] proclaimed that Belfast's AA defences were 'almost completely silenced – surprised by the power of the attacks ... their nervous erratic firing completed the picture of destruction that nobody will forget.' The crews actually participating often found it difficult to recognize Goebbels' description of the attacks they had just carried out and the raid of 4/5 May is probably a good example. Their individual assessments of the flak they had encountered tended to be subjective and influenced by what went on around them but none disparaged it. One described the fire as 'sustained and severe at 3000 metres'. Another said that the bombing run had to be made in the face of very accurate fire.

About 25 balloons, flying between 1500 and 2000 metres, were observed by the attackers but seem to have presented no problems for aircraft attacking from below those levels.

A further contrast to the night of 15/16 April lay in the addition to the city's defence capability made by the aircraft carrier *Furious*. On this occasion her four-inch and two-pounder anti-aircraft guns made a deafening contribution to the general pandemonium. The ship's log records that her guns opened fire at 0040 hours and that almost immediately she received a direct hit in the lower aircraft hangar. No information as to the extent of the damage or casualties is given.

No positive successes were claimed by either the shorebased or ships' gunners but 3 AA Brigade's Intelligence Summary issued the following day stated that there were 'several reports of crashed aircraft' but that no confirmation was available. There was, in fact, one bomber which could not be accounted for.

The 2nd Staffel of the Küstenfliegergruppe 106 (2./106) was normally engaged in maritime operations and the crews of its Ju88A-5s spent much of their time over the North Sea and the coastal areas of Northern Scotland. Towards the end of the night offensive, however, the unit was increasingly called upon to supplement the conventional bomber units. Commanded by Hauptmann Gerhard Hausmann, the staffel was unable as a rule to put more than five or six aircraft into the air on any single operation. On the night of 4/5 May, Hausmann led an unknown number of aircraft (possibly not more than four or five) in the attack on Belfast.[19] After taking off from Amsterdam-Schiphol, the staffel crossed the North Sea and reached the English coast at The Wash. At 0045 hours, one of them, commanded by naval officer Oberleutnant z. S. Metzger, was intercepted by an unidentified night fighter and caught fire after being hit. All four on board were able to bale out successfully but the aircraft crashed into a house near Bradford. Four civilians lost their lives. The remaining aircraft continued towards Belfast but one of them, under the command of Oberleutnant z. S. Wilhelm Pyrkosch met an unknown fate either before or after reaching the city. There appears to be no report from any RAF night fighter unit which would account for the aircraft's disappearance and the possibility remains that Pyrkosch and his crew did, in fact, fall victim to Belfast's anti-aircraft defences and crashed into the sea. Two nights later, Hausmann himself along with his pilot, Oberleutnant Coenen, lost their lives in an attack on Glasgow when they were shot down by a Defiant of No. 141 Squadron. The other two crewmen baled out and were taken prisoner.

THE FINAL HOURS OF DARKNESS

In the final stages of the raid, Belfast presented an awesome spectacle, both to the crews of the bombers and the horrified citizens sheltering on the surrounding hills. A dense pall of black smoke hung in the still air and merged in the glare of what now seemed like one single enormous fire.

Although he was unaware of it at the time, Hauptmann von Beust's bomb load was one of the last to contribute to this scene of devastation. The 12 Heinkels of his Gruppe, III/KG 27 from Brest, dropped 45 SC 250kg bombs, nine of them with LZZ long-time delay fuses, and 3456 BIEI 1kg incendiaries from between 3500 and 4000 metres. The last of his aircraft was over the target at 0308 hours and may, in fact, have been the last or one of the last to drop bombs on the city that night. The War Diary of 3 AA Brigade states that 'the engagement was finally broken off at 0340 hours'. However, explosions from bombs with time fuses would probably have created uncertainty about when the raid actually ended.

The time that it would take the last attackers to reach their home bases after the raid would depend on factors such as the winds aloft and throttle settings as well as the distance to be covered but, allowing for a ground speed of 300 to 320 km/h, it would have been safe to allow three hours for the He111s of III/KG 27 to get back to Brest. To have prolonged their attack beyond 0330 hours would have made the return landing time uncomfortably close to daybreak. Since fuel consumption was a prime consideration, aircraft would ordinarily take the most direct route home. This, however, tended to increase the risk of detection by night fighters. At this late stage, the 'Y' Service would be aware of the identity of all or most of the bomber units involved and the location of their bases. Night fighters could, therefore, be expected to concentrate on the airspace through which the homeward-bound aircraft would pass and, from time to time, some of them came to grief for that reason.

Further hazards awaited them in the vicinity of their airfields. Even if they escaped the attention of RAF fighters lurking around the landing circuit, they had to be careful not to stray into zones patrolled by German night fighters searching for RAF bombers going to and from targets on the continent.

Consequently, height restrictions were often imposed on returning aircraft. For example, KG 4 aircraft, on the final stage of their flight from Belfast to Soesterberg on the morning of 5 May, had to descend to below 1500 metres after crossing the Dutch coast in an attempt to distinguish themselves from RAF bombers. This apparently proved to be more difficult where German AA gunners were concerned and many crews complained bitterly about being fired on by their own troops, notwithstanding that they had signalled the correct code word of the day by lamp.[1]

Added to this was the all too frequent difficulty of finding the home airfield in bad visibility. At such times, the 'Y' Service monitors would overhear desperate calls from pilots short of fuel asking controllers for QDM bearings (a magnetic course to steer) that would bring them overhead their bases.

All these potential dangers, which applied with equal force to the men of RAF Bomber Command, had to be faced at the end of a long flight under conditions of extreme stress, when crews were almost at the limit of their endurance. Writing 50 years after he had taken part in the bombing of Belfast, Georg Aigner, the radio operator in *Ida Richard*, said: 'So much was asked of young men then'.[2]

Hauptmann Dietrich Peltz, who led II/KG 77 in the attack, would have been listening out on his radio for anything of interest as he flew across England on the way from Belfast to Amsterdam. The 'Y' Service log records that his unit was being controlled from Schiphol on 4130 kc/s.[3] Earlier in the evening, as he was crossing the Yorkshire coast near Bridlington on the outbound flight to Belfast, he had overheard one of his officers, Oberleutnant Baumann, making a distress call due to engine failure. Baumann reported that he was ditching in the sea. The ditching was not a success, however, and it was later learned that of the four on board only Oberfeldwebel Schieting, the air-gunner, survived the impact and was picked up by a passing ship. Peltz had a similar experience on the homeward journey. Shortly after 0400 hours, as he was flying across Norfolk, he heard Leutnant Kurt Obenhack, from his own staff flight, call Schiphol to report engine trouble and dwindling fuel.[4] Obenhack eventually made a relatively successful forced landing on the shore but the radio operator Unteroffizier Johann Simon was killed when the aircraft hit a sand dune. The other three on board suffered only minor injuries and were taken prisoner.

Peltz was to prove to be an outstanding officer. He was 26 years old when he led his Groppe on both the large-scale raids on Belfast. He flew with distinction on the Eastern Front when the night offensive against Britain came to an end and after a meteoric rise through the commissioned ranks, he became the youngest general in the Luftwaffe in October 1943 at the age of twenty-nine. He survived the war to become a senior executive in the giant German electronics firm of Telefunken.[5]

26 Dietrich Peltz, the Luftwaffe's youngest general

Luftwaffe losses in the night operation of 4/5 May against Belfast were light. Only two can be positively attributed to RAF night fighter interceptions. They are the Ju88s of III/KG 1 and 2./106 shot down over Yorkshire and Lincolnshire respectively. In view of the apprehension throughout the bomber units before the raid, these very modest losses must have come as a considerable relief. The weather conditions had been favourable for interceptions and, in view of the increasing effectiveness of the RAF's GCI radar installations and AI radar-equipped fighters, the story might well have been very different.

The large number of diversions to alternate targets which occurred on Easter Tuesday was repeated and while the raid could only be described as a success in the context of the damage inflicted. the effect was less than planned. Thirty-four bombers from Luftflotte 3 units bombed Liverpool as an alternate and 18 attacked a variety of widely-scattered targets. Most of them were attributed in crew reports to an inability to find the primary target, something that may seem surprising since other crews spoke of the fires at the target being visible for well over 100 kilometres. However, the weather data from stations on the coast of North Wales and Liverpool Bay confirm the presence of thick ground mist and 7/10ths cloud at midnight. This extended to the Isle of Man and could have created difficulties for the early attackers when the fires in Belfast had not yet taken a firm hold. The same weather reports show a significant improvement in conditions at 0300 hours by which time the raid had virtually ended. Whatever the reasons, the upshot was that 25 per cent of the force dispatched to Belfast failed to attack it, constituting another in a long series of demoralising frustrations for the Luftwaffe. It was a further reminder of the price being paid for the lack of a reliable target-finding aid but in more general terms there was a widespread feeling that the sooner the wretched night campaign was over the better.

The effect of the attack on Belfast was, by any standards, severe. Serious disruption to industries engaged in important war work, especially the shipyard, aircraft factory and port installations, occurred. The final assessment of the raid by the headquarters staff of Luftflotte 3 did not overstate the result when it said:

> Visual bombing conditions prevailed. Intense coalescing fires in the targeted areas developed and and a very good effect can be presumed.[6]

Measured in terms of civilian life the cost was heavy but significantly less than on the previous occasion. This was a reflection of a higher degree of preparedness on the ground and greater accuracy on the part of the attackers, which in turn could be attributed to the more favourable weather conditions.

Less than a week later, the OKW recorded that 600 bombers had attacked London on the night of 10/11 May – a maximum effort achieved by many aircraft having to make more than one sortie. At the time, an air raid of this scale seemed to represent the ultimate in total war but in just over a year's time, on 30/31 May 1942, the RAF launched its first 1000-bomber raid of the war against the city of Cologne. In the ensuing three years, the Allied air forces were to develop the concept of strategic bombing to hitherto unimagined lengths and lay waste entire cities.

The fires in Belfast continued to burn for several days. Thick acrid smoke hung over the harbour basin and the entire city in the almost calm conditions and added to the sense of desolation. At 2000 hours in the evening of the fifth, the *Furious*, her ammunition exhausted, slipped quietly away from her moorings and down the Victoria Channel on the way to Liverpool,[7] past the twisted and smouldering wharves of Harland & Wolff's where the corvettes *Bryony*, *Buttercup* and *La Malouine* under construction were almost completely destroyed. Lying nearby and also damaged was the training aircraft-carrier *Pegasus*, which had been at the yard for repair.[8]

That night, at 0029 hours, the sirens wailed again through the city. The war diary of 968 Balloon Squadron reported 'several hostile aircraft, mainly travelling north'. The AA batteries opened fire at 0155 hours at an unknown number of targets. During the engagement, a total of 221 heavy rounds were fired. Fourteen people were killed in the east of the city when what was thought to be a parachute mine fell in a residential area close to Belfast Ropeworks. It later emerged that 175 bombers of Luftflotte 3 bombed Glasgow and targets in the Clyde Valley that night. Many of them were tracked northwards along the Irish coast by the Irish LOPs and by the newly-commissioned radar station of the RAF's 77 Wing at Kilkeel, Co. Down.[9] The Irish LOPs reported that altogether 15 waves of aircraft passed up the east coast and that, in many cases, the aircraft were inside Irish territorial airspace. One group of five was known to have penetrated as far west as Kildare and Monaghan.[10]

The German files dealing with the operations of the night of 5/6 May make no specific reference to a raid on Belfast but there is evidence that the attack, although minor, was in fact planned. On the following morning, Radio Deutschlandsender announced that 'last night strong formations attacked Glasgow, Liverpool and Belfast'. It went on:

> Since the crippling of London docks and ports on the east coast, Liverpool, Glasgow and Belfast have been the main channels through which foodstuffs, raw materials and war materials have entered Britain ... Glasgow and Belfast moreover are important ship-building centres which have, for some months, been trying to cope with the continually increasing number of damaged ships which have been brought there for repair, quite apart from the building of new ships to replace, at least a small part of the tonnage sunk.[11]

A more explicit explanation for the bombing incident at Belfast that night is contained in a unit history of KGr100 based on war diary entries. This states that, on the night of 5/6 May, two He111s carried out a *Störeinsatz*, or 'nuisance sortie' against the north-west area of Belfast.[12] The description does not fit that of the district where the casualties occurred but the incident bore all the characteristics of a nuisance raid. This was a tactic employed by both sides during the war. One of its aims was to interrupt the emergency services in their dealing with the aftermath of a heavy raid and to spread further alarm in the civil population. In this way, two or three aircraft could bring an entire city and its industries to a standstill for several hours. In the closing stages of the war, the Allies developed the tactic to the point where a virtual 24-hour air raid alert was in force in places such as Berlin and the Ruhr valley. Workers in vital war industries were unable to function properly because of exhaustion and lack of sleep.

During the course of this minor attack, Squadron-Leader J.W. Simpson, the commanding officer of 245 Squadron at Aldergrove, claimed another victim in his Hurricane. He reported sighting three Ju88s flying in line astern near Ardglass at 0100 hours. He made a head-on attack and saw one of them catch fire and crash into the sea.[13] As far as is known, no wreckage or bodies were found and it is not possible to match the incident with any loss reported by the Luftwaffe that night. A Ju88 reported missing was later identified as belonging to II/KG 54. It had been on the way to bomb Dumbarton when it was intercepted and shot down by a night fighter at Chawleigh in Devon.

On the night of 6/7 May, for the third night in succession, a 'Red' alert sounded in Belfast. The AA defence opened fire at an unknown number of hostile aircraft over the city expending 235 rounds but no bombs were dropped.

This, in fact, marked the end of the 'Blitz' on Belfast. For the remainder of the war, most of the enemy flights over Northern Ireland were, in one way or another, associated with the Battle of the Atlantic. One such incursion in the summer of 1941 seems to have been a determined attempt to bomb an important ammunition dump.

On the night of 23/24 July, several enemy aircraft were plotted by radar over Northern Ireland. Shortly after 0200 hours, bombs fell in the Townland of Caddy, near Randalstown in Co. Antrim.[14] The circumstances are obscure, which is probably due to the anxiety by the authorities to preserve secrecy. Aircraft had been heard flying south over Ballymena followed by the sound of explosions a few minutes later. Depending on which of the official versions is accepted, anything from six to 13 bombs, two of which failed to explode, fell on agricultural land, apparently causing no damage. A witness stated that he had seen one aircraft coming from the Ballymena direction dropping bombs 'from almost tree-top height'.

One official explanation for the incident was that the bombs were 'obviously jettisoned'. Elsewhere in this account, however, it was admitted that they had fallen two miles from one of the most important military supply depots in Ulster. But even this bland explanation was less than frank. The bombs had, in fact, fallen short of Shane's Castle estate where one of the Royal Navy's largest dumps of ordnance for use in the war at sea, including mines and torpedoes, was located.

It is known that on the same night, several He111s of III/KG 40 (KG 40 had now been expanded to contain three Gruppen) were operating over and around the coast of Northern Ireland. It is significant that one of the unit's tasks was to bomb targets which had a direct bearing on the Battle of the Atlantic. In the event, what appears to have been an audacious attempt to cause destruction on a large scale had failed but the incident suggested that the Germans possessed reliable information about a well-concealed installation.

The attacks on Glasgow and Clydeside on 5/6 and 6/7 May were of major proportions and they were followed on the 7/8 by yet another in the seemingly endless series on Liverpool. But it was to prove to be the last large-scale attack on that much bombed city. The night was also to be the worst for the Luftwaffe in the entire night offensive, a confirmed 21 of its aircraft being lost to night fighters. The violent assault of 10/11 May on London brought the night offensive of 1940/41 to a close and over the next few weeks all but an estimated four bomber Gruppen vacated their bases in France and the Low Countries to return to Germany, Austria and Poland where they were to rest and re-equip for further operations 'in another theatre of war' which was not immediately identified.

The bombing of *Etappe* had no long-term impact on the course of the Battle of the Atlantic which had been its primary objective or on Britain's war effort as a whole. In the view of General Field Marshal Albert Kesselring the same could be said of the entire German night bombing offensive:

> Just as we went into the war with Poland unprepared, so were we not equipped for the economic war against England in all its intensity and diversity. Certainly, we made life difficult for the English on their island but we were unable to sever Great Britain's lifelines.[15]

The price paid for this futility was high. In Belfast, at least 900 people died and in Britain as a whole the final figure exceeded forty thousand.[16] And the campaign left its mark on the German airmen who waged it. There was a sense of failure throughout the Luftwaffe which was exacerbated by the loss of so many of its best young men. These feelings, tinged with bitterness, were eloquently expressed in a eulogy delivered by Oberleutnant (later Hauptmann) Herbert Wittmann, a Staffelkapitän in KG 53 who took part in the Easter Tuesday raid on Belfast:

Only those who flew in the battle against England can tell of the physical and psychological demands to which the crews were exposed. Crew after crew was lost. Only a few who had to ditch in the water were picked up and survived, others were taken prisoner in England and from then on spent the war in Canada. Out of the men originally in the staff squadron, only one crew with myself and Oberleutnant Bichowsky are still flying on operations. All the rest have been killed or are missing. But the willingness to fly on missions is still there, the spirit and the comradeship in the squadron is exemplary.

I would also like to record here that from the beginning to the end only military targets were assigned in our operational orders. An order for the bombing of an open city in any theatre of war was never given. Of course, sticks of bombs for harbour installations in places like London, Liverpool and Southhampton also fell in residential areas. Everyone should be in no doubt that where a stick of twenty 100kg bombs is aimed at a target some can fall over a distance of 400 metres away.[17]

It is likely that most airmen who flew in bombing operations in the Second World War – whatever their nationality – would have agreed with Wittmann that the targeting of civilians was not expressly ordered but unfortunately the reality was that many bombs were dropped, if not with the intention of killing civilians, then with the knowledge that they were probably not going to hit their targets.

CHANGING PERSPECTIVES

The lengthening days of spring brought changes in the war at sea which were to have significance for both parts of Ireland. The focus of the battle shifted away from the waters off her northern and western shores as Doenitz took delivery of more of the larger 500-ton and 750-ton U-boats and sent his packs further west into the Atlantic.

The fortunes of the U-boat fleet underwent a radical change in the first six months of 1941. From a low point in February when the force had a mere 21 boats in service, the number in commission by May had reached about a hundred. Of these, one-third were operational; the remainder were either working up or engaged in training. By June it was estimated that an average of 32 boats were attacking convoys in mid-Atlantic at any given time.[1] A small number remained to cover the area immediately to the west of the North Channel from where they could shadow the departing westbound convoys and report their progress to the waiting packs to the south and west of Iceland.

The German decision to move the battlefield further west had not been made entirely from choice.[2] Although the new larger oceangoing U-boats were able to confront the convoys in mid-Atlantic where the escorts were stretched to the limit, they had to devote more thought to their own survival. Hopes of a short war, born of the early successes, were ebbing away. There was a growing need to maintain a constant look-out for Coastal Command aircraft even away from the waters close to the Irish coast while travelling on the surface. This, in turn, led to more of them making night attacks, a tactic developed and refined by the now redundant Otto Kretschmer. Further evidence of the perils of life in a German submarine at the time can be seen in the Admiralty statistics of the period which record the number of recorded attacks on them. There were 50 in March, 59 in April, 64 in May and 82 in June.[3]

It is notable that the increase in the number of the boats deployed by Doenitz was not marked by a commensurate increase in the tonnage sunk by them. While the number of ships lost in March – forty, representing 238719 tons – rose to fifty-seven with a total tonnage of 296152 in June, this rate of success did not reflect the additional German input.[4]

Slowly and almost imperceptibly, the fury that had raged in the North West Approaches for almost a year began to abate. For Britain, a phase of unprecedented danger was coming to an end. Ironically, it is possible to say in retrospect that the watershed which signalled a modest improvement in Britain's fortunes came about not in the grim war of attrition against the U-boats but in the epic battle that ended in the destruction of the German battleship *Bismarck*. The sinking of this great warship belongs in the annals of heroic sea battles and is well documented but the desperate efforts of the Luftwaffe to help her are less well known.

At 1600 hours on 24 May 1941, a message was received in the headquarters of Luftflotte 3 in Paris to say that the *Bismarck* had been involved in an engagement in which the British battlecruiser *Hood* had been sunk and the battleship *Prince of Wales* damaged. The *Bismarck* had herself been damaged and was said to be making for St Nazaire but it later emerged that, in fact, her captain intended to try and reach Brest. The Luftwaffe was ordered to commit every available aircraft to cover her escape from the British fleet that would surely hunt her down. However, many flying units had already begun to leave their bases in France in preparation for the attack on the Soviet Union. Nevertheless, more than 200 He111s and Ju88s were assembled on airfields close to the French coast for the rescue operation but it went wrong from the start.[5]

At first, the Luftwaffe was unable to find the *Bismarck*. She was compelled to maintain radio silence for fear of revealing her position to her pursuers and moreover the searching aircraft were hampered by atrocious weather. A deep depression west of Ireland brought storm force winds and a cloud base down to sea level in places. The majority of the German crews engaged in the search had no experience of operating over water in such conditions. An equally telling factor was that the range limitations of the Heinkels and Junkers prevented them from operating more than 200 miles beyond the Irish coast. While the adverse weather conditions would give the *Bismarck* some welcome cover, the early signs for the aerial support operation were poor.

By the morning of 27 May the great battleship had been cornered and her fate was already sealed. The only German aircraft to make visual contact with her at this time were five Ju88s of the Küstenfliegergruppe 606 based at Brest, one of the few units with crews – apart from I/KG 40 – with any real experience of this kind of operation. The time was 0950 hours DBST. In a furious hail of anti-aircraft fire, they immediately made a dive-bombing attack on the British warships surrounding the stricken ship but all the bombs missed their targets.

The *Bismarck* finally sank at 1036 hours. Fifteen minutes later, 17 He111s from KG 28 found the British ships, including the aircraft carrier *Ark Royal*, and attacked with 500kg and 250kg bombs, again without success. One after another, the remaining German bomber units converged on the dispersing warships within 50 miles of the Irish coast. The RAF's 'Y' Service reported monitoring forty-three separate attacks on them between 1130 hours on the 28th and 0300 hours on the 29th at various points between Eagle Island, County Mayo and Cape Clear in Co. Cork. There were countless intrusions into Irish airspace as aircraft (probably including RAF machines) took the shortest route to and from their bases.

One of the British warships, the destroyer *Mashona*, was hit and sank 50 miles due west of Slyne Head on the morning of the 28th with the loss of 46 of her crew. The exact number of aircraft lost by the Luftwaffe in the engagements is not known. What is known is that all four of the Arado Ar196 floatplanes aboard the *Bismarck* were lost, each with a crew of two. They had either been destroyed by gunfire or in air battles with shadowing aircraft.[6] There were many reports of enemy aircraft over Northern Ireland. On the 28th a Ju88 belonging to the reconnaissance group of the Luftwaffe's Commander-in-Chief (2. Ob.d.L) was seen flying east at a position north of Inishowen Head. It was pursued across Scotland by fighters of No. 43 Squadron and shot down over East Lothian. Two of the crew of four were killed including the aircraft commander, Leutnant Fritz Gortan.

One of the German casualties survived to provide an interesting tailpiece to the story of the battle. On 24 May, a Condor of I/KG 40 received several direct hits when making a low-level attack on the British warships. The meteorologist on board, Gustav Schlarb, was killed and two other crew members wounded. One of them was the aircraft commander, Oberleutnant Heinz Braun, who lost an eye. He survived the war and in spite of his disability was accepted into the post-war Luftwaffe as a pilot and he continued to fly until his retirement.

June was a bad month for Doenitz. He lost four of his boats but only one of them in the North West Approaches. The *U-147*, commanded by Oberleutnant z. S. Wetjen, was sunk with the loss of all hands by the destroyer *Wanderer* and the corvette *Periwinkle* 100 miles north-west of Malin Head on 24 June.[7] The others went down to Royal Navy escort vessels further to the south and west.

By the end of May, four escort groups were operating from Londonderry and Greenock,[8] supported by an ever-increasing number of Coastal Command aircraft flying out of Ulster airfields and the flying boat base at Castle Archdale on Lough Erne. The westward movement of the U-boat packs was countered by a comprehensive system of convoy escorts operating from new bases in Iceland and Newfoundland that would provide 'end to end' cover all the way across the North Atlantic. The first convoy to benefit from this extended protection was the HX 129 which left Halifax on 27 May.[9]

Unknown to the American public, the US Navy began to undertake periodic sweeps along the convoy routes west of the 26 degrees West meridian during which they would shadow any Axis vessels they encountered and report their whereabouts to the Royal Navy. Later in the summer, US warships began to undertake positive responsibility for convoys west of the 30 West meridian.

Further evidence of conduct not befitting a neutral country was also emerging in Londonderry. The earlier German reports that American sailors had been engaged in some kind of activity there in January proved to be accurate. Work on the construction of a full-scale naval base was now in progress. This led to a protest from de Valera to the US government in July but the work continued apace notwithstanding and the next stage in the process was the stationing of US marines in the city to guard the installations. It was yet another twist in a bizarre situation in which Northern Ireland was at the centre of a dispute between two neutral countries!

Neutral status may have had some benefits in Eire but their ephemeral nature was again demonstrated on the night of 30 May when bombs fell on the North Strand in Dublin killing 34 people. Charge and counter-charge came thick and fast in the heated diplomatic exchanges between Dublin and Berlin that followed but there was no doubt that the bombs were of German origin. Several theories as to why the bombs were dropped have been advanced but the incident remains unexplained and, not surprisingly, the Luftwaffe records are of no help. If the bombing was intentional, the various unit war diaries would not have recorded the fact and, if it was accidental, an aircraft commander was unlikely to admit to such a blunder. If it was the latter, it is difficult to explain the incident away on the grounds of mistaken identity caused by poor visibility. Although the city's lights had been partially obscured as an air raid precaution there must surely have been enough light visible to alert an aircraft commander to the fact that he was not flying over a British city. Furthermore, the prevailing weather conditions were good. At 2200 hours local time, the Phoenix Park weather station reported 'night clear' with only 2/10ths cloud cover. A German aerial photograph of the Dublin docks taken on 24 October 1940 shows that the docks lie almost a mile from the North Strand even if an aircraft commander thought that he was bombing port installations somewhere else then his bomb-aimer was very wide of the mark.

The anger in Dublin at the loss of life coincided with another bad-tempered episode in this turbulent year which blew up when it became known that the British cabinet – urged on by the Stormont government – was apparently toying with the idea of introducing conscription in Northern Ireland. As it turned out, the opposition from within nationalist circles throughout Ireland and the advice from, amongst others, Sir John Maffey and David Gray, the British and American diplomatic representatives in

Dublin, ensured that the proposal never progressed beyond the stage of an idea.

The Dublin government had good reason to feel beleaguered at this time. While there was no evidence that the bombs that fell on 30 May were a manifestation of German exasperation, there was an awareness that Berlin had compiled quite a catalogue of unneutral activity which had been working to the advantage of the British. It was therefore ironic that the governing circles in Dublin should at the same time have cause to regard a British seizure of the ports as well-founded but there was always the danger that Britain might, for example, suffer a catastrophic loss of life at sea which could conceivably have been traced to a denial of the ports. In such circumstances, the British press would have reacted so violently that the War Cabinet might have found it impossible to resist calls for decisive action.

Fortunately for Eire, however, the spotlight gradually swung away from this contentious issue. Although the deep-seated British resentment surfaced publicly from time to time until the end of the war, the possibility of a seizure of the ports receded as the Battle of the Atlantic took on an increasingly far-flung character. Eventually, in November 1942, Churchill was heard to remark that 'the hour of the ports' importance had passed.'[10]

The twelve months that began with Dunkirk had been a time of trial for de Valera and his government. His policy had attracted the condemnation (much of it precipitate) not only of Britain and her Dominions but increasingly of the United States. The problems with the belligerents that arose with depressing regularity were compounded by American partiality. President Roosevelt's bias towards Britain since the fall of France had inevitably led to strain in Irish-American relations whenever Irish neutrality was thought to adversely affect British interests. Roosevelt's sentiments were well represented in Dublin by the American minister, David Gray. Not only was he openly pro-British but his poor personal relations with de Valera degenerated to the point where the relationship often seemed to be driving American policy.

It was a year when the fear of invasion was also very real in Eire. It would later emerge that the danger from the German side had in fact vanished with the abandonment of *Operation Sealion*, the planned invasion of Britain. However, there were occasions when it seemed as if the British Army was only hours away from crossing the border in a pre-emptive move that would have disastrous consequences. But the possible effect on American public opinion weighed heavily on British thinking and, on balance. it seems that this too was never imminent.

Outside Ireland, the perception of de Valera in many quarters was that he was rabidly anti-British and hoping for a German victory. But appearances were deceptive and there was a great deal going on behind the scenes which belied this image. Decidedly unneutral conduct that favoured the British was — for internal political reasons — concealed from the Irish public by the strict censorship regime and from the outside world by a need to avoid provoking the Germans. In his biography of de Valera, Tim Pat Coogan quotes the revealing observations of an American intelligence officer who operated in Ireland during the war without the knowledge of the Dublin government.[11] His assessment of de Valera's policy is cynical and shrewd:

> Much of the problem ... was grounded in the character of de Valera and of Churchill, each of whom hated the other from youth. Each was a kind of genius with one or more human flaws. For their personal political reasons, each said much to conceal the fact that Eire was a significant help to the Allies and was neutral in name only — a fact clearly known to the Germans and the Japanese.

If de Valera was obliged to remain silent about the manner in which his policy of neutrality was being implemented in practice, he would nevertheless have been in a position to point out that, aside from Britain and France (and their Dominions), no sovereign and independent country had yet declared war on Nazi Germany without first having been attacked.

In Northern Ireland, significant changes in the course of events were taking place. A month after the bombing of Belfast, its inhabitants were trying to come to terms with the harrowing events themselves and with the outlook in the medium to long-term. The protection given by the long hours of daylight had dispelled the fear of further raids in the near term but a factor of much greater magnitude was about to radically alter the course of the war in a completely unexpected way. On Sunday morning, 22 June, people awoke to hear the astonishing news that Hitler had launched an attack on the Soviet Union. It required little knowledge of logistics to see that this gigantic undertaking meant that the bombing of British cities would now have to assume a much lower priority in German eyes. In the event, Goering's bombers would not return to Belfast. In human terms, the city's wounds were grievous but its peripheral location and the enemy's deficiencies had spared it the further ravages that its strategic importance merited.

Unknown to the public, the relative tranquillity which descended on the city was in bizarre contrast to the relentless battle being fought out a mere 200 miles and less to the north-west. There, seamen of both sides lived in a permanent state of alarm but now the increasingly precarious existence on board the U-boats was also being experienced by the Condor crews. In addition to the growing number of escort vessels they had to contend with when attacking convoys, the arming of the merchant ships themselves had become a serious problem. On 19 May, the freighter *Umgeni* (owner unknown) was 300 miles west of Donegal Bay homeward-bound to the UK from

South Africa when she was attacked by a Condor commanded by Oberleutnant Hans Buchholz. The freighter replied with its 12-pounder gun and scored a direct hit on the aircraft which crashed into the sea. Buchholz and one of the radio-operators Oberfeldwebel Paul Schmidt were killed but the *Umgeni* picked up the other five members of the crew and proceeded to Belfast. It dropped anchor in Belfast Lough at 2230 hours where intelligence officers came on board to interrogate the surviving airmen.[12]

The loss of Condors from unknown causes in the summer of 1941 was a depressingly regular occurrence for the staff of I/KG 40 but one was particularly painful. Aircraft F8+AB had taken off from Bordeaux on the morning of 18 July with the familiar task of searching for shipping north-west of Ireland.[13] When approximately 340 miles west of Donegal the crew sighted the outward bound convoy OB 346* and made a low-level attack on one of the ships, the *Pilar de Larrinaga*. The ship was hit by one bomb but its gunners nevertheless opened fire with their machine guns and 12-pounder. Their concentrated fire blew one of the Condor's wings off and it crashed into the sea. There were no survivors. The circumstances of the attack were consistent with the near-cavalier exploits of its commander, an officer who had long been a thorn in the flesh of seamen round the coast of Ireland.

Hauptmann Fritz Fliegel had been a member of I/KG 40 since 14 November 1939 and had been continuously in action against Allied shipping since the unit moved to Bordeaux in July 1940. He assumed command of the Gruppe on 21 November 1940 when Edgar Petersen was appointed Geschwaderkommodore on the enlargement of the unit to Geschwader status. The surviving unit files do not record the number of vessels he sank or damaged but his reputation in maritime operations was unsurpassed.

Petersen's small force of Condors was further depleted five days later on 23 July when aircraft F8+BB commanded by Oberfeldwebel Heinrich Bleichert failed to return. Although it was not immediately known in Bordeaux, this aircraft had been shot down in an air battle with a Coastal Command Hudson belonging to No. 233 Squadron from Aldergrave. Bleichert had managed to ditch the badly damaged Condor and the crew were picked up by an escort corvette with the exception of the meteorologist August Dollinger who had been killed by a bullet.[15]

By the middle of July, the aerial mining of the approaches to Belfast and Larne had also ceased as part of the de-escalation of Luftwaffe activity over the British Isles. The minelayers of I/KG 4, which for a year had regularly

* It was reported that one of the convoy escorts had on board at the time the crew of an RAF Whiteley of No. 502 Squadron from Aldergrove, shot down by a Condor the previous day. That Condor (F8+CL) is believed to be that of Oberfeldwebel Hans Jordant[14] which itself failed to return to base on 17 July and may have been fatally damaged in the engagement with the Whiteley

27 Fritz Friegel (right) in conversation with Edgar Petersen shortly before his death

operated over the inshore waters of the Irish Sea were among the last aircraft to be withdrawn from their bases in the west. They moved to Königsberg in East Prussia on 17 July in preparation for their transfer to the eastern front.

In the Atlantic, the relentless battle between the U-boats and their pursuers would go on for four more years. With the formal entry of the United States into the war, January 1942 saw Doenitz unleash his packs off the eastern seaboard of the North American continent in an unpredecented orgy of destruction. In the ensuing year, the U-boat campaign reached its peak but would continue to the end of the war to exact a dreadful price in men and materials. The (as yet) unascertained number of wrecks of ships and U-boats that litter the sea-bed close to the shores of Ireland testify to the island's pivotal position in a desperate battle for supremacy. Seamen and airmen of many nations are numbered among the dead but two monuments serve to bear witness to the ferocity of the struggle and represent them all. At Tower Hill in London, a memorial has been dedicated to the 23765 men of the Merchant Navy who died, most of them in the Battle of the Atlantic. Across the North Sea, in Wilhelmshaven, another monument stands, this one in memory of the men of the U-boat service who were also lost. In this case, the exact number is not known but it is estimated to be in the region of 30000, that is, 70 per cent of all those who served in U-boats in the Second World War.

But in the summer of 1941, a perilous year when the island of Ireland had dominated the wall charts of the belligerents was coming to an end. Many crises in different theatres of the conflict were yet to come but, for Britain, it was a year that occupies a unique place in the history of the Second World War. There are divergent views of Eire's place in it, some of which lack objectivity. But Northern Ireland would in the end hear Winston Churchill's ringing praise for the role she played and when the Commander-in-Chief Western Approaches, Admiral Sir Maxwell Horton, formally accepted the surrender of more than 40 U-boats at Lisahally on Lough Foyle on 14 May 1945, it seemed a fitting place to mark the end of the Battle of the Atlantic.

NOTES

ABBREVIATIONS

BArch	Bundesarchiv, Koblenz
BdU	Commander-in-Chief, U-boats
GFM	German Foreign Ministry Archives
Ic	Luftwaffe, Operations Branch
Ir.MA	Irish Military Archives, Dublin
IWM	Imperial War Museum, London
KTB	War Diary (German)
Lfl.	Luftflotte (Air Fleet)
Ma.F	German Military Archives,Freiburg
Met Office	Meteorological Office, Bracknall
NAI	National Archives of Ireland
Ob.d.L.	Commander-in-Chief, Luftwaffe
Ob.d.M.	Commander-in-Chief, German Navy
Ops.	Operations
ORB	Operations Record Book (RAF)
PRO	Public Records Office, Kew
PRONI	Public Records Office, Belfast
Skl	German Naval War Staff
U-BArch	U-boat Archives, Cuxhaven
US Nat Arch	National Archives, Washington DC

Books providing sources and listed in the Bibliography are referred to in the notes by author's name only.

CHAPTER 1   (Pages 11 to 19)

1   PRO, ADM 199/827
2   Ma.F, RL7 Ic Lfl 3
3   PRO, WO 166/1727
4   PRO, ADM 199/371
5   Ibid.
6   Ma.F, RL 20/142
7   Information from Flt-Lt C.H. Goss
8   PRO, WO 166/1727
9   PRO, ADM 199/371
10   Ma.F, RL2 III
11   PRO, AIR22 24.7.1940
12   Ibid., Summary No. 340 8.8.1940
13   Gundelach, p. 90
14   PRO, ADM 199/371

CHAPTER 2   (Pages 20 to 30)

1   Ma.F, RL7 Einzelmeldung Nr 7
    13.9.1940
2   Barker, *passim*
3   *Belfast News Letter*, 14.9.1940
4   Author's interview with the late
    Tommy Ross
5   PRO, ORB 245 Squadron
6   Saunders, p. 64 et seq
7   Ma.F, RL7/91
8   PRO, ADM 199/371-2
9   Churchill, p. 353 et seq
10   Ibid., Appendix B
11   Stern, p. 5
12   HMSO, *Treaty Series No. 1* (1931)
    Cmd. 3758

13   Ibid., *Treaty Series No. 29*
     (1936) Cmd. 5302
14   Schmoekel, p. 23
15   U-BArch, Skl KTB, p. 232
16   Forde, pp. 69–73

CHAPTER 3   (Pages 31 to 40)

 1   U-BArch, Skl KTB
     September 1940
 2   Churchill, p. 530
 3   PRO, ADM 199/51
 4   U-BArch, Skl KTB p. 275
 5   Ibid., p. 287
 6   Ibid., KTB U-99 21.9.1940
 7   PRO, ADM 199/142
 8   Ibid., ADM 199/51
 9   U-BArch, *U-100* KTB
     22.9.1940
10   PRO, ADM 199/51
11   Ibid.
12   U-BArch, Skl KTB 30.9.1940
13   Churchill, op.cit.

CHAPTER 4   (Pages 41 to 53)

 1   PRO, WO 166/4293
 2   See Bibliography
 3   *Bangor Spectator*, 1.6.1940
 4   ORB No. 88 Squadron
 5   PRO, ADM 199/59
 6   Defence Regulations 1940
     No. 1883
 7   Identified by Mr Alan Watt
 8   PRO, AIR 27/2318
 9   Ma.F, RL7 Ic 26.10.1940
10   Guildhall Library, Lloyds lists
11   Churchill, p. 530
12   Ibid., p. 529
13   Ir.MA, G2 report 26.10.1940
14   US Nat Arch, T1022
     PG74802a
15   Ibid.
16   Ibid., T1022 PG33691

CHAPTER 5   (Pages 54 to 60)

 1   PRO, ADM 199/372
 2   Ibid., ADM 53/112247
 3   Ibid., ADM 199/59
 4   Ibid., AIR 15/173
 5   Irving (Milch diaries), p. 173
 6   Clark, *passim*
 7   PRO, ADM 199/59

 8   Ibid., ADM 199/112247
 9   Forde, p. 26
10   Just, *passim*

CHAPTER 6   (Pages 61 to 67)

 1   PRO, AIR 27/2318
 2   RUC Monthly Intelligence Report
 3   Ibid.
 4   Irving, p. 177
 5   Ibid.
 6   *Belfast Telegraph*, 23.12.1940
 7   Ibid., 21.12.1940
 8   Ir.MA, Defence Command Report
     21.12.1940
 9   *Irish Times*, 2.1.1941 et seq
10   GFM, Telegram No. 790
11   Ibid., unnumbered telegram
     18.12.1940
12   Ibid., Telegram No. 841
13   Ibid., unnumbered telegram
     25.12.1940
14   Ibid., Telegram No. 867
15   Information from Flt-Lt C.H. Goss
16   GFM, Telegram No. 222

CHAPTER 7   (Pages 68 to 79)

 1   US Nat Arch, T1022 PG32421–22
 2   Ibid., PG32419
 3   Ibid., PG30034/1–13
 4   Ibid., PG32419
 5   Ibid., PG30035/1–20
 6   Stephan, p. 114
 7   Goertz committed suicide in Dublin
     on 23.5.1947
 8   Stephan, p. 95
 9   Carroll, p. 65
10   US Nat Arch, T1022 PG32032
11   GFM, Telegram No. 116
12   Ibid., Telegram No. 207
13   NAI, Cabinet papers May 1941
14   GFM, unnumbered telegram
     23.1.1941
15   Ibid., Telegram No. 144
16   US Nat Arch, T1022 PG33691
17   Ibid.
18   PRO, ADM 199/371
19   US Nat Arch, T1022
     PG 33691

CHAPTER 8   (Pages 80 to 90)

 1   Ir.MA, G2 report 6.2.1941

2   PRO, AIR 15/171
3   US Nat Arch, T1022 PG74802a
4   Bekker, p. 369
5   Young, pp. 73–4
6   Ma.F, RL7 Ic 28.1.1941
7   Churchill, p. 564
8   Doherty, p. 18
9   Richard Doherty to author
10 Churchill, p. 530

CHAPTER 9   (Pages 91 to 96)

1   GFM, Telegram No. 786, 5.12.1940
2   Ibid., Telegram No. 726, 10.11.1940
3   Carroll, p. 13
4   GFM, unnumbered telegram
    13.3.1941
5   Greiner, OKW KTB extract
    19.11.1940
6   GFM, Telegram No. 786
7   Ibid., Auswärtiges Amt DII Bd393
    5.2.1941
8   Ibid., Telegrams Nos. 57, 62 and 79

CHAPTER 10   (Pages 97 to 110)

1   BArch, KTB OKW/WFSt/1
2   Ibid., OKW Staff papers 1940–41
3   Ibid.
4   Irving, p. 95 et seq
5   Greiner, quoting from Weisung Nr. 17
6   Irving, passim
7   Ibid., p. 209 et seq
8   Baumbach, p. 117
9   See Bibliography
10 Stahl, p. 123 et seq
11 Ma.F, RL7 Lfl 3 Ic 7/8.4.1941
12 Ibid., RL10 Lfl 2 8.4.1941
13 Ibid., RL10/36
14 PRO, AIR 22 log 7/8.4.1941
15 Ir.MA, Wireless plots 7/8.4.1941
16 Röthke, correspondence with author
17 Ibid., Kriegsbericht Nr. 1372/Do/26
18 Met Office, weather data 7/8.4.1941
19 Letter to author 19.1.1990
20 Ma.F, RL7 Ic Einzelmeldung Nr. 17,
    8.4.1941
21 PRO, ORB No. 245 Squadron
    8.4.1941

CHAPTER 11   (Pages 111 to 122)

1   Bekker, p. 144
2   Churchill, Appendix C, p. 640

3   Ma.F, RL10/516
4   Ibid., RL2 III daily loss reports
    13.4.1941
5   Ir.MA, Wireless plots 14.4.1941
6   PRO, WO 166/2392
7   Ir.MA, ante
8   Ma.F, RL20/241
9   Ibid., RL10/37
10 Met Office, weather data 15/16.4.1941
11 Ma.F, RL10
12 Ibid., RL10/37
13 Ibid., RL7/88 Bd II
14 Dierich, p. 164
15 Ma.F, RL10/37
16 Ibid.
17 Georg Aigner to author
18 PRO, AIR 25 ORB 10 Group 16.4.1941
19 Ma.F, RLIO/127
20 Ir.MA, wireless plots 15/16.4.1941
21 PRO, AIR 27/2318

CHAPTER 12   (123 to 142)

1   Walther Siber to author
2   Ma.F, RL2 III daily loss reports
    16.4.1941
3   Frau Christa Hörenz to author
    1.11.1988
4   PRO, WO 166/2392
5   Interview with Norman McSween
6   Ma.F, RL10 Ic KG53 15/16.4.1941
7   Ibid., RL10/37
8   PRO, AIR 25 ORB 12 Group
    15/16.4.1941
9   PRONI, Ministry of Public Security file
10 Ma.F; RL10/37
11 Information from Flt-Lt C H Goss
    to author
12 Ma.F, RL2 III daily loss reports
    17.4.1941
13 PRO, WO 166/2392
14 Ma.F, RL7/98 Bdll Ic
15 Ibid., RL10/563
16 Ibid., RL10/37
17 *Newtownards Chronicle*, 8.2.1989
18 PRO, ADM 199/2064
19 Ma.F, RL2 III daily loss reports
    16.4.1941
20 Gerhard Baeker to author
21 PRO, WO 166/2392
22 Ma.F, RL7/98 Bdll Ic
23 Met Office, weather data
    15/16.4.1941
24 Ma.F, RL7/98 Bdll Ic

25 Ibid., RL10/576
26 Ibid.
27 Ministry of Home Security
     statistics 1939/45
28 Churchill, p. 309

CHAPTER 13   (Pages 143 to 149)

1   Churchill, Appendix B, p. 639
2   *Das Archiv* Heft Nr. 4
3   Macintyre, p. 39 et seq
4   Ibid.
5   Ma.F, RL2 III daily loss
     reports April 1941
6   PRO, ORB No. 252 Squadron
7   *Irish Times*, 1 January 1991
8   GFM, Telegram No. 111
     6.2.1941
9   Ibid., curriculum vitae
     Eduard Hempel
10 *Irish Times*, ante
11 Tony Kearns, Dublin,
     quoting eyewitnesses
12 GFM, Telegram No. 174
     24.7.1941
13 *The Army Air Forces in
     WWII*, University of
     Chicago Press, 1960
14 Coogan, pp. 577–8
15 Churchill, p. 510
16 PRO, WO 166/2224

CHAPTER 14   (Pages 150 to 169)

1   PRO, WO 166/2224
2   Stahl, pp. 49–147
3   Order in Council (1941
     No. 476)
4   Met Office data 4.5.1941
5   Greiner, p. 147
6   Dieter Lukesch to author
7   Gerhard Baeker to author
8   Georg Aigner to author
9   Extract supplied to author by
     Joachim Herrfurth
10 Met Office data supplied
     4.9.1993
11 Ir.MA, wireless plots
     4/5.5.1941
12 Irish Meterological Service, monthly
     data for May 1941
13 PRO, ADM 53/114290
14 Ma.F, RL7/99 Bd12

15 PRO, WO 166/2224 Intelligence
     Summary No. 5
16 PRO, AIR 22 'Y' Service summary
     5.5.1941
17 Summary dated 22.3.1956
18 PRONI, CAB 9CD/207
19 Ma.F, RL20/241

CHAPTER 15   (Pages 170 to 177)

1   Stahl, p. 133
2   Letter to author
3   PRO, AIR 22/487 et seq
4   Ma.F, RL2 III daily loss reports
     5.5.1941
5   Brütting, p. 67 et seq
6   Ma.F, RL7/99 Bd12
7   PRO, ADM 53/114290
8   IWM, Admiralty Preliminary
     Narrative Vol II Jan-Dec 1941
9   PRO, AIR 26 ORB 77 & 79 Wings
10 Ir.MA, wireless plots 4/5.5.1941
11 PRONI, CAB 9CD/207
12 Balke, p. 77
13 PRO, ORB 245 Squadron 5/6.5.1941
14 PRONI, Ministry of Public Security
     file 24/25.7.1941
15 Ma.F, RL10 statement undated
16 HMSO, Official War History Series
     (Civil Defence)
17 Kiehl, p. 125

CHAPTER 16   (Pages 178 to 186)

1   Roskill, Volume II
2   Ibid.
3   IWM, Admiralty Preliminary
     Narrative, ante
4   Ibid.
5   Bekker, p. 372
6   Ma.F, RL2 III daily loss reports
     27.5.1941
7   IWM, Admiralty Preliminary
     Narrative, ante
8   Roskill, ante
9   IWM, Admiralty Preliminary
     Narrative, ante
10 Coogan, p. 599
11 Ibid, p. 592
12 Poolman, p. 85
13 Ma.F, RL2 III daily loss reports
     18.7.1941
14 Ibid, 17.7.1941
15 Ibid, 23.7.1941

BIBLIOGRAPHY

A. ARCHIVAL SOURCES

Auswärtiges Amt, Bonn, Series D: Documents on German Foreign Policy 1936–41 relating to Ireland.

Bundesarchiv-Militärarchiv, Freiburg: RL files relating to Luftwaffe operations.

Deutsche Dienststelle, Berlin: Record of casualties.

Guildhall Library, London: Lloyds shipping lists.

Imperial War Museum, London: Admiralty records; German military text books.

Irish Military Archives, Dublin: G2 reports; wireless plots 1940–41.

Militärgeschichtliches Forschungsamt, Freiburg: Luftwaffe technical data.

Public Record Office, Kew, Richmond, Surrey: Records relating to British armed forces, ADM, WO and AIR files.

Public Record Office of Northern Ireland, Belfast: CAB and HA files.

U-boot Archiv, Cuxhaven: War diaries of naval staff (Skl) and individual U-boats.

Volksbund Deutsche Kriegsgräberfürsorge e.V., Kassel: Burial records of German war dead.

National Archives and Records Administration, Washington, DC: Captured German naval records for the period 1940–41.

B. BOOKS

Balke, Uwe, *Kampfgeschwader 100 'Wiking'* (Motorbuch Verlag, Stuttgart, 1981).

Barker, Ralph *Children of the Benares* (Methuen, London, 1987).

Barton, Brian, *The Blitz: Belfast in the War Years* (Blackstaff Press, Belfast, 1989).

Bekker, Cajus, *Angriffshöhe 4000* (Deutscher Bücherbund, Stuttgart, 1961).

Brütting, Georg, *Das waren die deutschen Kampfflieger 1939–1945* (Motorbuch Verlag, Stuttgart, 1986).

Carroll, Joseph T., *Ireland in the War Years* (David & Charles, Newton Abbot, 1975).

Churchill, Winston, *The Second World War, Volume II* (Cassel, London, 1949).

Clark, Wallace, *Rathlin - Disputed Island* (Volturna Press, Portlaw, 1971).

Clayton, Aileen, *The Enemy Is Listening* (Crecy Books, London, 1993).

Coogan, Tim Pat, *De Valera* (Hutchinson, London, 1993).

Dierich, Wolfgang, *Kampfgeschwader 55 'Greif'* (Motorbuch Verlag, Stuttgart, 1975).

Doherty, Richard, *Key to Victory* (Greystone Books Ltd., Antrim, 1995).

Forde, Frank, *The Long Watch* (Gill & Macmillan, Dublin, 1981).

Greiner, Helmut, *Die oberste Wehrmachtführung* (Musterschmidt Verlag, Göttingen, 1959).

Gundelach, Karl, *Kampfgeschwader 'General Wever' 4* (Motorbuch Verlag, Stuttgart, 1978).

Hoyt, Edwin, *The Death of the U-boats* (Grafton Books, London 1989).

Irvine, David, *Die Tragödie der deutschen Luftwaffe* (Verlag Ullstein, Frankfurt, 1970).

Jones, R.V., *Most Secret War* (Hamilton, London, 1978).

Just, Paul, *Vom Seeflieger zum U-boat-Fahrer* (Motorbuch Verlag, Stuttgart, 1979).

Kiehl, Heinz, *Kampfgeschwader 'Legion Condor' 53* (Motorbuch Verlag, Stuttgart, 1983).

Kurowski, Franz, *Seekrieg aus der Luft* (Verlag A.S. Mittler, Herford, 1979).

Macintyre, Donald, *U-boat Killer* (Weidenfeld & Nicholson, London, 1956).

National Archives and Records Administration, *Records relating to U-boat warfare 1939* (Washington, 1985).

Nowarra, Heinz, *Focke-Wulf Fw200 Condor* (Bernard & Graefe Verlag, Koblenz, 1988).

Poolman, Kenneth, *Scourge of the Atlantic: Focke-Wulf Condor* (Macdonald & Janes, London, 1978).

Price, Alfred, *Luftwaffe Handbook, 1939–45* (Ian Allan, Shepperton, 1971).

Ramsey, Winston G., (Ed.), *The Blitz. Then and Now Battle of Britain Prints International* (London, 1988).

Roskill, S.W., *The War at Sea* (HMSO, London, 1961).

Saunders, Hilary St George, *Valiant Voyaging* (Faber, 1949).

Schmoekel, Helmut, *Menschlichkeit im Seekrieg* (Verlag E.S. Mittler, Herford, 1987).

Seamer, Robert, *The Floating Inferno* (Patrick Stephens Limited, Wellingborough, 1990).

Smith, David J., *Action Stations; Military Airfields of* (inter alia) *Northern Ireland* (Wellingborough, 1985).

Smith, J.R. and Kay, Anthony, *German Aircraft of the Second World War* (Putnam, London, 1972).

Stahl, Peter, *Kampfflieger zwischen Eismeer und Sahara* (Motorbuch Verlag, Stuttgart, 1985).

Stephan, Enno, *Spies in Ireland* (Macdonald, London, 1963).

Stern, Robert C., *U-boats of World War 2 Vol. I* (Arms & Armour Press, London, 1981).

Wheal, Elizabeth-Anne, Pope, Stephen and Taylor, James, *A Dictionary of the Second World War* (Grafton Press, London, 1989).

Young, John M., *Britain's Sea War* (Patrick Stephens, Wellingborough, 1989).

INDEX